Psychedelic mushrooms don't pose a risk to public health and should be made legal.

—Dutch Health Inspection Service

No one should be punished for what they put into their bodies.

—Ethan Nadelmann, Drug Policy Alliance

Anything that can make vomit pretty is certainly worth taking.

—Radio talk show host Michael Jackson

MAGIC
Mushrooms
and Other
HIGHS

From Toad Slime
to Ecstasy

Edited by Paul Krassner

TEN SPEED PRESS
Berkeley | Toronto

Ten Speed Press
P.O. Box 7123
Berkeley, California 94707
www.tenspeed.com

Originally self-published in 2003.

Distributed in Australia by Simon and Schuster Australia, in Canada by Ten Speed Press Canada, in New Zealand by Southern Publishers Group, in South Africa by Real Books, and in the United Kingdom and Europe by Airlift Book Company.

Cover design by Paul Kepple
Cover illustration by Kalynn Campbell
Interior design by Jeff Puda
Creative fuel by Dennis

Visit Paul Krassner online at www.paulkrassner.com

Library of Congress Cataloging-in-Publication Data

Magic mushrooms and other highs: from toad slime to ecstasy / edited by Paul Krassner.
p. cm.
ISBN 1-58008-581-4
1. Drug abuse—United States—Popular works. 2. Drugs of abuse—Popular works. I. Krassner, Paul.

HV5825.M323 2004
362.29'0973—dc22

2003068711

First printing, 2004
Printed in Canada

1 2 3 4 5 6 7 8 9 10 — 08 07 06 05 04

Dedication

If the words "life, liberty and the pursuit of happiness" don't include the right to experiment with your own consciousness, then the Declaration of Independence isn't worth the hemp it was written on.

—Terence McKenna, 1946–2000

Magic Mushrooms is dedicated to the memory of McKenna and his Magic Mind—one of the most vibrant minds I've ever encountered—and so it was with karmic irony that he died of brain cancer. He had a tumor, which he described as "the size of a quail egg," three inches behind his right eye. It had to be cut out immediately, under local anesthetic. He was conscious during the entire operation.

"Guys," he joked with the doctors, "let's keep the 'Oops' factor to a minimum here."

Later, his son asked the surgeon, "So, this tumor, it's thinking?"

The doctor thought for a while, and then he said, "Oh, yes, it's thinking about *something*."

Two weeks later, Terence said that he kept looking into his mind trying to see what difference there was. "And," he mused, "I'm trying to figure out *what* it was thinking about that I'm not thinking about any more."

CONTENTS

Introduction

Five years ago, I began collecting material for a book I planned to call *Funny Dope Stories*. However, not all the stories turned out to be funny, at least not funny ha-ha, or as they say in cyberspace, all the stories weren't exactly LOL. Some were poignant, others were bizarre, but they were all true experiences.

Although the tales told of encounters with a variety of plants and chemicals, in a shrewd marketing move, the publisher, *High Times'* book division, decided to limit the material just to marijuana and to change the title to *Pot Stories for the Soul*. But who could have predicted that it would win a Firecracker Alternative Book Award and become a Quality Paperback Book-of-the-Month Club selection?

Then came the sequel. I wanted to call it *Acid Trips for the Soul*. The distributor insisted on a different title—*Psychedelic Trips for the Soul*—which was fine with me. And, although there was a great deal of material about all kinds of hallucinogens, I decided to include only the stories about LSD.

Meanwhile, the publisher of *Chicken Soup for the Soul* threatened to sue *High Times* if they did not cease and desist. So *Psychedelic Trips for the Soul* turned into *Psychedelic Trips for the Mind*, and it too became a Quality Paperback Book-of-the-Month Club selection.

The moral of this story is that, although the human soul can not be located, it can be copyrighted. However, a twenty-year-old man did attempt to sell his soul on the Internet, auctioning it off to the highest bidder for $400.

So now you hold in your hands the third book in this trilogy—not *Magic Mushrooms for the Soul* as originally planned—and, who knows, that might have been changed to *Magic Mushrooms for the Body*—but instead it's *Magic Mushrooms and Other Highs: From Toad Slime to Ecstasy*, featuring stories about anything folks have used to get high except for marijuana and acid. It's as though *Pot Stories* had been an amoeba which split in half to reproduce itself in the form of *Psychedelic Trips*, which in turn bifurcated to reproduce itself in the form of *Magic Mushrooms*.

This book was originally self-published, and I sent a copy to contributor Todd McCormick, then in federal prison for growing medical marijuana. It was rejected by the warden "because on pages 259–261, it describes the process of squeezing toads to obtain illicit substances which could be detrimental to the security, good order, and discipline of the institution." McCormick commented, "I wonder how much we pay the person who actually sits and reads every book that comes in for offending passages." I then sent another copy, with a note to the warden pointing out that the offending pages had been removed, but it too was returned, marked "Unauthorized." Obviously, McCormick was being punished simply for being a prisoner. Furthermore, in December 2003 he was released to a halfway house, where all his books and magazines were confiscated as "paraphernalia."

The stories in this book are told in many different voices with a wide variety of styles along the spectrum—from hilarious to frightening, from naive to sophisticated, from schmaltzy to jaded, from sacred to profane-but what all these contributors have in common is the fact that they have chosen to explore and enjoy their own consciousness with substances that are not manufactured by corporations or advertised on TV by pharmaceutical pushers trying to persuade you to "Ask your doctor" for prescription drugs with deadly side effects.

My favorite is Pravachol, which promises to prevent your first and second heart attacks. Which means that when you have your first heart attack, you'll think it's really your third.

On October 4, 2001, the U.S. government released the results of the 2000 National Household Survey on Drug Abuse. Roughly one million Americans were considered current users of hallucinogens if they had used LSD, mushrooms, mescaline, Ecstasy, peyote, or PCP during the month prior to the interview.

Although the study didn't mention scorpions, according to a Reuters dispatch from Quetta, a small but growing number of people in strife-torn Pakistan deal with their woes by smoking scorpions. Users dry the scorpion's stingers, grind them up, light the powder and suck in the smoke. "When I smoke scorpion," said Ghulam Raza, "then the heroin is like nothing to me." Addicts in Quetta tend to hang out at a local cemetery, where outsiders will not bother them, though there is an occasional problem with "enstupored persons" falling into partially dug graves.

Meanwhile, psilocybin has made its way into mythology.

Dr. Ian Edwards, head of education at the Royal Botanic Gardens in Edinburgh, claims not only that the bright color of magic mushrooms may have inspired the traditional red coat worn by Santa Claus, but they may also help Santa Claus to fly. He told the *Daily Telegraph* about a story originating in Lapland, where the people used to feed the hallucinogenic fungi to their herd of reindeer.

"They used to feed red and white fly–agaric mushrooms to their reindeer, then drink the animals' urine. Drinking the urine would give them a high similar to taking LSD.

One of the results was that they thought they and their reindeer were flying through space, looking down on the world."

Speaking of which, you might want to lick the bottom right-hand corner of page 23. Go ahead, it's all right. No one will ever know.

And you won't be indirectly providing any drug money for weapons to the terrorists, either.

—Paul Krassner
January 2004

MAGIC MUSHROOMS

Further Weirdness with Terence McKenna / Paul Krassner

The first thing you notice about the naked men and women soaking in the outdoor hot springs overlooking the Pacific Ocean is that they all seem to maintain excellent eye contact while engaging in casual conversation.

They have come to the Esalen Institute—a New Age human–potential resort in Big Sur, California—to participate in various weekend workshops. The group in this particular tub includes Terence McKenna, who will be conducting a workshop titled "Pushing the Envelope." With his curly brown hair and beard, a twinkle in his eye, and a lilt to his voice, he could easily pass for a leprechaun.

"I'm convinced," he is saying, "that probably for most people, the most important thing in a workshop situation is nothing that I will say or do, but who you might meet here."

Of course, those who are at Esalen for McKenna's workshop have come mainly to meet him. He is a psychedelic adventurer and a visionary author (his books include *True Hallucinations, Food of the Gods,* and *The Archaic Revival)* who serves as a missing link between botany and technology.

He took his first acid trip in the '60s when he was a student, majoring in shamanism and the conservation of natural resources, at UC Berkeley, where he became active in the free-speech and antiwar movements. He was influenced by Aldous Huxley, Timothy Leary, and Ram Dass, and now he has become a countercultural icon himself.

He handles that role with intelligence, grace, and humor. In person, he is spontaneously charming and effortlessly witty. He loves language, and though he is glib without being speedy, he chooses his words carefully. He communicates with the precision of an architect and the passion of a poet, speaking in a friendly, entertaining twang. He is, in short, a Mr. Rogers for grown-ups, and the neighborhood he welcomes you to explore is your own inner space.

A woman approaches our tub from the walkway to tell McKenna that it's time for his massage. When he rises from his sitting position in the water, I can't help but notice that not only is he fairly well hung, but also that he's much too tall to be a leprechaun.

I continue to soak for a while, replaying in my mind the incident that brought me here.

A few months previously, on the morning of April 1, I flew to San Francisco, where I had lived for fifteen years. It remains my favorite city, and I jump at any excuse to return. My excuse for this visit: I was scheduled to emcee a benefit for Beat Generation novelist Jack Kerouac's daughter, Jan, who had been on dialysis treatment for the last few years.

On that sunny afternoon, I was standing around stoned in Washington Square Park, wearing my *Mad* magazine jacket that my daughter Holly had given me the previous Christmas. The smiling face of Alfred E. Neuman—stating his renowned philosophy, "What—me worry?"—graced the back of my jacket. That's exactly how I felt that day, like a harmless innocent.

I was waiting for the arrival of the annual Saint Stupid Day Parade, led this year by Grand Marshal Ken Kesey and his Merry Prankster sidekick, Ken Babbs, in an open-topped convertible. The event was sponsored by the First Church of the Last Laugh. Their sound equipment was surrounded by yellow plastic tape warning, "Police Line—Do Not Cross." Somebody in a clown costume handed me a three-foot section of that tape and, April fool that I am, I graciously accepted.

The celebration featured music, comedy, and a traditional free brunch, along with such favorite rituals as the Sock Exchange and the Leap of Faith. Kesey, also in town to speak at the benefit, was in fine form. He delivered an optimistic pep talk to the audience sitting contentedly on the grass.

"It ain't over," he concluded, "until the fat lady gets high!"

Then he led a gong bong, where everybody stands up, forms a circle, holds hands and, as a single unit, takes a dozen long, deep breaths, letting out the final exhalation with upraised arms and a group wail of exultation. During this moment of spiritual hyperventilation, a young woman fell to the ground and broke her nose. She was a casualty of peace.

That night, at the benefit for Jan Kerouac—held, let's face it, only because she happened to be the daughter of a ground-breaking literary celebrity, even though he had abandoned her mother when she was pregnant with Jan—I pointed out that "It's not enough any more just to be a sperm donor." Backstage, someone I knew handed me a baggie of what I assumed to be marijuana. I thanked him and put it in my pocket. Ah, yes, one of the perks of the benefit biz.

Later, as the final members of the audience were straggling out of the theater, I was sitting with my friend Julius in his car, in the parking area at Fort Mason center. He was busy rolling a joint in a cigar box on the dashboard with the map light on. There was a police car circling around in the distance, but we foolishly ignored it. Suddenly, a moment later, there was a fist knocking heavily on the passenger-side window and a flashlight shining in my eyes. Shit! Fuck! Caught!

We were ordered outside and, with our arms outstretched against the side of the car, searched. As I was being frisked, I realized that the cop was facing the back of my jacket, with the face of Alfred E. Neuman smiling at him and asking, "What, me worry?" And, indeed, the cop was worried. He asked if I had anything sharp in my pockets.

"Because," he explained, "I'm gonna get very mad if I get stuck," obviously referring to a hypodermic needle.

"No," I said, "there's only a pen in this pocket"—gesturing toward the left with my head—"and keys in that one."

He found the coiled-up three feet of yellow plastic tape warning, "Police Line—Do Not Cross," and said, "Where'd you get this?"

"At the Saint Stupid Day Parade."

"What's it for?"

"To keep people away."

But then he found the baggie. And, to my surprise, it contained psilocybin. He examined it. Then, reeking with sarcasm, he said, "So you like mushrooms, huh?" Under the circumstances, it was such a ridiculous question that I almost laughed, but I realized that, from his point of view, this was a serious offense.

Whereas Julius was given a fifty-dollar citation for possession of marijuana, I was arrested on the spot, handcuffed behind my back, and read my Miranda rights. I stood there, heart pounding fast and mouth terminally dry, trying to keep my balance on the cusp between reality and unreality.

That cop's question—"So you like mushrooms, huh?"—was asked with such archetypal hostility that it kept reverberating inside my head. *So you like mushrooms, huh?* It was not as though I had done anything which might harm another human being. This was simply an authority figure's need to control. But control what? My pleasure? Or was it deeper than that?

This need to understand the basis of my plight became the impetus for my decision to meet Terence McKenna. He was, after all, the Head Mushroom Guru.

I contact McKenna in Hawaii, where he lives in happy isolation. "My website is on a machine in the Bronx," he says, "although I administer it from the big island." However, he is coming to the mainland, and he invites me to attend his workshop at Esalen. We meet on a Friday evening in the dining room just as a fellow sitting next to him is leaving the table.

"If you see him again," McKenna advises me, "cover your wallet with one hand and your ass with the other."

"Why? What's he selling?"

"A videotape claiming that this guy Hudson has discovered a cure for cancer, the elixir of immortality, and the philosopher's stone, but he needs investors to just dot a few i's and cross a few t's."

After dinner, the workshop convenes with an introductory session. There are thirty-five participants, sitting on cushions in a circle against the walls of a cabin in the woods. Everybody has arrived with their own personal agenda, and each will hear McKenna through their own individual filter. One by one, we introduce ourselves.

Here, a woman who's a professional raver. There, a man who strolled the streets of Paris with a lobster on a leash. Here, a mother and her son, whom she has brought as a gift for his twenty-first birthday. There, a woman who will spend the entire weekend sucking on a little straw coming out of the top of a plastic water bottle in the shape of a large, pink erect penis. She introduces herself as "a hooker from LA I'm here to party with the elves." McKenna turns to the person sitting next to her and says softly, "Top that."

Someone tells him, "I heard you're one of the greatest minds in the universe."

McKenna responds, "More outlandish claims. We'll compare notes at the end."

Someone else publicly confides to him, "If my life were a ride through the fun house at Disneyland, you're like one of the characters who keeps popping up."

McKenna confesses, "I'm an epistemological cartoon."

When these formalities are over, he begins his rap, a swirling kaleidoscope of speculation on the influence of another dimension and what's happening at the end of the twentieth century to fracture our understanding of reality. This weekend turns out to be much more than I bargained for. Mushrooms are only a starting point.

"Why," McKenna asks, "is there so much social tension over this psychedelic issue? Nobody who has informed themselves claims that great criminal fortunes are being made or that kids are being turned into psilocybin runners in the ghetto. We know that all the stupid reasons given for suppressing psychedelics are in fact some kind of lie.

"And then the more naive on our side therefore assume [that, well, shortly, some with reason will climb to its zenith,] and all these things will be made legal—not. Because this phenomenon is a dagger pointed at the heart of every social system that's ever been in place, from the grain tower at Jericho to modern fascism in China.

"No social system is so confident of its first premise that it can tolerate this. But we don't live for the greater glory of social theories and institutions. We live because we find ourselves, as Heidegger said, *thrown* into being, and we have to sort that out on an individual basis."

And this is where McKenna's concept of novelty comes in. Novelty is the absolute core of his quest. The ultimate battle is between the increase of novelty as opposed to habit or entropy.

"Look at the history of the universe," he says. "Novelty has been increasing since the Big Bang. We need to undergo radical deprogramming before the eschaton—the last thing. We are on the brink of moving into the domain of the imagination. Novelty is maximized and preserved. It changes our position in the cosmic drama, the cosmic accident. We're damn lucky to be here as spectators, we are told by science. Suddenly we matter. We still have freedom to act, to create.

"The bottom line, the final true message of psychedelics—the positive input that comes to you if you accept change—is the message that the culture outside of psychedelics is so keen to deny with materialism, everything from the calendar to theories of democracy. But nothing lasts, not your friends, enemies, fortune, children, not even you. Nothing lasts.

"Well, if you live your life in denial of that, then it's essentially like being dragged kicking and screaming sixty years to the yawning grave. Strangely enough, the way you cheat the grim reaper is by living as fast as you can, because all time is the seriality of events, and the more events there are, the more time you have, so awareness becomes very important, and even, as the Buddhists say, awareness of awareness."

There is a sculpture of Buddha in the middle of the vegetable garden at Esalen, with a small bench nearby. That night, I take a walk there and just sit under the stars, listening to the sound of wind chimes tinkling in the breeze as I compose a contemporary haiku. The traditional haiku is three lines: five syllables, then seven, then five again. Ordinarily, I'm one for breaking tradition, but I figure that if you don't stick to traditional form in this case, then it's not really a haiku, it's merely free verse. And so I wrote:

Aspirins and Prozac,
Tums, Nytol, Pepto Bismol,
Just say no to drugs.

❧

Saturday morning at Esalen. Fresh fruit and vegetables galore. Hot cereal and stewed prunes. People will be passing gas all over the place, and I remember with fondness my deaf uncle who once, when somebody farted, struggled to say, "I can't hear it, but I can smell it."

At the first session that day, McKenna maintains that "There are not good beliefs, there are just bad beliefs, because they inhibit human freedom. A belief is a closed system. Psilocybin, like all psychedelics, has this quality of dissolving preexisting mental and behavior patterns. This ability to entertain possibilities is what starts us on the road to free will.

"Our legacy is the legacy of the children of the stoned monkeys. And the chaotic element that a psychedelic introduces into the mental structures of a population is an inevitable precondition for the overcoming of habit and the production of novelty. We are dysfunctional because we have been away from this symbiotic relationship to mushrooms for such a very long time.

"We have got to make a transition to some kind of higher consciousness. If yoga can do it, great. If transcendental meditation can do it, great. The pope and the Dalai Lama, fine. But in my experience, the only thing that changes consciousness as fast as we're going to have to change it is psychedelics. We have to change it on the dime, because the processes that we have set in motion are going to drag us down.

"If we *don't* make this higher ascent within fifty years, all the easily extracted metal will be gone, petroleum supplies will be dwindled, and there will be epidemic diseases, fascism, and the erosion of any knowledge by most people with a historical database. We're just turning ourselves into victims of our own processes. That's why I think this is the choke-point. The next twenty years are make or break for the human enterprise. It's a forward escape into a world we can barely conceive of, but the only choice is grim death and extinction.

"We are all very toxified and poisoned by the society we live in, we're critics of it, but nevertheless we're products of it. We need to unify heart and head in the presence of super technology. The culture is being left behind by the technology. We have to re-engineer ourselves.

"Fortunately, I have managed to transcend the idea that politics or some social reformation or some messiah is going to bail us out. The reason I'm an optimist is because I think that nature is about some very complex business here, and we are its instruments, and ten thousand years of our discomfort is, from the point of view of the planet, a small price to pay for what is going to be achieved. I don't know about a god, but the laws of physics favor the production of novelty."

Someone asks, "If psychedelics are such a valuable tool, how do you explain the disappointment of the '60s generation?"

"If psychedelics are so great," McKenna responds, "then what's so great about us? Are we better than these poor people who have never taken psychedelics? Are we morally better? Are we wiser? Or are we just some kind of screwball cult like Mormons, who congratulate themselves on having achieved this supreme understanding, and yet to everybody else they just look like geeks? And we look like geeks. This really is a problem I carry with me, because I've advocated psychedelics my entire life, yet I often see incredibly bad behavior and stupidity and cruelty and insensitivity committed by psychedelic people.

"The bottom line of psychedelics is not how good it makes you feel but how creative you are, and the acceleration of creativity that is taking place is immense, and if you can get off with the people who are responsible for most cutting-edge phenomena, they will admit that they began with psychedelics. I mean all cutting-edge science, art, literature, is driven from those places.

"I really believe our evolutionary past holds the key to our evolutionary future, and drugs and computers are just two ends of a spectrum. The only difference between them is that one is too large to swallow. And our best people are working on that.

"So I really see recovering ancient values through modern technology and a reconstruction of our lifestyles and our relationships to each other. This is how to make the ride to the singularity of the end of time a more pleasant and palatable experience. If you don't do this, the ride to the end of time will proceed at the same rate, but you may lose it.

"It may go from a white-knuckle ride to truly terrifying, because the change that lies ahead is going to require a great deal of flexibility and open-mindedness and a willingness to transform in order to take place without generating a megadose of anxiety.

"Anxiety is already rising. For most governments in the world, their entire function is simply to manage catastrophe at this point, because they have no plan, they have no vision, they're utterly clueless. Basically, they're waiting for flying saucers or the Second Coming to somehow cancel the nightmare that their own institutions and methods have made inevitable."

Jesus, I think, what if McKenna wasn't an optimist? And what if he were not so charismatic? Would he then be just another guy with a long white beard, wearing a toga and sandals, walking along the sidewalk and carrying a big signboard to remind us, "The End of the World Is Coming! Are You Prepared?" Only, McKenna has a specific date for it.

"The end of the Mayan calendar," he says, "is the same day that I had calculated. Well, this is not a reason for believing my theory, for you, but for *me* it was a reason. Too weird a coincidence. The only thing that I have in common with the Mayan civilization is that we both used psilocybin, and it's almost as though when you purge the virus off your disc, there is at the bottom line, written in assembly code that cannot be expunged, a discard date that says, 'Abandon this locality before December 21, 2012 AD.'"

So, kids, be sure to mark that date on your calendar. Circle it in red.

On Saturday, before the afternoon session begins, participants make small talk with Terence.

Someone asks, "How'd you like your massage?"

"It was cool," he replies. "I mean like I'm right out of the oven. I should just slip into sleep and meditation, but no hardship is too great."

Someone else asks, "What book are you currently reading?"

"I'm reading a book, it's a hoot, *Time Machines: Time Travel in Physics, Metaphysics and Science Fiction* by Paul Nahin. It's published by the American Institute of Physics, so you need not hang your head in the subway."

Another person asks, "How's your website going?"

"I'm just so damned proud of having hacked it in the first place. The things we're discussing here, if you go there and download, it's all there in high detail, and you can take your time. I think of it—in terms of my intellectual life—it's more who I am than who I am sitting here, because I might forget a reference or skip over something. On the Web site, we got it right."

Except that on the website you can't appreciate McKenna's speech pattern. He would pronounce pat-tern, as though his inner dictionary were separating his syllables, certainly a shat-tering experience.

"The great principle that I've tried to enunciate," he tells the group, "is that nature conserves novelty."

Somebody asks, "Is nature conscious?"

"Seems more reasonable to me than the idea that all of this complexity is just for the purpose of you to run around and have a career for a few years, and then it all is given back to chaos. We're not the chance existential witnesses to a cosmic accident, we are Hamlet. The play is about us. And so our struggles to attain justice and decency among ourselves are not simply a why-not proposition as Camus thought, but in fact somehow the tone of the universal process is cast by human decisions.

"Nature is not mute, nature affirms the conservation of novelty and is incredibly interested in our efforts to make something more of it. The conservation of novelty lays an obligation upon us to preserve what has been achieved and to go beyond it and to make a contribution to it. So if there is an ethic derivative of the psychedelic experience, I think this is it.

"It's really not entirely for our benefit. I think we are like atoms in some enormous process that is taking place. If there are aliens, they don't talk to people in trailer courts; species are addressed. Aliens don't talk to individuals, they talk to species. And they don't say things like, 'Be vegetarian,' they say things like, 'Now do language. Now physics.' Ultimately, everything is a mystery. And it's good, after such an exalted, plodding journey toward explanation, to remember that nowhere is it written that higher apes should be able to divine cosmic purpose.

"What wants to save itself is biology, and we're simply a kind of specialized cell that can work at high temperatures or can encode data, and so we've been deputized. I'm sure we're as expendable as any other species and as clueless. The problem is that so much novelty will be lost, and the universe doesn't like that. It wants to conserve novelty at all costs. That seems to be more important to it than conserving biology. It will sacrifice biology if necessary to save novelty. Novelty is the top of the value hierarchy, as I see it, and biology, culture, technology, physics—all are simply means to an end."

I remember the first time I came to Esalen, in 1970, for a workshop with John Lilly. He played a tape loop of one word being repeated continuously, but after a while you would begin to hear other words.

"When faced with repetition," Lilly explained, "your human biocomputer automatically programs in novelty."

At sundown, I keep my eyes focused on the precise instant that the sun disappears over the ocean's horizon, and there is a flash of green. I'm sure there's a logical explanation for it, having to do with refraction of color, but until I saw the green flash with my own eyes, I had always thought it was a myth. And, to quote Terence McKenna, "The truth is more important than anybody's opinion or myth or story or hope or fear about how the universe is put together."

Our evening session is devoted to demonstrating the results of his work on a computerized timewave of novelty in history, which originally developed out of a mathematical analysis of the deep structure of the I Ching.

"At this stage in my life," McKenna admits, "I became a burden to my friends and a joy to my enemies because I knew—[laughing with self-deprecation, then mimicking a critic] 'the way they always *do* know'—I knew that this was a map of time, and that the history of the universe was here, and a helpful person pointed out a passage in Gurdjieff, whom to that point I had always written off, but since it supported my delusion—there's a passage which says, in the future there will be a diagram invented which people will simply unroll and look at, and they will understand everything.

"Finally, after I had alarmed a number of people, and my friends were meeting, speaking of intervention—on an *idea,* for god's sake—Ralph Abraham came to see me on his own, he wasn't delegated by the interventionists, and said, 'The problem here is that you have an occult diagram. Only you understand it, and only you can interpret it, and therefore it's not very persuasive.'

"Three years passed, and I basically prayed, and then one day I was sitting in my parlor, and I had twisted a fattie—no, I did not abuse an obese person, it means I had smoked some cannabis—and I was thinking about the great unsolved problem, as I always was in those years, and it was just like, *plunk,* and I saw the solution, I saw how to do it, I saw it from end to end, from side to side, in a single moment, and here comes a great piece of good news that you should greet with tears of joy streaming down your face—I'm not going to explain it to you.

"I did it, and the result is the timewave which is totally straightforward and makes extremely precise predictions about where novelty should be found in history. What the computer software is allowing us to do is to move around inside it and see any amount of time at any level of magnification. We could look at something as huge as the condensation of the planet—there it is—or we could look at something as small as the Kennedy assassination, or even smaller. We could concentrate into a single minute and say where the novelty was and where the habit was.

"For me, this is sort of the payoff of doing these weekends. In the other parts of the weekend, I basically function as the nutty professor. This is so personal that no one has ever tried to steal it. That's how uniquely and wholly and totally mine it is. So if it's malarkey I get all the blame, and if it's true I get all the credit. On a basic level, the cosmology that I'm proposing is this: that the universe should be thought of as a kind of struggle, or competition, between two enormous forces. We'll name them habit and novelty.

"Habit is repetition of pattern already established, it's conservation of traditional values, it's path of least resistance, it's momentum. Novelty is an equally easy concept to grasp. Novelty is what's never been before. Novelty is emergent. Novelty is new. Novelty makes connections where they were never made before.

"And any span of time—a millisecond, a million years—has within it a struggle between habit and novelty and potentially a signature of how that process proceeded. Like a stock market. The shifts between habit and novelty are like the shifts between high and low prices of commodity.

"The good news in all of this is that novelty is winning, and novelty will triumph absolutely at a certain future moment in time. Let me lead us into the future here, and all mysteries will be revealed. Isn't this fun? You see, it's not so much whether you believe it, it's that this causes thinking."

And then, as the group gathers in front of a computer, McKenna takes us on a guided tour of novelty in history.

"We're now at six million years, and this is the story of the evolution of the higher primates, and these are solar energy cycles, glaciations, we're still moving in the realm here of large-scale cosmic input . . . this is a domain of high novelty, a very long period, longer than the time that separates us from Moses . . . this may be where that partnership paradise occurs, the early influence of psychoactive plants on consciousness . . . now we're under a million years. And remember, it wouldn't have any of these correlations if the end date were different . . . this is the last 62,000 years . . . 42,000 years . . . this is the mushroom paradise back here . . . the crucifixion is here . . . this is the fall of Rome here.

"This is the birth of Muhammad here, this is the consolidation of Islam—570 to 630, Muhammad's birth and death—the world had never seen anything like Islam. These guys were desert tribes dealing water to each other for millennia at the edge of organized civilization. They were desert barbarians, and suddenly one guy, Muhammad, not only founds a world religion but claims the allegiance of 700 million people, and he founds a political order, too. Buddha didn't pull that off, and neither did Christ. There's a book, *The One Hundred,* that seeks to list the hundred most influential people in human history, and number one, Muhammad, built a political and religious and philosophical order that maintained its coherency."

However, novelty is not necessarily a good thing from the human point of view.

"What happened in 1355?" McKenna asks. "Within eighteen months, one-third of the human population of Earth died—Bubonic Plague—and no one knows how many died in Europe. It's an interesting signature. It certainly is novel to have one-third of the population drop dead." Because McKenna's predictions of the past are in accurate accordance with history, he is able to extrapolate into the future. "I predicted the fall of the Berlin Wall, Tiananmen Square, Chernobyl—I predicted all of these things—I didn't say what would happen, but I said the day. 'This day will be the most novel day of this year.'"

The journey through time continues.

"This is 1440, Gutenberg invents printing . . . 1492, Columbus . . . the American revolution begins at a symmetry break at the top of a slide into novelty. It succeeds. The French revolution begins at the bottom of a novelty trough on an upturn into habit, and fails . . . January 1, 1900, symmetry break occurs, and this is the signature of the twentieth century, an almost continuous descent [ascent, in a sense, but depicted in this computerized graph as descent] into novelty from 1900 to 1905, the special theory of relativity, 1906, flight, radio, World War I, the Russian revolution, Dada, surrealism-it's the 20th century, for crying out loud—Hitler, big-time novelty . . . World War II, culminates with the atomic bomb, the end of the war, and the return to normalcy . . . 1950, invention of the hydrogen bomb.

"For those of you who are true fans of predictive accuracy, the day of the Human Be-In, January 13, 1967, is the day we go over the hump. Isn't it wonderful that it validates-well, but hell, it was the symmetry-breaking moment. And then, just after that, the landing on the moon and the cascade into novelty. Saddam invades Kuwait . . . Tiananmen Square, three million, the largest crowd in human history . . . we're right about here. This is the pause before the storm. This is the most habituated moment that we will know for maybe the rest of time."

Boy, was I exhausted. Talk about your long, strange trips. Maybe it's all really just self-fulfilling prophecy, but you have to admire McKenna, if for nothing else, for just how far out on a limb he is willing to go.

"Hell," he says, "I *live* on a limb."

Sunday morning is our final session. Judging by rearranged seating and body language, a couple of new liaisons—this friendship, that romance—have developed over the weekend. Or what's a workshop for?

"I suppose if I were a different kind of personality," McKenna observes, "I would haunt the hallways of major universities and try to drag these guys into my theory. But for some reason, I think the timewave itself empowers a certain kind of fatalism, and I just say if I'm right, I'm right; if I'm wrong, I've probably told enough people already.

"It is a remarkable thing for a nonmathematician to have created, and I know how little I knew when I started. If it's true, I really don't think we'll have to wait till 2012. If it's true [and this has become my mantra, in McKenna's voice], the world is going to get *nut-tier* and *nut-tier* and *nut-tier*. Eventually it will get so nuts that those at the top, in charge of managing all these interlocking systems, will begin to ask, first themselves and then others, 'What is going *on*?'

"It's a done deal, folks. I feel like I am inside an enormous joke. And that to some degree, each of you is too, to the degree that you understand what's going on here, what's *really* going on here. Then all you can do is act with style and a certain panache, and try to carry things forward, keep everybody happy, keep the levels of anxiety under control. It's a huge, huge joke of some sort, and the real belly laugh is beyond the yawning grave, and then you just look back and say, 'Why didn't I see it? It was in front of me all the time, and I lived my whole life in anxiety and doubt and frustration.'

"So the kind of laid-back, chilled-out quality of psychedelic people is simply that they've been there, they've done that, and now they're just living without the illusion of history. It is not the eschaton that is the illusion, it is history that is illusion—three-dimensional space, causality, the structures that we allowed our languages and our science and our mathematics to put in place, to delude us over the last several thousand years.

"As we get closer and closer to the eschaton, there's going to be a lot of panic, uncertainty, unhappiness, because everything in the world is going to change, nothing will survive in recognizable form, into the new modality, and this is good news, but it may be taken for bad news.

"And the task of psychedelic people, I think, is to act as midwives for this collective birthing of a new *ontos* of being that is going to rend the shell of three-dimensional space and time, and create a new level of novelty and organization in the universe, as has happened so many, many times before. But this is the first time that human beings will be witnesses to and participators in the action, at least since the invention of language. So keep your powder dry and your will protected, and I'll see you, if not before, at the end of the world."

I had a suggestion for McKenna. "You could become like the Unabomber, just send psilocybin in the mail to these professors and insist that the *Washington Post* and the *New York Times* publish your thesis on the stoned monkeys."

"Good, well, you can be my advance man. Then they'll believe me."
"Oh, right. I have less credibility than you."

For all his pursuit of mysticism, Terence McKenna is essentially a scientist. He may have a cult following, but he is not a cult leader in the sense that he encourages challenge rather than forbids it. "A scientist's job," he says, "is to prove that he's wrong. You don't get that at the ashram or up in a monastery—[mimicking what such a guru would not say] 'Well, we crushed that hypothesis to smithereens.'" So, naturally, I had some follow-up questions for him, in person and by email.

Q. I would feel incomplete if I didn't ask for your comment on the recent news story about the Heaven's Gate cult.

A. Like most people, I haven't sorted out the San Diego mass suicide. I imagine that on the mainland, the soul-searching and efforts to determine everyone's collective guilt and complicity are in full cry. But from the slopes of Mauna Loa, it looks like simply the latest Southern California psychodrama with attendant obligatory media jack-off. I encountered Do (then Bo) and Peep in 1972. They were contemptible, power-crazed new age creepoids then, and apparently things didn't get better.

Q. During the workshop at Esalen, you talked about not knowing where the mind is. Do you think that the mind can function without the brain?

A. I have not made up my mind on this, but think of the mind as a hyperspacially deployed organ that is ordinarily invisible. As to whether or not it can exist independent of the brain, I am not sure. If the physical world is conceived as a 4-D manifold, it is logically impossible for a physical thing, a 4-D solid, to move or otherwise change. It must be our state of consciousness which changes as we become successively aware of adjacent cross-sections of the 4-D manifold. But this makes sense only if we, the observers, are not in space-time. This would imply that our minds exist on a level beyond anything that physics can tell us about.

Q. You also mentioned how, posteschaton, we'll look back from the grave and laugh at the futility with which we struggled through life. Were you implying that you believe individual consciousness can survive after physical death?

A. Not really, only that life will show its pattern and plan when we look back on it, and that will redeem some of the weirdness of having to live it essentially without a clue.

Q. You mentioned in the workshop, in terms of the coming apocalypse, that people should do things fast. Now, I thought that doing things fast was one of the problems that brought us to this place and that the antidote would be to slow down and savor the implications of what we do. Maybe you and I are saying the same thing?

A. Well, I didn't really mean do more and more things, I said more and more will happen. I think the thing to do is to eliminate foolishness, having your time vampirized. I agree with you, the goal is not to just jam in as much stuff as possible. Basically, one strong motivation for moving to Hawaii was just to escape the silliness, the triviality, of it all, and I've discovered there was apparently no information loss. I can keep up with an O. J. Simpson discussion even though I only spent three minutes a week keeping track. The people who watched every day of the testimony, my God, they must be slow learners. And it's amazing how many fields you can participate in as a fully empowered player without investing much time.

As pleasant as it is, I can't hold the whole thing in my mind in the states, as we citizens of the sovereign state of Hawaii refer to your country. I just feel like I've been parachuted behind enemy lines, and this is no time for philosophy; let's blow up the damn bridge and get out of here. But in Hawaii, I can look at it all and see trends and tendencies, and pontificate about it in my rain forest, and it all makes sense. Somebody said, "Yeah, well, it all makes sense because you never talk to anybody else." Probably some truth to that

➡ **Q.** At Esalen, you stated: "The technological push that has seemed so relentless and so brutal and so diffcult to deflect is, in fact, we are doing the right thing, and the only question is whether we'll make it in time, and it looks like it's going to be a flash photo finish. We basically have until 2012 to figure out how to download all human DNA and other forms of DNA on this planet into some kind of indestructible storage mode. Then there's a chance to ride out this catastrophic wave of extinction."

Now, my question is, in view of the recent news which has placed human cloning on the border between science-fiction and reality, might not cloning be an answer to the question posed by your statement? How does cloning fit into your theory of the need to prepare ourselves for the apocalypse?

A. In spite of the cloning of Dolly, we still have a great deal to learn about DNA. What was remarkable about the Dolly episode was how far the research team got without really understanding why they were succeeding. There is still a great deal to understand about the cloning process and how it works. Which does not mean that it will not be applied before it is fully understood. But at this point, it is a kind of stunt. Clones are simply people with a strange family history, and who among us does not fit that description?

The interesting thing about the recent cloning news, both regarding Dolly the ewe and the two cloned monkeys, is that both fated births occurred right around the same time, July–August 1996. That was a time that my timewave had long predicted would be a period when there would be some enormous scientific breakthrough.

I was very excited, therefore, by the announcement, at the time, of the discovery of microfossils in a Martian meteorite. Now, with the news of the clones, I am more convinced than ever that my prediction of a period of novelty and scientific breakthrough was correct. As for the clones themselves, I am reminded of *Brave New World*, Aldous Huxley's distopia of clueless clones. More scary than *1984*, that is for sure. And more likely, long run. So corporate, so elegant.

➡ **Q.** What are your visions of alternative scenarios that are upcoming, either in December of 2012 or before?

A. Well, I've spent a lot of time thinking about this, although I realized about a year ago that, in a sense, it's not really my issue. The funny thing is, here I have this wave, it predicts every second between here and December 21, 2012, I show it to people and their first question is, "So what happens afterwards?" It doesn't address that. It addresses all moments *before* that. Nevertheless, I feel the force of the question, and I've created a series of scenarios in ascending weirdness which answer the question.

A low weirdness answer would be, suddenly everyone begins to behave appropriately. This is kind of a Buddhist, Taoist approach. Now, the interesting thing about that scenario is, the first thirty seconds of that we can predict—appropriate behavior would probably be to take your foot off your neighbor's neck. Step back from what you're doing.

And then I always imagine—for some reason, I don't know why—that everybody would take off their clothes and go outside. But after that I can't figure—that's only the first thirty seconds of appropriate behavior. If you change the context of reality so radically that predicting what would be appropriate in the next thirty seconds is impossible, we would just dissolve into appropriate behavior. Since we've never had that, we can't imagine what it would be like.

Then there's the transformation-of-physics scenario, which basically says, "All boundaries dissolve." What that would probably be like, the first hour of it would be like a thousand micrograms of LSD. After that we can't imagine or predict, because again it would have so totally changed the context that you could no longer predict it.

Then there are the catastrophic scenarios that revolve around the question, "Death, where is thy sting?" And probably the most effcient of those is the planetesimal-impact scenario. A very large object strikes the earth and kills everybody, and that's it.

➡ **Q.** A blunt object?

A. It's a blunt solution. Sort of in that same category is the blue star in Sagittarius. And then a kind of intermediate between those two-the sun will explode. That would certainly clear the disc and fulfill the whole thing. The planet vaporizes, and collectively we and all life on earth move into the shimmering capsules of the post-mortem realm, whatever that is. Novel, novel.

When I worked with the timewave, I argued strenuously that it reflects all ebb and flow of novelty, but somebody will come up with something like the release of the *Sergeant Pepper* album or the O. J. Simpson trial, and then we see that it's lost in the noise. What the wave seems most pristinely to predict, or what parallels the wave most closely, is the evolution of technology, and I think technology is something that we haven't really understood. In a sense, technology is the alchemical journey for the condensation of the soul and the union of spirit and matter in some kind of hyperobject.

The rise of the Web has been a great boost to my fantasies along these lines, because now I can see with the Web from here to the eschaton. Apparently, it's a technology for dissolving space, time, personalty, and just releasing everybody into a data stream, something like the imagination. Then that's why the ultimate technological fantasy along this line of thought is what is conventionally called a time machine.

There's an interesting aspect to the time machine. The wave describes the ebb and flow of novelty in time, but then you reach a point when it's so novel that it fails beyond that point. Well, a time-traveling technology would cause such a system to fail, because it's a description of the unfolding seriality of linear events, which a time machine would disrupt.

So it may be that it isn't the explosion of the sun, or the coming of the aliens, or the descent of the second person of the Trinity, it's simply that a technology is put into place that destroys linear time and, from thence forward, when you give your address you have to say not only where but when. There are some problems with this.

And then here is a slightly more interesting and woo-woo scenario. The thing that's always held out against time travel, especially time travel into the past, is that what's called the grandfather paradox—somebody pointed out it's not called the father paradox because apparently you want to avoid an Oedipal situation—and it's simply the following objection: If you could travel into the past, you could kill your grandfather. If you killed your grandfather, you wouldn't exist. Therefore, you couldn't travel into the past. Therefore, time travel is impossible.

One idea I have for an end-of-history scenario: Time travel becomes more and more discussible; finally there are laboratories working on it; finally there is a prototype machine; finally it's possible to conceive of a test; and so on the morning of December 21, 2012, at the World Temporal Institute headquarters in the Amazon Basin, by a worldwide, high-definition, three-dimensional hook-up, the entire world tunes in to see the first flight into time. And the lady temponaut comes to the microphone and makes a few brief statements, hands are shaken, the champagne bottle is smashed, she climbs into her time machine, pushes the button and disappears into the far-flung reaches of the future. Now, the interesting question is, what happens next? And I already established for myself that you can travel backward into the past, but you can't travel further into the past than the invention of the first time machine, for the simple reason that there are no time machines before that, and if you were to take one where there are none, you get another paradox.

So what happens when the lady temponaut slips into the future? Well, I think what would happen a millisecond later is tens of thousands of time machines would arrive from all points in the future, having come back through time, of course, to witness the first fight into time. Exactly as if you could fly your Beachcraft back to Kitty Hawk, North Carolina, to that windy morning when the Wright brothers rolled their flier out and fueled 'er up. And that's as far as the road goes. That's the end of the time road.

But the grandfather paradox persists. One of those time travelers from 5,000 years in the future, on their way back to the first time-travel incident, could stop and kill his grandfather, and then we have this whole problem all over again. So I thought about this for a long time, and I think I've found my way around it. But, as usual, at the cost of further weirdness.

Here's what would *really* happen if we invented a time machine of that sort. The lady temponaut pushes the button, and instead of all time machines appearing instantly in the next moment, in order to preserve the system from that paradox, what will happen is, the rest of the history of the universe will occur instantly. And so that's it. I call it the God whistle.

This is because you thought you were building a time machine, and in a sense you were, but the time machine isn't what you thought it was. It caused the rest of time to happen instantaneously, and so the furthest-out developments of life, matter, and technology in the universe come right up against you a millisecond after you break that barrier, and in fact you discover that traveling time is not traveling time, it's a doorway into eternity, which is all of time, and that's why it becomes more like a hyperspatial deal than a simple linear time-travel thing.

There's been a parallel development which has caused me to feel even more confident. We're now beginning to build this parallel world called the World Wide Web. And you can bet that long before we reach 2012, the major religions of the world will build virtual realities of their eschatological scenarios. There will be the Islamic paradise, the Christian millennium, the Buddhist shunyata—these will be channels that you tune into to see if you like it and want to join, so in a sense guaranteeing we will have a virtual singularity.

It's all very well to try to understand the end point, but recall that where we are relative to the end point is in resonance with the year 950 AD. We're like the people in 950 AD trying to understand the Web, the hydrogen bomb, and the catscanner. How can we? My God, we don't even have calculus yet. Newton hasn't been born yet, let alone Einstein. I mean we're running around—essentially we're primitives, is what I'm saying. We don't have tools yet to conceive of the object of 2012. We must build those tools between now and then. And good places to start are with the Web, psychedelic drugs, whatever is the most cutting edge and most far out.

▶ **Q.** So that saying, "May you live in interesting times," is supposed to have been a Chinese curse, but if the ruling class had control of the language, it was a curse to *them,* but it was a blessing to the people who *made* it interesting times.

A. I think it's saying the same thing as the Irish toast [heavy brogue], "May you be alive at the end of the world."

▶ **Q.** Meanwhile, my Chinese fortune cookie predicted that you and I will cross paths again and also that I will enjoy another Chinese repast soon.

A. We must meet in a Chinese restaurant and save the oracle unnecessary embarrassment.

Jan Kerouac had met her father only twice. The first time she was nine. The second time, six years later, he sat drinking a fifth of whiskey and watching *The Beverly Hillbillies.* Jan died of kidney failure at the age of forty-four, never having fulfilled her fantasy of becoming drinking buddies with her father, who died when she was a teenager.

As for my psilocybin bust, I was lucky. With the aid of a terrific attorney, Doron Weinberg, I got off with a $100 fine and nothing on my permanent record. But I finally understood what that cop had meant when he snarled, "So you like mushrooms, huh?" What was his *actual* message? Back through eons of ancestors—all the way back to those unstoned apes—this cop was continuing a never—ending attempt to maintain the status quo. He had unintentionally revealed the true nature of the threat he perceived. What he had really said to me was, "So you like the evolution of human consciousness, huh?"

Well, yeah, now that you mention it, I do. I mean, when you put it like that—*So you like the evolution of human consciousness, huh?*—sure, I do. I like it a whole lot.

Video of My Mind / Roslyn Cristiano Payne

I grew up in Los Angeles and was taught not to eat the mushrooms that grew on the lawn, since they might be poisonous. My only experience with mushrooms was Campbell's cream-of-mushroom soup. I spent the '60s in New York City making films with Newsreel, a documentary political film collective. In 1970, I moved to Vermont to live in a commune.

One day, Pierre Biner, the Swiss mycologist and member of the Living Theater, came to visit. We went into the woods, and he taught me about the mushrooms that which his father had taught him. I learned about the most delectable edibles, such as *Boletus edulis* or porcini, Chanterelles, *Agaricus campestris* or meadow mushrooms, and morels. We ate them cooked—in white cream sauce, in butter, or with eggs—simple dishes that would not hide the taste of the mushroom.

Pierre knew that psilocybin mushrooms grew on lawns fertilized by cow manure. One day he picked some mushrooms and I asked him, "How do you know what they are?" He said, "I just know." I was unsatisfied and scared, as I knew so little. I would walk past hundred of unknowns called LBMs or little brown mushrooms. "What a waste," I thought.

One day, while sitting on the lawn in City Hall park talking to friends, I began to eat raw, freshly picked, beautiful mushrooms that I thought were a close cousin of the store-bought mushroom, *Agaricus campestris* or meadow mushrooms. I spent the next few hours vomiting and having an upset stomach. The need to know more was evident—I did not want to poison or kill myself.

That summer, while looking at a class catalog of the University of Vermont, I spotted a course in mycology taught by Dr. Thomas Sproston. I showed up the first day of class with a basket of freshly picked mushrooms and asked if I could sit in. Dr. Sproston smiled and said, "Yes." I was the only one in the class that had brought mushrooms.

We learned how to identify mushrooms by the color and shape of the spores under a microscope. Our two textbooks had no pictures, just written descriptions of spores. I had to learn how to choose the correct brown-color spore deposit out of a possible 30 shades of brown. I worked hard, but I just couldn't get it.

Dr. Sproston paid us one dollar for every *Amanita virosa,* Destroying Angel, that was turned in. Experiments were being made to find an antidote to save folks from dying when they ate it. In the woods, I was great. I could spot and pick baskets full of deadly white *Amanitas.* I told Dr. Sproston to keep the money in exchange for allowing me to sit in the class.

That summer, I went into the woods many times and began to learn. Returning home, I laid the mushrooms out on newspaper and tried to identify them from the black-and-white pictures in my identification book by Dr. Alexander Smith. I learned which of the *Amanita* mushrooms were deadly poisonous, and I began to eat some of the edibles like the beautiful and delicious *Amanita caesarea,* which were named after Julius Caesar.

I was young and often foolish in the early '70s. One day at the lake, I picked a mushroom that I thought was edible, popped it into my mouth, and chewed it, but not well. Shortly after, I began to feel sick, dizzy, and nauseated. I tried to walk to my friends, who were fishing a short distance away. I couldn't move my legs very well, and I fell to my knees. My body felt like I was drunk. Quickly, my vision began to darken. I was in a long black tunnel with no end, I felt scared and alone, and needed help. I thought I was going to die.

As I tried to make my way back to the car, I vomited and immediately began to feel better. Later, when I examined my vomit, I found that it contained large pieces of the mushroom that I had not chewed well. I had not eaten an *Amanita muscaria* after all. At that moment, I learned that there is a fine line between poison and hallucinatory mushrooms and death. What some folks call poison, others call mind-expanding.

Perhaps I ate an *Amanita phalloides, verna,* or *virosa,* one of the deadly mushrooms that kill people every year. I felt I was saved because I had not chewed the mushroom into little pieces where it could have entered my body system more quickly and caused my death. Never again. Sometimes a little information is worse than none. A friend of mine ate a variety of *Amanita* that she thought was *muscaria* and spent the next six hours lying in bed, drooling, sweating, feeling horrible, not able to talk, and then slowly came back to life.

In the '70s, Dr. Andrew Weil wrote for the *Journal of Psychedelic Drugs,* published by the University of Michigan. He wrote a series of letters about mushrooming which later appeared in his book, *The Marriage of the Sun and the Moon.* I had read the letters and liked the way he talked about mushrooms. He was familiar with the writings in the '50s of Gordon Wasson, who had written about Soma and magic mushrooms.

I wrote to Andy Weil and told him about my experience. He had been one of my mushroom heroes for years. He wrote back, telling me that the true *Amanita muscaria*— a beautiful blood-red color with white specks—did not grow east of the Rocky Mountains, but there were some look-alikes.

We emptied our big chest freezer, which was filled with the orange-red mushrooms, and watched them defrost. We had also been drying the *Amanitas* in our oven. As they dried, the smell was making a number of our commune members sick. I came to the conclusion that the *Amanita muscaria* or magic mushroom did not grow in eastern North America, and if it did, I didn't want to have anything to do with it except to admire its beauty.

As the years passed, I learned more about mushrooms by attending lectures, conferences, teaching, and spending time in the woods picking. I became one of the "experts" in my state, receiving phone calls from poison centers at hospitals, from strangers whose children were found with half a mushroom in their hand and the other half in their mouth, or perhaps already chewed up and swallowed.

People called, asking me to help them identify mushrooms over the phone. I had to say, "I am unable to identify over the phone—I need to see the mushroom." Coming home, I would find, on my back porch, paper bags filled with mushrooms and notes with names and phone numbers asking me, "Which are the good ones?"

For fifteen years, I taught mycology and history at a small community college in Vermont and was a cofounder of the Vermont Mycology Association. I spend hours walking, climbing, and crawling in the woods near my home in search of mushrooms. Wherever I go, my eyes are scanning the ground, tree trunks, old firewood, in search of fungi. I have spotted mushrooms growing out of cracks in the sidewalks of New York City, in basements of friends' homes, around edges of bathtubs, and in the middle of gravel roads.

A bird-watcher friend once said, "Roz spots mushrooms the same way we see birds." Mushroom clubs, societies, associations, and local groups throughout the world present events, fairs, conferences, lectures, gatherings, forays, and dinners where mycologists gather to share information and to go into the woods to pick, to identify, to cook, and to eat mushrooms.

In 1975, a group of mycologists—including Gary Lincoff, author of the Audubon mushroom book and mycologist at the Bronx Botanical Gardens; Dr. Andy Weil, the now-famous author and lecturer; Dr. Manny Salzman, a well-known medical doctor with a specialization in mushroom poisoning; Dr. Alexander Smith, the author of my first mushroom book-organized a conference on identifying poisonous mushrooms, held in Aspen, Colorado.

A conflict occurred between those interested in all mushrooms, including psychedelic mushrooms, and those who wanted to exclude psychedelic mushrooms. They split into two groups. The group that wanted to include psychedelic mushrooms was excluded from the conference the following year, so they started their own "Educational Conference on the Study and Cultivation of Wild Mushrooms," which settled 24 years ago in Telluride, Colorado. Telluride was known for being one of the most beautiful mountain towns having large quantities of Chanterelles, *Boletus,* and *Amanitas.* No mushroom was discriminated against, and all mushrooms were treated with equal rights.

"You are invited to attend the first potluck brunch and meeting of the Vermont Mycology Club," was the ad that ran in the events section of our local newspaper. On a warm day in May, twenty people showed up at my house, bearing various mushroom dishes. Included were creamed morels in baked puff pastry, *Bolitus edulis* (porcini) pizza, cream-of-eighteen-mushroom soup, pickled honey mushrooms, clumps of oyster mushrooms cooked in olive oil and butter, hedgehog-tooth mushroom salad, Chanterelle omelet, *Amanita caesarea* on toast, *Marasmius* toasted with pine nuts, *Agaricus* fried with chicken, puffball lasagna, juice, espresso, wine, and beer.

At the meeting, we introduced ourselves and described our relationship to the mushroom world. We signed up to take turns in leading forays into the woods during the summer and fall. After the meeting, Dennis, who commercially grew organic oyster mushrooms, said, "Roz, you need to go to the wild mushroom conference in Telluride." I liked Dennis so much that I signed up and bought my airplane ticket for the last weekend in August.

The plane landed in Telluride. Slowly I got used to the altitude and registered in the mushroom tent for the Telluride Wild Mushroom Conference. The first evening, there was a great potluck dinner and opening ceremonies. During the following three days, I attended lectures, meetings, and forays. I met people that talked my mushroom language and felt the way I did. Mushrooms and politics merged together.

Gary Lincoff, the author of the Audubon book, told me that I didn't need to know the "correct" name of a mushroom as long as I knew the mushroom. He made me feel good. I met and grew to love Joanne and Manny Salzman, founders and organizers of the conference, and became friends with their children and grandchildren. In the evenings during the conference and after the lectures, we would hang out and talk while some ate mushrooms. Year after year for the next seventeen years, I returned to Telluride to visit with my mushroom friends.

One year, we had gathered in the evening after a lecture in a suite of rooms at a condo on the first anniversary of the death of Jerry Garcia. Someone from Ben & Jerry's had donated pints of Cherry Garcia ice cream, and someone from the Evergreen area of Washington had brought hot fudge sauce. It was delicious, we ate and ate, talked and talked.

At some point, I realized that someone was talking and no words were coming out of his mouth, and his spine began to melt. It turned out that the hot fudge sauce had bits of chopped-up psychoactive mushrooms in it, and I had overeaten. My friend from Ben

& Jerry's had left, and I was alone with a roomful of people. Someone said, "I know why he left. He left because our ice cream is better than his."

I wanted to leave but did not know how to. I opened the door of the condo and looked down the long white hall with too many doors. I had no idea how to get to the street or which way was up and which way was down. I closed the door. People wanted to talk to me. I didn't want to talk. I just wanted to go home to my little room at the Oak Street Inn at the other end of the same street. I kept asking folks if they would walk me out of the building so I could get to the street where I thought I would be able to walk home.

After what seemed like a long time, two sisters were leaving to walk their father, a doctor, home, and they agreed to help me. I followed them through a maze of halls, down a set of stairs, to the outside of the condo. Once outside, I found myself inside a fractal. I was in the midst of various color beams of light crystals which shot down from the heavens and surrounded me. I had no idea how to walk, and the street was gone.

One of the sisters took my arm, while the other sister took her father's arm, and we walked down the street about five blocks or so, toward my room. We passed a policeman sitting in his parked car in the elementary-school parking lot. I got that "There's-a-cop" rush. One of the sisters said, "It's okay, just keep walking," and I did. About a block from my room, I must have been making sounds of gagging, and I heard a sister say, "It's okay, just throw up." I had no idea I was feeling bad, but I threw up at the curb and felt much better.

Arriving at my room, one of the sisters took my key to unlock the door, as I did not know how to use a key. I sat down on my bed. The bathroom was across the hall, and I asked for a bottle to be filled up with water and for the wastebasket to be brought close to the bed in case I got sick. The Oak Street Inn had the cheapest rooms in town. In the old days, it was a youth hostel with shared girl-and-boy bathrooms in the hall and a common TV room.

Besides being cheap, I liked it because it was the closest hotel to the mushroom tent. The mushroom tent was a gathering place where, during the day, folks met to identify the mushrooms they had found on forays. There were workshops on how to identify poisonous and edibles, how to use mushrooms for dyeing wool and making mushroom paper, and the potluck dinner was held there.

My hiking boots were tied with a double knot. I tried to untie a boot but could not understand how a knot worked. As I pulled at it, one of the sisters said, "It's okay, I'll do it." I said, "No, just cut it off." She untied my boots and asked if there was anything else I wanted or needed before she left. I thanked her and said goodnight.

Finally alone, with my door locked, I was safe in my room. I put on my long white cotton nightgown, laid back on the bed and looked around. My safe harbor turned out to be an ugly small room with whitish, yellowed walls of a smooth lumpy stucco type of material. I had never really looked at the walls before. The walls were breathing, each pore slowly moving and pulsating. I began to see the walls for the first time, amazingly clear, so beautiful. Native American patterns began to merge with East Indian dancers who had appeared, and they melted into each other.

I watched for a while until I decided that I needed to capture the beauty. I took out my Sony minidigital video camera and began to shoot the living, breathing wall. My history of documentary filmmaking took over. It was important to capture what I was seeing. The evening was long, and I wanted to remember by recording all that I saw. As I shot the wall and panned to the right, I captured my reflection in the mirror, me in my long white nightgown, holding my video camera.

I began to talk quietly, describing what I was seeing. I videotaped the walls so I would remember. It was late, I was tired, and I turned off the video camera and the lights. I lay down on the bed, listening to the sounds of the bars closing on Main Street, the drunks in the alley, and the workers throwing out the trash, as I retreated into mushroom dreams and finally slept, feeling safe, knowing that I had the mini-digital video of my mind.

Later, when I returned home and showed the tape to my friends, we all laughed at my footage of blank stucco walls.

Pilgrimage to Palenque / Bill Weinberg

February 1983. Magic mushrooms at Palenque. My first time in Mexico. I hardly spoke a syllable of Spanish. I couldn't have told you the name of the president of Mexico. I couldn't even have told you that I was in the state of Chiapas, where there is now a revolution going on. I couldn't have told you that I was on the northern edge of the Lacandon rain forest. I was just a hippie vagabond down there to take mushrooms with Lauren K., and running, once again, from a broken heart.

There was a wistful tone to this ecstasy, because we were out of money, and Lauren (who had subsisted on a lifetime of bland New England food) was starting to get sick, and after one exquisite day tripping on the ruins, we would have to turn around and head north. But what a day. Bathed in sunlight, melting into the jungle, gazing at these strangely beautiful but mysterious and alien structures, and wondering . . . what kind of intelligence built this?

I knew, instinctively, that I had eaten the same mushrooms which had been used ritually at this ceremonial center a thousand years ago. We went down into the dark, cool belly of the pyramid, and I saw the same sarcophagus lid which had intrigued me as a kid in Queens when I read Von Daniken's *Chariots of the Gods*.

We went into the smaller temples, and I wondered what rituals and ecstasies had taken place there. I was entranced all the more because I didn't understand anything that I was looking at; the beauty that transfixed me was incomprehensible. And I knew then that I would have to come back. I would have to study these strange, intricate rock-carved symbols and know something of what they were meant to communicate, know something of the culture which had left this behind. The vision of that afternoon haunted me for two years before I made it back down there.

The following year, I started planning and saving money for my journey to Central America. Back in Chiapas in '85, I studied at the Na Bolom Library in San Cristobal de Las Casas, immersed myself in Mayan cosmology, went into the Lacandon Selva to see the remote and only semi-excavated ruins of Yaxchilan and Bonampak, and met some of the Lacandon Maya, Mexico's last unconquered, un-Christianized Indians. There were rumors of guerrillas in the jungle.

Ten years later, those rumors would be proved true, and I would travel back to that jungle to meet them. Just about everything really important that I have done with my life since then can be traced back to that afternoon at Palenque.

Bill Weinberg is the author of *Homage to Chiapas: The New Indigenous Struggles in Mexico.*

The Timely Tea Party / Todd McCormick

One cold and rainy night in Amsterdam, my friend phoned to invite me to a party at a night club called Mistair 2000. He told me that there was going to be a celebration of the passing of the new law.

"What law is that?" I asked.

"The Dutch government had just declared psilocybin an ecodrug. Magic mushroom stores are popping up all over the city. Tripping on 'shrooms is completely legal!"

At first, I couldn't believe my ears. Having grown up in America, where so many good things are banned, I was suddenly feeling so good realizing that I had yet another free-dom to explore. I mean, really, to be able to walk in the store and pick up a new book, some incense, and when the clerk asks the age-old question while you are checking out—"Can I get you anything else?"—you reply, "Yes, I'd like an ounce of Liberty Caps." Only to be asked, "Fresh or dried?" Does this sound like utopia or what?

I accepted my friend's invitation without hesitation. He told me they would be serv-ing potent tea, so I would not need to bring anything to get high with. I interpreted this as meaning I would only need nine or ten grams of my favorite Kali Mist, and about the same amount of Afghan hash.

Nights out in Amsterdam can easily last into the next day. Most clubs don't close until 5 a.m., and then there is always somewhere else to go. I have literally walked into a club in daylight at around 10:30 p.m. (the city is so far north that summer sunsets happen quite late) and left at 5:30 a.m., only to walk back out into sunlight. That was weird.

After a short bicycle ride, I met up with a friend. We locked our bikes and went inside. Upon entering, we couldn't help but notice the beautiful and well-lit bar. But, unlike a typical bar, this one served no alcohol. Instead, it served herbal mixes and energy drinks. We walked past the bar and sat at a table. The atmosphere was very laid back and relaxed. People were talking to people at other tables, laughing, and openly rolling joints. After all, this was Amsterdam.

Right away, we were brought two glass mugs and a pitcher of tea, and told to sip carefully after the first cup. As I looked around for a familiar face, I noticed every table had a pitcher of tea. That's when I realized how wild it was going to become when the high from the psilocybin kicked in. I poured each of us a cup, and we toasted to freedom. It didn't take long to feel the laughter creep up on us. Suddenly it seemed that everyone was laughing. The only sound I could hear was happiness. After that first wave hit us, the entire place began to chill out.

There were a few chuckles here and there when someone shouted, "How could this stuff have ever been illegal?" At which point we all began laughing at the absurdity of prohibiting something that caused us to feel this great.

After that wore off, some folks took to the center of the room with djambys and assorted instruments and began to play a very tribal-sounding rhythm. I swear the beat of the music increased my high. Everyone seemed to get pulled to their feet and began to dance. You just had to move. The moment was simply too strong to resist.

The music put us off onto the perfect vibration for the orgy of conversation that followed. It felt like everybody got to talk to everybody else, and the conversations were all so profound. I have no idea how much tea I drank, but I do remember the pitcher being refilled multiple times. The evening turned into a long song, every note a little more perfect.

Sometime in the night we became hungry, so we went to find food. Still tripping and trying to eat, we ended up in a cafe in the middle of the city. Everything I tried felt so spongy, I realized I was still way too high to eat. I have no idea how I made it home, or when, for that matter.

The next day I woke up, got dressed and went out, only to realize I had no idea where my bike was. I couldn't remember if I had left it at the club or in the city center. After I few phone calls, I reached my friend, who was by chance standing outside his apartment, wondering where the hell his bike was. We came to the conclusion that our bikes must still be at Mistair 2000. When we met there, we decided to go to a mushroom store and see what was available. He told me the store was in the gay district, which I thought was a wholly appropriate place to eat happy food.

When we arrived, I was amazed at how modern a place it was, as well as how many different types of fungi there were to choose from. We ended up getting a couple of ounces of some strain we had never tried, as well as a closet grow-kit that we were told would produce two ounces twice within a month. At twenty-five guilders, it seemed like a bargain we couldn't refuse.

Everything seemed to change completely in the world of mushrooms back in the winter of 1996 in Holland. It still seems so weird that I'm back in America and surrounded by ignorant law makers. When, I wonder, will Americans come around to demand such simple freedoms?

Since then, I've heard that Holland changed the laws and has disallowed the sale of dried mushrooms. You now have to buy them fresh or grow them yourself, then dry them. Which is a rule that is easy to live with.

Todd McCormick served five years in federal prison for growing marijuana. Like Ed Rosenthal and the late Peter McWilliams, he was not permitted to testify that it was intended for medical purposes at cannabis clubs that are legal under California state law.

Psilocybin with the Poets / Ken Weaver

In 1966, Ed Sanders suggested we go to Gloucester to visit Charles Olson. I jumped at the chance to meet the Lord of Projective Verse, Maximus of Gloucester, and to travel north of Fourteenth Street for the first time in a year. So we flew up. Olson obviously held the belief that "a man's home is his landfill"—his was filled with drifts of manuscripts and books—a variation on the theme of decor by the Brothers Collier.

After Ed introduced us, Charles suggested we go to one of his favorite restaurants for dinner and then proceed on to Panna Grady's house, where we were all to spend the night. We settled in at our table and listened, enraptured, to Olson holding forth on a variety of subjects. He discussed a local seafood dish—muddled cod's head—which was not available, so he settled for haunch of manatee or something equally filling.

I grew up on the Gulf of Mexico, and we compared notes on the similarities of coastal people. I felt that the mellow weather of the Texas gulf coast made my peers more laid back than the Northeast variety, except for Saturday nights, when they sometimes shared a talent for knife-fighting and other bar-room brawling techniques.

I treated my cholesterol deficiency with steak, rare, and Ed ate his usual vegan fare, muttering, "Sin, sin," through his drooping gunfighter mustache at us filthy Scythian flesh-eaters. Ed was a strict vegetarian and used to dine, in his Peace Eye Bookstore and Scrounge Lounge, on strange concoctions of canned mushrooms and garbanzos, right out of the can, au chambre. These dishes had little nutritional value, but on the positive karmic side of the account, no sentient beings higher than fungi and legumes had to die that Ed might live.

My motto was "Kill 'em and eat 'em," and occasionally I'd come in with deep-fried pig ears, a toothsome Puerto Rican delicacy, just to disgust Ed, particularly when they still sported clusters of deep-fried bristles. I would pretend to use the bristles as organic toothpicks and would munch away to the sound of Ed gently moaning and retching.

So after dinner we repaired back to Olson's where I broke out my Jack Daniels sipping whiskey (which we did not sip) for postprandial chugs and to put a touch of fire to the ass of the evening and get things cranked up. We drank while Ed and Olson talked about deep (to me) shit: Hesiod and other poets, history, poetics, projective verse.

We were getting lit up quite nicely when Olson (a huge man, as big as Howlin' Wolf, six foot seven, a Kodiak bear with a neatly knotted samurai queue) lumbered over to his refrigerator, plucked out a small bottle of clear liquid and offered it. "LSD?" We assumed he wanted us all to take a shot of it, like liquor. One drop would have been an immeasurable dose of acid, but the mood of the evening, and the times, was such that it was tempting to take a shot and wash it down with Black Jack. It would have been like diving into the Abyss Uncharted.

By 1966, I had quit counting acid trips and never cared how many micrograms I took, as was the wont of some of the more clinical psychedilettanti. I recalled visiting the loft of a guitar-maker friend of Steve Weber (who, along with Peter Stampfel, were the Holy Modal Rounders) in 1965, before LSD had been criminalized. No one was home, and the door was unlocked. We went in and found a couple of cookie trays filled with sugar cubes fused together into solid rectangles of sugar, a couple of square feet each.

The narcs had come in and found the sugar cubes, each dosed with a drop of acid. They poured water into the trays to dilute the acid. By the time we arrived, the stuff had dried and hardened, so we took it with us into the streets, munching great chunks of the Sweet Absolute Elsewhere and handing out pieces to anybody who wanted any. By the time it had all been disposed of, we were getting messages from sidewalk cracks, like Trashman comics.

But here in Gloucester, not wishing to dive into brainmelt just yet, we demurred. Olson turned back to his well-stocked larder and brought out a bottle of what looked like small orange M&Ms. The name Sandoz was printed on each and every piece of goody. Well, now. Pure lab psilocybin.

I had first read about psilocybin in, of all places, the *Reader's Digest*, when I was twelve years old. The story had been written by a couple of scientists who had taken the mushrooms in a hut in Mexico. The hut had been transformed into a "cave of diamonds," and it seemed that the scientists had enjoyed themselves immensely. So the twelve-year-old me wrote the word "psilocybin" down on a scrap of paper and tucked it into a corner of my Roy Rogers billfold. If I ever met anyone who had some, the paper would remind me, and I would take it.

So Olson counted out a dozen of them for each of us. We knocked them back, and Jack Daniels chased them home. We talked, waiting. A few minutes passed, and the psilocybin hit both Ed and Charles simultaneously. They beamed down at me from up behind the ceiling light, floating up there like a couple of Oobies (Out of Bodies). I still awaited my chemical epiphany, so Charles said, "Well, you're a big boy; have a few more," dumping five more caplets into my hand. I took them and waited to join them in psilospace.

In accordance with our plan, we got ready to go to Panna Grady's house. We piled into Olson's car, a beat white 1956 Chevy station wagon, and began driving over, Charles at the wheel. I was riding shotgun and still feeling no effects from the psilocybin. Ed had the back seat to himself. Charles was fully loaded and was driving slowly, slowly. I looked at the speedometer and could see that we were oozing along at a smooth four miles per hour.

Traffic was stacking up behind us, and our followers were furious, honking their horns, waving their fists in a demonstration of proto–road rage. "Fucking Nazis," Olson shouted back at them. Ed, in the full grip of mushroom analog, thought Olson was Poseidon and that the Nazis were real, perhaps members of the notorious SS "Fiancees of Death," and curled up on the back floorboard, screaming in paranoid terror.

We turned off on a side street, and the helldrivers went their way. We passed a formation of large gray boulders which delighted Olson, who stopped to ogle. "Look at the elephants!" More cars passed us, horns honking, drivers hollering. I was still not high and glad of it.

We crawled along and I saw a traffic sign bearing the warning, Dear Child. Neither Charles nor Ed saw this one, and I implemented the "need-to-know" rule and said nothing to them. If they had seen this one, we would have been there all night, weeping and calling for the poor kid, searching the woods.

Somehow we found the house. The instant Olson switched off the ignition and we were safely there, the psilocybin enveloped me—all of it—and I was sharing the Absolute Elsewhere with Charles and Ed. We crawled out of the car and made it to the front door. Olson fished the house key out of his pocket, but there was no keyhole. Somehow, under the influence, I knew to flip up a piece of the wrought ironwork on the door, and there was the keyhole.

We achieved ingress. Ed and Charles talked unraveledly for a bit, and then Ed careened out the door, into the darkness, for a walkabout in the forest. Charles and I drank more whiskey and talked—not about Hesiod, but about the raw and violence—driven peculiarities of Texas redneck speech.

Charles sat down at the dining-room table and began writing. I watched tiny comets and solar flares shoot out of his head. Ed, hollering in the woods outside, provided a loony counterpoint to the quiet of the house. I wandered around the house, went into the bathroom and pissed a rainbow. I talked tenderly to my dick—I was calling him "Vlad the Impaler" in those days.

I found an abalone shell and wept like a maudlin drunk at the beauty of it. The house became the Temple of Poignance and was filled with delicious sadness. I drank some more whiskey, but could no longer feel any effect from alcohol. There was a well-stocked liquor cabinet, and I thought about drinking everything in it, but Charles advised that this might not be such a good idea. Somehow he knew that our brainpans had reached their elastic limits.

I wandered about the house some more, stepping into my old friend the bathroom again. Mayan ticker tape passed silently across the bathtub floor. I went into the kitchen and looked in the refrigerator. There was a science-fiction movie inside, things shifting and flowing suspiciously, but only in my peripheral vision. Snoid City.

Time noodled by in a pleasant blur, and late in the night someone pounded at the door. We opened the door and there was Ed, with night-vision pupils, leaves in his hair, accompanied by a puzzled local constable. "I, uh, found this guy out there. He seems to be a little confused. Is he with you?"

We told the officer that, yes indeed, Ed was with us, and that he'd probably had a bit too much to drink just leave 'im here and we'll take care of him thank you and good night. The young cop seemed satisfied with this thin explanation, but seemed not to know whether he should leave or investigate us further. It was, remember, only 1966, and the Freak Juggernaut had not accelerated to full speed.

The young cop had probably been born here, graduated from high school here, and simply and decently migrated into the local police force. Now he finds this raving maniac in the woods wearing a red vinyl vest, red pants and shirt, red everything, looking like the young Mark Twain, but howling in the woods with twigs in his hair, his pupils smooth obsidian discs.

After what must have been a high Dada question-and-answer session, they had found their way back to the house, only to find more bizarre life forms: Charles Olson, a white giant, his eyebrows twin ravens perched on his eyeglasses, silver samurai hair knotted in a bun, and me, in Viking drag, sans horned helmet.

The cop must have smelled the Jack Daniels and let that be all the explanation he needed, or wanted. He bolted. Ed explained that he had been transformed into an Arcadian brick maker in the forest. Perhaps the cop had found him searching for straw.

The next day, Ed and I returned to New York. I saw Olson for the last time a couple of years later in San Francisco, when Janis Joplin took me to dinner with Charles and Ed. We ate Chinese food, and later Ed, Janis, and I played pool. Janis won.

Ken Weaver was a member of The Fugs.

The Ghost of Mushrooms Yet to Come / Cat Simril Ishikawa

In the early '80s, I was living in a small city in Chiba Prefecture and working in Tokyo, an hour away by train. On winter nights, I had taken to dropping by a tiny bar near the station on my way home. A hot glass of sake made the fifteen-minute walk home a lot less chilling.

Eight thin people could squeeze into the bar. Perhaps two sumo wrestlers. It was rarely full, but when it was, the bartender sometimes brought in her sister to fill our glasses.

One day, some mushrooms arrived in the mail from their Southeast Asian point of origin. A visiting friend and I consumed them, and then began our journey to Tokyo, him to his home on the other side of the city, and me to a meeting I didn't have to attend but I decided to go anyway because it would be a pleasant trip.

The express subway from Nishi-Funabashi into the center of the city where I worked would fly across Chiba at its sunset best, with views of Mount Fuji creating postcards from my window. Then we'd plunge into Tokyo Bay and all the enjoyments of the night. A fun way to go to work, and with the mushrooms, oh, so much more so.

Funabashi is a huge train station with a city built around it. From my Chiba town and from throughout the prefecture, we streamed into Funabashi station in search of the best route into Tokyo. My friend went on his way to his chosen line, and I sought mine through the maze of stairs and railroad possibilities.

And then I saw her. She saw me, and waved. On that vast stone staircase, the ghost waved at me and called my name! In horror, I ran back to my previous train, and instead of Tokyo, I returned home, and hid under the futon.

My wife and daughter asked what I was doing.

"A ghost! A ghost! I've seen a ghost," I shrieked.

The woman from the bar. My neighbor said she was dead, but There She Was. Mushrooms opening up a hole into the universe of the dead? Fills me with dread to recall now.

My wife asked the neighbor, the source of my initial information, and he told her that the sister was only metaphorically dead, having moved to a bar in Funabashi and thus "dead" to her old fans at our bar. Not dead, just beyond my linguistic ability. The mushrooms were off the hook.

[I hope they don't sue me.] If only we all had that opportunity to move from real death to story, to metaphor, a possibility only of sprouting mushrooms, not crushing reality. I've never eaten a magic mushroom nor seen a ghost since that day. I'm not entirely sure that is a good thing.

Solo Performance / Tom

A bunch of us headed down to Charlotte for the October 5, 1984, Grateful Dead show. In the early '80s, most venues did general admission, so if you got there early enough (a few hours was usually plenty in those days), you could get the seat you wanted. We always liked the railing seats on stage left. In any arena these seats were usually just above stage level and afforded us a great view of the stage, facing the guitar players.

Anyway, we got inside and got our front-row-on-the-side railing seats, and everything was great. The first set was really good, and then came the break. We had all gotten fungicized, so when the lights came up it was a bit nerve rattling, but we settled down and got into the break and were talking about how glad we were that we weren't on the floor because it looked so crowded.

All of a sudden, about twenty feet in front of the stage, a circle started to open in the crowd. We assumed that someone threw up or some such thing, but as the circle got bigger we saw that it was a guy, on his knees with his pants pulled down around his ankles, jerking off with the biggest smile on his face we'd ever seen! He was obviously *really* tripped out and having a blissful time masturbating in front of 13,000 people.

This was very hard to handle in our condition. We basically had a front-row seat for this, and it was very weird. By this point the circle was fifty feet in diameter because no one wanted to go near this guy. He just continued on with his business. A girl I knew standing next to me said, "Why doesn't someone go out and help him?"

"Be my guest," I said.

I have no idea if he even realized where he was. The cops were laughing and wouldn't go near him. Well, he finally shot his wad to great applause, and someone threw him a bandanna, and he started wiping up the floor. Then the cops went out and got him and gently carted him off to who knows where, but he never stopped smiling.

The Day the Lampshades Breathed / Ed McClanahan

Like everybody else who lived in California during the 1960s, I went through a phase. I grew me a mustache and a big wig, and got me some granny glasses and pointy-toed elf boots and bell-bottom britches (which did not, Charles Reich, author of *The Greening of America*, to the contrary, turn my walk into "a kind of dance"; nothing could turn my walk into a kind of dance). I threw the Ching. I rocked and rolled. I ingested illicit substances. I revoluted.

But this was not my first attack of *mal de Californie*. I'd been through it all before.

By way of explanation, let me go all the way back to 1952, just long enough to say that after an uninspired freshman year at Washington and Lee, I moved on for three more uninspired years at University of Miami in Ohio, where I majored in beer and blanket parties on the golf course and published uninspired short stories in the campus lit mag. In 1955, I went to Stanford, to try my hand at creational writage in graduate school.

Stanford was too much for me. I lasted just two quarters before I received a note from the chairman of the English department inviting me to drop by to discuss my highly improbable future as a graduate student. I declined the invitation but took the hint, dropped out, and slunk back home to Kentucky to conclude a brief and embarrassingly undistinguished graduate career at the state university in Lexington. Then to Oregon, and four years of honest toil at Backwater State College, in the freshman composition line.

But California had left its mark on me. For I had gone West the blandest perambulatory tapioca pudding ever poured into a charcoal-gray suit, and I came home six months later in Levi's and cycle boots and twenty-four-hours-a-day shades and an armpit of a goatee and a hairdo that wasn't so much a duck's-ass as it was, say, a sort of cocker spaniel's-ass. I had been to San Francisco and seen the Beatniks in North Beach; I had smoked a genuine reefer; I had sat on the floor drinking cheap Chianti and listening to "City of Glass" on the hi-fi. I'd been Californified to a fare-thee-well, and I'd loved every minute of it.

So when I weaseled my way back into Stanford—and California—in the fall of 1962, via a Wallace Stegner Fellowship in creative writing, it was a case of the victim returning to the scene of the outrage, eager for more. Immediately, I sought out my old Stanford roommates, Jim Wolpman and Vic Lovell, who were now respectively a labor lawyer and a grad student in psychology, living next door to each other in a dusty, idyllic little bohemian compound called Perry Lane, just off the Stanford campus.

Among their neighbors was Ken Kesey, himself but lately down from Oregon, whose novel *One Flew over the Cuckoo's Nest* had been published just a year ago and was in fact dedicated to Vic—"Who told me dragons did not exist, then led me to their lairs"— for having arranged Ken's enrollment as a test subject in a drug-experiment program at the local VA hospital. And the neighborhood was fairly crawling with writers and artists and students and musicians and mad scientists. It was just what I was looking for: a bad crowd to fall in with. I moved in a couple of blocks down the street and started my mustache.

In a lot of ways, it was the same old California. We still sat on the floor and drank cheap Chianti, though now we listened to Sandy Bull and called the hi-fi a stereo, and the atmosphere was often murky with the sickly-sweet blue smaze of the dread devil's-weed. The manner we'd cultivated back in the '50s was sullen, brooding, withdrawn but volatile, dangerous—if not to others, then at the very least to ourselves. Its models were Elvis, James Dean, Marlon Brando in *The Wild One*. The idea was to seem at once murderous, suicidal . . . and sensitive.

Locally, our hero in those days had been, improbably enough, the president of the Stanford student-body government, George Ralph, who'd campaigned in sideburns and *Wild One* leathers, behind the sneering slogan, "I Hate Cops." George's campaign was a put-on, of course—between those sideburns was a dyed-in-the-wool Stevenson Democrat—but he had the style down cold, and he beat the cashmere socks off the poor fraternity row creampuff who opposed him.

But six years can wreak a lot of changes, and by 1962 the future was already happening again on Perry Lane. "We pioneered," Vic was to write years later, with becoming modesty, "what have since become the hallmarks of hippie culture: LSD and other psychedelics too numerous to mention, body painting, light shows and mixed-media presentations, total aestheticism, be-ins, exotic costumes, strobe lights, sexual mayhem, freakouts and the deification of psychoticism, Eastern mysticism, and the rebirth of hair."

Oh, they wanted to maintain their cool, these pioneers, they wanted to go on being or seeming aloof and cynical and hip and antisocial, but they just couldn't keep a straight face. They were like new lovers, or newly expectant mothers; they had this big, wonderful secret, and their idiot grins kept giving it away. They were the sweetest, smartest, liveliest, craziest bad crowd I'd ever had the good fortune to fall in with. And their great secret was simply this: They knew how to change the world.

Think of it this way," my Perry Lane friend Peter, who never drew an unstoned breath, once countered when I mentioned that my TV was on the fritz: "Your TV's all right. But you've been lookin' at it wrong, man, you've been bum-trippin' your own TV set!"

For a while there, it almost seemed as if it might really be that easy. The way to change the world was just to start looking at it right, to stop bumming it out (ah, we could turn a phrase in those days!), and start grooving on it—to scarf down a little something from the psychedelicatessen and settle back and watch the world do its ineluctable thing. Gratified by the attention, the world would spring to life and cheerfully reveal its deepest mysteries. The commonplace world would become marvelous; you could take the pulse of a rock, listen to the heartbeat of a tree, feel the hot breath of a butterfly against your cheek. ("So I took this pill," said another friend, reporting back after his first visit to the Lane, "and a little later I was lying on the couch, when I noticed that the lampshade had begun to breathe . . .")

It was a time of what now seems astonishing innocence, before Watergate or Woodstock or Vietnam or Charles Manson or the Summer of Love or Groovy and Linda or the Long Hot Summer or even, for a while, Lee Harvey Oswald—a time when wonder was the order of the day. One noticed one's friends (not to mention oneself) saying "Oh wow!" with almost reflexive frequency; and the cry that was to become the "Excelsior!" of the day-glo decade, the ecstatic, ubiquitous "Far out!" rang oft upon the air.

The first time I ever felt entitled to employ that rallying cry was on Thanksgiving of 1962. That evening, after a huge communal Thanksgiving feast at the Kesey's, Ken led me to his medicine cabinet, made a selection, and said matter-of-factly, "Here, take this, we're going to the movies." A scant few minutes later, he and I and three or four other lunatics were sitting way down front in a crowded Palo Alto theater, and the opening credits of *West Side Story* were disintegrating before my eyes. "This is . . . CINERAMA!" roared the voice-over inside my head as I cringed in my seat. And though I stared almost unblinking at the screen for the next two hours and thirty-five minutes, I never saw a coherent moment of the movie.

What I saw was a ceaseless barrage of guns, knives, policemen, and lurid gouts of eyeball-searing color, accompanied by an ear-splitting, cacophonous din, throughout which I sat transfixed with terror—perfectly immobile, the others told me afterward; stark, staring immobile, petrified, trepanned, stricken by the certainty, the absolute *certainty,* that in one more instant the authorities would be arriving to seize me and drag me up the aisle and off to the nearest madhouse. It was the distillation of all the fear I'd ever known, fear without tangible reason or cause or occasion, pure, unadulterated, abject fear itself, and for one hundred and fifty-five awful minutes it invaded me to the very follicles of my mustache.

Then, suddenly and miraculously, like a beacon in the *Dark Night of the Soul,* the words "The End" shimmered before me on the screen. Relief swept over me sweet as a zephyr. I was delivered. The curtain closed, the lights came up. I felt grand, exuberant, triumphant—as if I'd just ridden a Brahman bull instead of a little old tab of psilocybin. If they'd turned off the lights again, I'd have glowed in the dark. Beside me, Ken stood up and stretched.

"So how was it?" he inquired, grinning.

"Oh wow!" I croaked joyfully. "It was fa-a-ar out!"

And in that instant, for me, the '60s began. Characteristically, I was about two years late getting out of the gate, but I was off at last.

Ed McClanahan is the editor of *Spit in the Ocean #7: All about Kesey.*

stickin with the natural / original okie

This story is set in the mid to late '80s we lived in a kinda bad neighborhood and our place got the nickname of the animal house see we used to have some pretty wild parties and invariably someone would usually get drunk and start a fight says a lot for the legal drug of choice alcohol doesn't it well anyway I don't know if we got the nickname from that or from the fact my mom usually kept four or five dogs in the house no matter how much we bitched anyway we were all sitting around gettin high and our stash was just about out so when these guys showed up carrying a brown paper sack we thought alright some more weed well turns out the sack was full of shrooms they ask if we want to do some with them and being young crazy and fearless we say sure dude anything for a high so we eat a few well i'm here to tell you it was a great high slightly psychedelic ya dig my brother showed me that you could put your hand close to the wall and see a sort of aura around its shadow cool but if you rotated your hand the aura would change colors green yellow etc super cool i watched the grass that was cut to within a half an inch of the ground it looked like it was four inches tall and waving in the wind of course there was no wind blowing either well anyway by this time we had run out of shrooms so this guy says you want to go with me to pick some more hell yes we do so we sneak into this feedlot in between this bar and this farmers house and fill up three laundry baskets full of shrooms man you should have seen the eyes light up when we got back so after two or three days of no sleep and eating shrooms we are all sitting on the front porch laughing like hyenas and what happens some uptight prick of a neighbor calls the cops on us for disturbing the peace well the cop shows up and usually i can maintain in this kind of situation but this time i cant quit laughing well the cop gives us the talk you know neighbors called in we're disturbin the peace so we gotta quiet down or he'll be forced to arrest us well let me tell you bro we didn't quiet down i mean we just couldn't quit laughin and by the time the cop left still telling us to quiet down he was bustin a gut so bad he had tears rollin down his cheeks and i was afraid he wasn't even going to be able to drive so i always say stick with weed and shrooms ya dig go natural it's the best stay free and stay high y'all come back now ya hear

Laughing Fit / Stacy Stapp

It was April 20 and some friends and I decided to get some mushrooms to celebrate the occasion. Our friend Ron said his mom was going away for the night and we could hang there.

So the five of us put our money together and got a fat baggie, along with an ounce of good green. We decided to make tea with most of it and leave the rest to munch on throughout the night.

So we drank the tea and started feeling fine, when all of a sudden there was a loud knock at the door. We were sure it was the cops coming to take our dope. Being very stoned and with the tea quickly giving me a buzz, I did the only logical thing I could think of and ate the rest of the 'shrooms on the table.

Ron opened the front door and it wasn't the police, it was his mother. She had forgotten her house keys and came to get them. She knew we were going to be hanging out there, and she knew we smoked pot—but that was all she knew—so she wasn't surprised to see us all there with big smiles on our faces. I got a bit nauseated from all the 'shrooms I had just scarfed and stood up to get some air.

I never made it outside, though, because I started laughing hysterically. Ron's mom said something like, "Must be some good stuff." My vision was jumping all around and I just sat back down. All of a sudden we heard a scream. Our friend Matt, who had been sitting on the floor, was now half-sitting, half-standing, with the palm of his hand pressed on the floor. His hand just sunk in the ground. That just threw me into another laughing fit.

Luckily, Ron's mom was already in her room looking for her keys when that outburst occurred. She found them and left, saying we were very weird. Once she was gone, my friends all started yelling at me for eating all the 'shrooms. Little did I know that I had a giant stem stuck in the gap between my two front teeth the entire time.

I don't remember much after that, seeing as the rest of the 'shrooms started kicking in around that time, but I do know, from what I was told, that it took them fifteen minutes to get Matt's hand off the floor.

Fuzzy / Pat Mormino

Me, I'm a tripper. I love trippin' on acid. Me and two of my other friends were getting drunk one night, and we decided we needed some dank nugs. My friend called up a friend of his to see if he had any. I was buzzin' off of the alchy when I heard him say to his friend, "You're selling 'shrooms?" I had never done 'shrooms before, and I was highly eager to try them.

We only had an eighth of 'shrooms among four people (my brother being the fourth). We put a few caps on saltines with peanut butter and ate them. Me and my friend were feeling the 'shrooms, but my brother and other friend kept saying they weren't feeling shit, and it was really bringing down my trip.

It was a really weird trip. I felt really happy and scared at the same time. One thought that kept entering my mind was that if my room lit up on fire I wouldn't have the coordination to put it out. We were watching *Natural Born Killers* and I kept thinking that 'cause I was watching it while tripping, I would be brainwashed into becoming a killer.

Everything was fuzzy, the walls were breathing, my body was tired, but my head was wide awake, and there was a lot of fucked-up shit. We had a little bit left and I thought, "This is a nice trip, but it's not that hard." I love trippin' hard, so I ate a little more.

Now, it wasn't like I ate the whole eighth, I only ate like two-fifths of that bag, and I still had some left.

My friends were yelling at me, like, "You're gonna OD. Why'd you do that?" And whenever I'd say, "You guys are fucking morons, I ate such a little amount," they would retaliate with, "Yeah, that's what people say before they OD." It really pissed me off and ruined my trip. I actually wasn't trippin' that hard, but it was a fun trip. I'd definitely take 'shrooms again if the chance rolled along.

The Honeymooners to the Rescue / Eliezer Sobel

One day I had the brilliant idea to take mushrooms in my New York City apartment. Realizing I was God, I proceeded to empty the contents of my medicine chest into a wastepaper basket, declaring aloud to my bewildered cat, Zorba, "God does not need ointments and creams. God, the All-Powerful Creator of the very heads which might ache, does not need aspirin."

Later that day, my miserable girlfriend Greenbaum helped me retrieve all the stuff from the garbage, and I reluctantly replaced them in the cabinet. From that moment on, however, I silently chastised myself if I so much as applied some Vaseline to a chapped lip, for it meant I was buying into a vision of myself as merely human, a denial of the God-Realized state that appeared self-evident on mushrooms. My creams and ointments were blasphemy in the face of the Divine.

There was more to the trip: I turned the radio on and heard a news broadcast about an event occurring in Poland, and there was mention of "men with bayonets."

"Do you mean to tell me," I asked Zorba, "that as I sit around, comfortable in my little apartment, having a psychological crisis about a crummy tube of chapstick, that there are actually men with bayonets in Poland pointing them at other men without bayonets?"

"That's precisely what I mean," Zorba meowed.

I suddenly understood the meaning of the word "duty," and felt myself called into action. I would travel overseas, become a missionary, sneak up behind the men with bayonets and trip them. Teach naked black people about Christ, impoverished Indian farmers how to make Rice-Krispie marshmallow treats. I began contemplating a nationwide bake sale to raise funds.

There was no time to lose, and I started dashing around the apartment, frantically, madly throwing clothes around, emptying drawers. What would one take on a mission of this sort, on such short notice? I finally decided to bring nothing at all apart from what I had on, which happened to be turquoise drawstring pants, a purple shirt, a bright green wool hat and plaid scarf, a Mexican poncho, and some sneakers.

I exited the apartment, headed for India. In all the excitement, I forgot about Poland. First I had to say goodbye to Greenbaum, and so I got in my car to head uptown to her place. This was a major error in judgment.

As I drove up Third Avenue, life suddenly began appearing to my consciousness and perception as simply a meaningless collection of noises, pictures, energies, and colors, materializing for no reason in the middle of nowhere. It seemed to me that were I to run over a pedestrian, it would have as little consequence as stepping on a leaf. It wouldn't be killing anyone, it would simply be moving energy around, squeezing it out of the little container and letting it float around in the big one, like wind.

Then it occurred to me that this would apply to myself as well, and I scared myself with the thought of blowing my own brains out. Fortunately, I was now parked in front of Greenbaum's apartment, and I managed to buzz her, and she came down and sat in the car while I sobbed, telling her, "I killed myself. I'm already dead, and I can't come back."

"No," she said wisely, "you're on a drug, and you will come down from this experience."

"No," I replied, "I know I'm on a drug and will come down. But I'm also already dead."

(Looking back now, I realize I was experiencing the shock that my consciousness was already spirit, and that this would remain true in life and death, on mushrooms or not. I just didn't have the vocabulary for that experience, which left room for only terror instead of awe.)

Greenbaum escorted me upstairs, spoon-fed me miso soup and insisted that I watch an episode of *The Honeymooners*. This was a good move, although I took the show very seriously.

"Ed Norton is my living spiritual master," I told her. "Ralph Kramden is the Antichrist. Alice and Trixie are angels. I am restored by this visitation."

Eliezer Sobel is the editor of *Wild Heart Journal*.

Embarrassing Moments / anonymous

I had some mushrooms on hand and spent several weeks reading psychedelic literature to prepare myself for what could happen. I took all the advice to heart about "set and setting." A veteran of countless trips, good and bad, I felt as if there was nothing that could arise which I couldn't handle. And if worse came to worse, I had some Xanax on hand which would sedate me.

I prepared a cozy, safe space in our meditation room—I had blankets, food, and water, soft Zen music and a candlelit altar. I was alone, but knew my wife would be returning within two hours or so, and she knew of my plans. Everything seemed ideal for jour-neying in the solo warrior tradition of Terence McKenna.

The trip began gently, and I experienced floating on a magic carpet, as the ceiling of the room opened up to an infinite expanse of space and stars. I lay down with eyes closed and saw the familiar and colorful interior fractal visions. At one point I was feeling some-thing incredibly painful digging into my side, and I was wishing it would go away.

Then I realized I was using this powerful electric massager we have—the Thumper—and all I had to do was turn the machine off and take my hand away. The realization that I had been hurting myself and could just stop was hilarious to me. But then there came a complete *time gap*.

I don't know how or why I left my safe haven, but the next thing I remember, I was lying on our kitchen table downstairs, etching my last, dying words into the wooden table: "I'm dying, I'm sorry, I love everyone, next time I'll try to be a Bodhisattva . . ."

I then calmly walked over to the phone and did something I may never fully under-stand. I dialed 911 and informed the woman on the line that "I believe I may have overdosed on mushrooms; I can't breathe or swallow, and everything hurts." She put me on hold for a moment and then came back and said, "So what were you saying? You can't breathe?"

This enraged me, and I screamed, "You're not helping," and I hung up on her.

Then things went from bad to worse, as I found myself lying on the living-room floor, screaming at the top of my lungs in our quiet country neighborhood, but I soon rec-ognized that it was all for naught. I had entered what I would later learn is a standard tripper's hell realm, a place of Eternal Torment and Suffering, in which nobody and nothing anywhere or anytime could possibly help me.

Even if someone came, I knew they would merely be part of the problem. I was in hell and would never, ever get out. And somehow, the Nazis seemed to be part of this scenario as well. Next thing I knew, my neighbor was sitting over me, with two cops and seven guys from the rescue squad standing behind him. I vaguely heard him explain-ing to them that I was generally normal and sane.

He told me the next day that I asked the rescue people if they wanted to "fuck me in the ass" and that I had my finger up my butt. Apparently there were no takers. Then I asked if they would massage my feet, and he asked the cops if they wanted to do that, and they said, "No, sir, we don't."

I was in a state of delirium, wondering if there was such a thing as "another person" and touched one guy's cheeks to see if he was real. They carried me out on a stretcher, throwing up on the lawn as I went, and they put me into what I absolutely experienced as a helicopter, although I was informed the next day it had been an ambulance. But I have vivid memories of flying in an open-air plane of some sort, wondering if I had wings, looking through the cockpit, the pilot needing me to be quiet so he could land safely, and the Nazi sitting with me being very mean.

In the ER they stuck an IV in me, and I was returned to normal within an hour or two. By this time my wife had returned home just as an ambulance was leaving our premises, and the neighbor's kid informed her that I had OD'd, which to her meant I was dead. When I awoke in the hospital, she was next to me, studying for GREs.

I still can't explain all this-it has been suggested that perhaps I really did simply overdose—they were such small mushrooms, with very few caps. Based on past experience, it seemed like I hadn't taken that many. But most puzzling, I still have no idea who it was in me that chose to call 911 and bring the police to my house rather than take a Xanax, a bath, or any number of other options that might have helped.

Luckily, the police took my neighbor aside as they carried me away and told him, "We're not going to press charges—he's suffered enough already."

When I wrote this to a friend of mine, she responded with, "I think we can agree that the key point in this whole story is, 'He's suffered enough already.'"

Tea and Sympathy / Dead Joe Jones

It was a couple or eight years ago, and I was again attempting to disguise myself as normal and hold a steady job as a territorial representative for a major air freight corporation. My daily route covered most of the southern half of Arkansas and part of north Louisiana. Where, as you may or may not know, there are a lot of snakey and hairpinned roads.

During my daily travels, I repeatedly noticed a pair of small signs on the right side of the road that stated that I could find Ed's Repair if I were to take the next right and travel one and a quarter miles down the road. Well, these signs were eleven miles apart from each other along the main highway. After passing them for several months, it finally dawned on me that if I were to cut down the gravel road to Ed's Repair, I'd be able to discard eight and a half miles from my daily toil.

So, one fine morning I did just that. It was rough and dusty, and I guess that was Ed who waved to me as I passed Ed's Repair. I pass a slight curve just past Ed's and then a straight stretch with woods on the right and a pasture on the left. As I was rolling along, I glanced to the left, and just past the fence I noticed a mess of familiar looking golden brown caps scattered about over the entire field.

Contrary to saving time and mileage, I just had to stop and check it out. I didn't even have to jump the fence. I just reached through the wire and picked one and waited for the effects of oxidation to tell me what I needed to know. Seemed like mere moments passed before I detected the purple yes that told me I was holding a psilocybin mushroom.

I picked what I figured would be a good dose, about fifteen or sixteen of the little boogers, and went on my merry but scheduled way. As I was driving along, I couldn't resist knocking the cow crap off of the stem of one of the smaller ones and nibbling on it. I figured for a very mild buzz—it was, after all, only one little old mushroom.

Twenty-three miles down the road and I was starting to get that magic feeling and the colors of the world were looking just a little brighter. Six more miles and it was my first delivery stop. I got out of the van with a grin that wrapped around to the back of my head and walked into the building, thinking I can handle it. As I walked in the door, the receptionist looked up and said, "Hey, Joe." I opened my mouth and for a full thirty seconds nothing at all would come out. Then I puked. It was spectacular.

Ten minutes later I was cracking one-liners at them, letting 'em know it was the rotten chicken smell that emanated from their plant that caused the hurlage. I never let on that it was the normal gut reaction to the 'shroom. Nor did I let 'em know that in the last twenty minutes I had picked up some really nifty brain powers. The rest of the day ran fairly smooth, considering my mental state and the general meltiness of the people I had to deal with.

Needless to say, the previous was mild compared with late that evening after I had brewed the rest of the fungi into a tea that had me spending the wee hours of the night lying on the floor talking to dead people while blood oozed from my forehead. It was great.

Never been sure what to think about this one. With your permission, I would like to ask you to walk with me now, back in time. Fall of '73 or spring of '74. Location, an old house on Irving Place we (or just Lucy, I think) had dubbed the House of Madness in that way that we have of chronically naming everything under and including the sun.

It's a Friday afternoon. Actually what we call evening around here. Earlier in the day we had been out patty scouting and had managed to fill two grocery sacks with our favorite pasture product. The better part of the third paper gang were hanging in the kitchen plotting out our collective evening. The majority vote was to go out to some friends' place where they were to have a band playing. I chose to hang at the house and sample the fungi.

As everyone else was preparing their outing, I selected a baker's dozen of the more delectable looking 'shrooms and put them on to boil down for tea. I drank my tea and everyone else left for the evening.

I sat in the quiet of the living room and read some book or another until the words started to get a little squiggly, and I knew that the alkaloids in the mushrooms had made contact with my brain. I decided to go upstairs and listen to some tunes on the good stereo in the sunroom. I played several different things that should have set a positive tone to things but didn't.

Then I remembered this piece by Curved Air by the name of "Vivaldi." I put it on and lay back on the couch to listen. Apparently it was the very thing needed. From the opening notes I could feel a stirring. As the tune reached its crescendo I leapt onto the window sill and peered out into the darkness.

Then, leaning out too far, I, I, I—well, instead of falling—I spread my wings and coasted to a branch across the back yard. I observed the scene around me and noticed that there were no small rodents visible anywhere within 360 degrees of my current location. I did what any predatory bird would do, I flew off in search of live food. Found it, too. Seems like that was all I did for the next sixty hours.

When I flew back to my nest for a rest, I tucked my head under a wing and closed my eyes, only to wake hunkered down in a corner of the sofa. I looked out the window at the sunrise and thought, What a trip. I went downstairs to the kitchen, and Butler asked, "Where have you been?"

"Upstairs on the couch," I said.

"Bullshit," was his response. To which he added, "We have been looking for you high and low ever since Saturday morning."

"Say what? *This* is Saturday morning."

"No, Joe, this is *Monday* morning," Butler said.

"You're joking, you've got to be."

"No. Look at the date on this morning's paper."

I did, and sure enough it was a Monday morning paper.

Now, close to a quarter of a century later, I still wonder, did I actually turn into a bird for two days or were my friends just fucking with my head after a mighty powerful dose? The practical realist side of me says my friends were just fucking with me and I was just blown out on the sofa for the duration. The lazy minded fool in me continues to think that for sixty glorious hours I actually was a free flying predatory bird.

Extra Ranch / Mary Mistretta

Last May, three of my buddies and I took a trip down to Myrtle Beach, South Carolina, for a couple of days. After losing our keys on the first morning, we couldn't drive anywhere until my keys got FedExed, which really sucked for the girl with the badly sprained ankle. It turned into the big joke of the trip, everyone saying they wouldn't give the keys back till it's time to leave. Something bad had to happen, and thank the Lord it was just a mysterious disappearance of keys. It wouldn't be us if shit like this didn't happen.

Since we had to walk everywhere, we were strolling the strip looking for some munchies. We found this really nice place. It sat right over the ocean and had an amazing view. So we had dinner there and went back to our room. The following night we decided to eat the 'shrooms we brought with us but didn't know how we wanted to go about it.

Everyone knows that something grown in shit tastes like shit, and things that taste like shit tend to make people puke. These 'shrooms also happened to be moldy from improper dehydration, so it was hard not to think of that when they were going down. We had some peanut butter, which cures the taste like you would not believe, but my girl with the busted ankle had a weak stomach when it comes to 'shrooms and insisted she'd get sick either way.

So we had to come up with a better plan. Remembering the awesome restaurant we were at the previous evening, we decided to cut the mushrooms into small pieces and sprinkle them onto our salads, getting extra ranch dressing to cover the taste. This worked out excellently because it wasn't too crowded—which could have been really bad if someone saw us sprinkle magic on our food—and our ocean view was incredible.

As three of us devoured our salads like starved pigs, our fourth companion wasn't doing so good. She couldn't get past the thought of the mold and ended up spitting some chewed-up 'shrooms and salad in her napkin (which I later made her eat, for I will not tolerate drug abuse). She started picking out all the 'shrooms off her plate, separating the vegetables onto another, which our waiter found very amusing. I still say he knew what we were up to.

When the food finally came, the three of us inhaled it before our fourth friend even finished her salad. We were tripping before we left the restaurant and went on to walk through Ripley's Believe It Or Not Museum, which was the funniest because we couldn't stop laughing the whole time, and Ripley's has some really crazy shit. "Extra ranch" will never be the same again.

The White Elephant and Disneyland / B. Load

A mind is a terrible thing to waste. Or, as America's former (and no doubt most quotable) vice president, Dan Quayle, so aptly put it, "What a waste it is to lose one's mind. Or not to have a mind is being very wasteful. How true that is." Besides the fact that Dan isn't exactly the brightest bulb on the tree, his comment is actually more ignorant than it sounds. Because "losing one's mind" is not a waste at all, so long as one loses it only temporarily. In fact, sometimes "not to have a mind" can be the best thing of all.

A buddy of mine had a cabin on a little alpine jewel of a lake, nestled in the pine forests of Crestline, California, in the San Bernadino Mountains. The cabin was nicknamed the White Elephant because inside there were elephants of all shapes and sizes (candles, paintings, crystal figurines, stained-glass windows, wooden carvings, you name it). We would lose our minds there quite often.

Luckily for us, we always found them again, and lo and behold, they were usually better off than before. Mushrooms will do this to you (or for you, depending on your point of view). I think Aldous Huxley said it best about excursions to the other side: "One comes back more confident, yet less cocksure." That's the plan, anyway.

We'd arrive at the Elephant around noon with a cooler full of cold beers, water, fruit, and granola bars, and for the post-trip portion of the evening, yogurt, ice cream, chocolate milk, and cookies. After sharing some wicked skunk from his infamous "natural wood" pipe and a cold beer down by the lake, we'd head back up to the cabin around 3 p.m. to prepare for the festivities, or as we liked to say, "Set the controls for the heart of the sun."

We were pretty serious about tripping. Well, maybe not serious, but we were sober to the fact that we planned on transporting ourselves into other realms and that our sense of selves would probably go bye-bye for what might seem like quite a long time. While not Boy Scouts by any sense of the word, we felt that when it was most likely that we would lose our senses of time and place, it was best to be prepared.

Around 4 p.m., we'd light up some sage and incense and put on some Stones or Doors (usually *Goat's Head Soup* or *Strange Days*) while making sure that all the music and any other accoutrements (nitrous oxide tanks, kaleidoscopes, light sticks, *The Wall* or *2001: A Space Odyssey*) were accessible for a smooth and easy come-down when we returned hours later.

Then we'd suit up for the evening, making sure we had the proper shoes, and jackets and gloves if it was winter. We would then divvy up the fungus into equal piles, grind them into small pieces, and place them in a bowl with a small spoonful of honey and a touch of milk or ice cream, and then whip the concoction into a smooth texture. One of us would then offer a small prayer or invocation of thanks and protection to the Great Spirit, and around 5 p.m., it was down the rabbit hole.

Once consumed, we'd put on Jimi Hendrix's *Electric Ladyland* and head out to the deck overlooking the lake, surrounded by a forest of pine, oak, and cedar. We'd have another beer, throw some horseshoes, and talk about whatever was going on at the time—girls, the NFL, the Lakers, friends, family—we just wanted to keep our minds in a good space and not really focus on what was happening in our bellies. This was a good thing, because although we normally made sure our stomachs were fairly empty before ingestion, I'd usually start to feel sick to my stomach and become totally immobilized as the 'shrooms began knocking on the door.

By the time the "Voodoo Chile" Slight Return signature refrain wafted out to the balcony, our fungal friends would be seriously kicking in, the sun would be dipping below the tree line, and we would head down toward the lake where we'd sit on a wooden bench next to the shore. We had a perfect view of six massive jets of water that arced outward in giant streams over the far end of the lake (we were never really sure what these were). With the sun dropping behind the mountain and our minds beginning to melt, they looked like some magnificent sparkling display of red, yellow, and orange fountains you might see at the Bellagio in Las Vegas. It was a beautiful sight.

We would sit there for a long while, watching the sun go down and the stars and moon come up. Laughing, talking, or usually just being silent, caught in the machinations and wonderment of our innermost thoughts and the wonders of nature. Eventually one of us would motivate the others, and we would begin to walk the path that led around the lake. It was a decent sized lake, about eighty-six acres. Since in our condition time didn't really exist, we would measure our trip by where we were on the lake. From experience, we could figure out how long we'd been out.

There were definite stops along the way. One small clearing always offered a perfect view of the moon framed among the pines. We would stop and stare as its mountains and canyons created strange leering faces and swirling images through the distortion of 239,000 miles of distance. The clearing gave way to a small slope that led up to another bench overlooking the lake, next to a tall pine tree that was always glad to share its energy with anyone who simply gave it a great big hug. Another smaller, felled pine created a bridge across the water. The reflections of the stars shimmering across the lake played in our minds as we walked across the old pine, careful not to fall into the lake.

Around a second curve was the "city of stones," huge boulders that had fallen naturally in such a way as to appear to the hallucinating mind as a city built by the gods. We could crawl up into spaces that seemed carved out of the stone, and at the top was a large flat slab that provided a perfect view of the lake and the shore beyond. We'd sit here, flat on our backs, and look up at our piece of space. Cold stone underneath, crisp mountain air all around, planets and stars above, taking millions of years to send their light through the vast expanses of the universe to our eagerly awaiting eyes.

Our minds would become as one, and nobody needed to say anything. We just knew. Knew that even through all the bullshit we were all brothers, knew that everything was going to be okay, knew the universe was a vast and wondrous place, knew there must be some kind of plan, even if none of us had any clue as to what it might be. Just small specks of flesh, here for a brief moment in time, riding the planet as best we could.

We didn't know that our body wouldn't live to see another summer. We had no way of knowing. Like so many things, it just happened. I haven't been back to the lake since; I think his family sold the place, I'm not sure. But the memories that were created there, with some special help from our friend the magic mushroom, will last a lifetime.

I have a particular group of friends that really enjoy traveling to the other side via psychedelics, especially magic mushrooms. This itinerant band of heads takes the fungal sacrament seriously; we truly believe in its powers of divination and universal discovery. Of course, we're also a bunch of stoner knuckleheads that just like to have a lot of fun.

When occasions such as these arise, we often head off to Disneyland to see what Mickey Mouse may have in store for us. I don't know if the by-product of Walt Disney's unique world view combined with Michael Eisner's drive to make a buck really makes it "The Happiest Place on Earth," but after ingesting a few caps and stems, it surely is one of the most special places on earth. And the *churros* are tasty, too.

Anyway, we decided to take one of our strange journeys to Anaheim, becuase two of us were in Los Angeles (Group A) and two of us were in Long Beach (Group B), so we decided to just meet there. I arranged for the roots, but as the pick-up spot was closer to Group A, I asked them to grab the goodies, and we would divvy them up at the Magical Kingdom. No problem.

When we got to the parking lot to ingest, there appeared to be a major shortage. "What's up?" I inquired. My friend said, "Oh, your boy only had this much left." Bummer. It wasn't really enough for four guys to achieve proper peakage. We were all about the same size, and none of us had eaten a lot, but oh, well, we were there, so we split what we had four ways, smoked some bowls, and hoped for the best.

After about an hour in the park, and a run through some early *Steamboat Willy* footage and the rush of Space Mountain, the boys of Group A seemed to have really blasted off and were peaking hard. But oddly, those of us in Group B, although happily coming on, weren't really tripping. In fact, it semed like this was going to be a mellow affair.

We forged our way through Adventure Land and, after one of those incredibly good orange-glazed doughnuts by the Tiki Room, we decided to hit the Pirates of the Caribbean. As we cheerfully floated through cannon explosions, musty treasures guarded by bleached skeletons, and scenes of debauchery and pillage, we went under a bridge where a pirate was sitting, swinging his leg back and forth.

"Dude, look at the *mud* on that pirate's heel, what attention to detail," said a member of Group A, with a little too much gusto. Something was not quite right here. I mean, yeah, that was cool, but considering the amounts we had taken and their mild effects, it wasn't *that* cool. He was obviously way more whacked out than he should be.

As we exited the ride in the French Quarter, the street sign read Blue Bayou. One of the Group A trippers looked over at me and said, "B-Load, that's a lot like what I do to you on the hoop court," and he and his Group A cohort started laughing hysterically. "Blew by you," he said, "get it?" "Yeah," I replied sarcastically, "that's really funny." Whatever.

We hopped on the ferry and headed over to Tom Sawyer's Island. Group A was still giggling like small girls as we exited near the shore. Suddenly, in a 'shroom-induced flash, it came to me. "You no good dogs," I said, "you busted into the bag before you got here, didn't you?" My Group B companion was shocked. "No wonder you're tripping so much harder than us, you bastards!" The other guys first looked indignant, then confused, and then they just started laughing wildly again, slapping each other on the backs.

"Uh, yeah, well, ahh . . . sorry, dude, but he who holds the bag, reaps the rewards," they said. I really wasn't that mad, but acted like I was. "What! I set up the whole thing *and* paid for them." The Group A boys didn't seem to share my indignation—until one of them, who was doubled over and laughing hysterically, lost his balance and fell into the lake.

Now it was the boys of Group B's turn to start laughing. "Yeah, you sure are reaping the rewards," we mocked. The other member of Group A raced over to help our buddy out of the water as we sat there in hysterics. About a minute later, a park employee showed up (how the hell do they know everything that's going on so fast?) and began dragging them toward the exit.

As they walked by us, I cackled, "He who holds the bag, goes for a swim!" the Disney guy shot us a death stare and asked if we knew them. We both gave our most completely innocent look and said, "Never seen them before in our lives, sir."

Group B enjoyed another few hours strolling leisurely through Fantasy Land, soaking up the double meanings of Alice in Wonderland and Mr. Toad on our mild but enjoyable high, and while the obviously whacked-out boys of Group A barely talked their way into convincing security that it was an accident, we dried off, and left the park.

They spent the next two hours trolling the Disney Hotel, one of them trying to get dry and the other trying to come down enough so they could drive home. They were doubly pissed when they discovered that we still had the buds (apparently, more than one bag can be held by fine friends). It seems Mickey Mouse always has a way of making things right.

As If True / Fly Agaric 23

I will explain a little about my first run-in with the little people in London. At sixteen years old, I swigged back some bitter cold mushroom brew as if getting pissed on cheap, nasty cider. After about fourty minutes, everything got bright. One hour later, my friend and I were talking in what now seems like an Arabic dialect, a new syntax or visual language which only adepts at drinking cider and rebelling when sixteen could understand.

Next I remember lying on my back screaming while doing the dying fly, seriously excited and ultrachildish, but happy. Then I felt a warm sensation upon my chest suddenly get hotter and hotter, like my young soul rising out of its fleshy body. I let out a cry and then noticed my poorly-rolled spliff had ejected its contents on me, which were burning my chest. Very surreal.

After two hours, we made a trip to our local American-style super shopping mall called "Merry Hill." Here we stumbled around, laughing and grinning like mad pranksters. I remember that everybody I set eyes upon had a bright white light core upon their chest which exploded into stars if I looked too long.

Afterward we continued drinking cider and acting foolishly, until I made the quantum leap into the worlds of mythology and folklore. Here I found evidence that what's real can be written about and experienced as if true.

Chub Chub / David Mark Dannov

The plan was to drive to Laguna Beach, eat some mushrooms, and trip out in the hills. So, Trent, Glen, and I packed up our things one day, hopped in Trent's car and took off down the street. When we arrived, Trent parked the car on the side of the road. It was a beautiful, sunny day—sometime in the early afternoon—the ocean to the right, bright green hills to the left.

"Okay," Trent said, handing each of us a bag of mushrooms. "Lunch time."

We ate that stuff in between peanut-butter sandwiches. It was horrible. I almost puked trying to swallow that shit. After all, 'shrooms grow from cow dung. Luckily, I brought some orange juice to wash it down. After we finished eating the 'shrooms, we grabbed our backpacks, closed the doors of the car, then walked across the street toward the grassy hills beyond. We were hiking up one of those hills when the mushrooms began to ooze through my blood.

"Man," Glen said, "I'm already feeling it."

"Me, too," I agreed, smiling at the sun.

As we walked, the grass eventually died out into this yellowish dry mud. That's when we found ourselves in a small ravine, almost like a ditch. I looked down at my shoes and listened to the crackling earth. It sounded like eggshells breaking. My hearing was completely heightened. I even heard a helicopter approach in the distance. Actually, I wasn't sure what it was at first. It kept getting louder and louder until it flew above our heads. The noise was spectacular, chaotic. It echoed down to my ears like machine-guns shooting from all directions.

"Run!" I shouted, the goose bumps zinging down my arms.

We all started running, charging through that trench with our backpacks flopping up and down. Our lives were at stake. We needed to find cover! It was war! Minutes later, the sound of the machine-guns slowly drifted away as the helicopter disappeared from our sight. We were relieved; we all looked at each other and laughed. What a crack-up— we actually thought we were being chased, in a trench war, at that! Good 'shrooms, we all agreed. We kept on going, trudging up that ditch like tired infantrymen. It seemed like it was never going to end.

"Jesus," I shouted. "How do we get outta this fuckin' thing?"

Right when I said that, the ravine suddenly came to a stop. We climbed up its crumbly side and—badabing!—there we were in paradise: green grass and rolling hills everywhere the eye could see. The ocean was behind us, of course. All we had to do was turn around and there it was, stretched below the hills. The sun reflected against the distant water like golden flakes of liquid fire. We all stood there, speechless as the sky above our heads.

Walking up a slope, I suddenly sat down in the middle of a grass mound and said, "I've gotta stop right here." The mushrooms had really kicked in. There was no way I could walk any further. My brain was a tide pool of chaos and blood. Glen stepped up to me. "What's going on, Dave?" He looked like a man stretched behind a crystal ball.

"He's peaking," Trent said, walking up to Glen's side.

Glen bent down to get a closer look. His face ballooned out like a reflection in a funhouse mirror. "Dave. You all right?"

Sure I knew he was talking to me. But he didn't make sense. I wasn't there anymore. I was somewhere else, drifting in a wind above his head. "Who's this Dave guy?" I asked, my voice sounding like a ghost from another man's throat. They started laughing.

"What do you mean?" Trent asked. He looked at me with a smile that blended into the clouds behind his head.

"I mean, who the fuck is this Dave guy?"

"C'mon," Trent said, a little spooked. "You know it's you."

"That's not my name," I insisted.

Trent and Glen looked at each other. They were amused.

"Okay," Trent said. "Then what do you want to be called?"

"Something simple. Something like . . . Chub Chub."

They burst into laughter. "Chub Chub?" Trent said. "You've gotta be kidding!"

"Okay," I said. "Then how about . . . Shrub."

"Forget it," Trent scowled. "I'm not calling you Shrub, either."

"Neither am I," Glen agreed, and they both marched off.

I was left alone, sitting there like a bush in the dirt. Okay, I admit, I knew they were stupid names. But I couldn't think. Nothing was coming to mind but sounds, images, the way I felt. Chub Chub, Shrub, soil, grass, bones, roots. I wanted to be it all. That was the problem. I was too aware, too alive in the moment, like a rock with a heart pumping beneath its shell. Names didn't exist anymore. They didn't matter. I was the earth in all its living glory—and no one, not even the sun, could tell me otherwise.

Now that my peak was over, my bones finally felt limber enough to move. Of course, I was still tripping, but at least now I could function in a somewhat rational manner. When I stood up, I looked around for Trent and Glen. They were nowhere in sight—

just hills and the silent ocean in the background. So I began to walk. They must be somewhere around here, I thought, as the breeze floated across the land.

That's when I saw Trent about one hundred yards ahead. I could see him through this tall, yellow grass that stuck out from the ground like some kind of African prairie. That's when my imagination took over. I was a lion ready to pounce on my prey. I couldn't help myself. I always wondered what it was like for an animal to look at another animal and want to hunt it down for the kill. I began to focus on my breathing, and I was doing it really fast now. In and out my lungs went, as a sort of grunt noise came along with it.

And then I was off, charging through the field like a monstrous thing. Trent saw me coming. He didn't know what to think. His eyes just stared in a panicked lock. But I didn't care. I had no sympathy. He was my victim, and the closer I came, the faster my heart pumped away. My blood was in a frenzy now as I imagined ripping Trent's flesh apart, eating his insides, and biting at all his bones. But that was as far as I took it. I quickly snapped myself out of it and stopped, dead in my tracks.

Trent was standing a few feet in front of me. His eyes were statues of fear. "What the fuck are you doing, Dave!"

"Jesus," I sighed, looking down at the ground. I brushed my hands through my hair. "That was freaky."

"You're telling me. You looked like you wanted to eat me or something!"

I didn't know what to say. Neither did he. We left it at that.

Family Values / Sadie Leon

Acquiring illegal substances through dealers was not an option. Isolated in a small boarding school in the winter woods of northern Michigan, we were forced to have our supplies shipped in from various hometowns. On one shady afternoon, a note was left in my mailbox. It simply stated, Package at the front desk. Anticipation pulsated through our sixteen-year-old veins. We opened the box, and the mushrooms lay naked in all their glory. Confused, we simply stared.

"What the hell do we do with these?" Katie asked. "How much do we take?"

"Who cares?" Rob replied. "Let's just do some fucking mushrooms!"

And we did, at my home. Luckily, my parents had gone upstairs and could not hear any of this—or had chosen not to, which was usually the case. They were frequently "not hearing" our teenage evenings. We were safe.

When Rob entered the darkness of the living room, he noticed that everyone's pores had begun to breathe. Katie, his ex-girlfriend, shouted, "You are the blackest of the black," tears streaming down her flushed cheeks. Rob then tiptoed to the kitchen, hoping to escape her wrath, only to find Sam and Maggie huddled together on a singular white square of the checkered floor.

"Come join our egg," Maggie blurted out. "It's great in here. We even have cable." Rob didn't hear that. He didn't hear anything. He just looked as all of their limbs fell onto the floor.

I was busy making snow angels on the blue shag carpeting in the back room. Through the use of my breath, I was filling the room with spider webs. I wanted to laugh, but forgot how. I could hear Katie scream from the other room, calling Rob Romeo and referring to herself as Juliet.

Rob couldn't feel his skin. He wanted to go into the kitchen, but couldn't stand up. His legs hurt, or did they? "Was somebody touching me? Is everyone pointing at me? Did I just take off all my clothes and masturbate on the floor? Is that my mom sitting in the chair across from me? Does anybody know that I'm here?" Apparently, we had eaten enough mushrooms.

He walked into the kitchen. Sam and Maggie were still in their egg. Ignoring them, he exclaimed, "Refrigerator, that's it," slapping his hand on his forehead. He opened the door of the fridge. "Butter. Now *that's* it. Now *here* is something reliable. If there was anything you could ever count on, it's butter." Artistic urges flaring, he decided that what the kitchen was missing was a touch of butter. Using our entire stash of butter, he smeared all four walls with the slimy mess.

Helena (our "sober" friend—we all need one, right?) entered the dining room. Maggie was now crouched at the head of the table, furiously scribbling on my mother's best linens. "I've found it," she said, still composing despite the fact that her face was nowhere near her "manuscript."

"Found *what*, sweetie?" Helena responded.

"The answer." Maggie'e eyes were scanning the room as if searching for an FBI bug. "I know where God is. He has been hiding for a long time, but I know. I saw."

Hearing parental footsteps on the stairs (as a teenager, it is very easy to distinguish), Helena dashed to the kitchen. She quickly assessed the room's condition. There was butter. Everywhere. My father was two feet from pushing the swinging door open. "No time," she mumbled. "We are totally busted."

My dad had an annoying habit of coming downstairs during all hours of the night, searching for the oddest things—a flashlight, chlorine for the pool, even sunglasses. Wandering over to the refrigerator, underwear half hanging off, he opened the door and stood there staring. Helena couldn't move. Deciding on bread, he placed a slice in the toaster. He turned to Helena, who was still in ice-sculpture mode.

"Where's the butter?" he asked, as calmly as if we were in church. "I thought I had bought some earlier." Helena just stood there, gaping.

Meanwhile, Rob found himself in the dining room. He sat down at the table, trying to figure what he could do. He decided that if he could feel urine on his leg, he was alive. Thus he peed, and not only on himself—needing to feel the warmth of urine, needing to remember how normal peeing was—but all over the dining-room rug as well.

"Wait, bathroom," he realized. Still peeing, he made the journey from the living room to the bathroom. Upon arriving, he saw Sam, who was busy at the sink. He was rocking back and forth, splashing water on his face, reciting *Hamlet*. Rob, still peeing, looked on in awe.

By this time, my father had compromised with jelly and was making his way back up the stairway. This left Helena gaping in the kitchen, Katie screaming in some dark corner, Rob urinating all over the dining-room rug and himself, Maggie looking into the eyes of God, Sam delivering various Shakespeare excerpts, and me marveling in my room of spider-webbed breath.

All in all, not bad for some kids whose previous knowledge of magic mushrooms was that they look like monkey feces and smell like wet dog food.

"Do you have any drugs?" I can ask my aunt and uncle anything.

"You mean other than pot?" I told you they're cool.

"Yeah. Anything that you guys don't want, that is." It takes very little to faze them.

"Check the freezer," my aunt said. "You never know what might be in there."

My uncle is a comedian, and he sometimes receives presents from fans in the audience, pockets full of goodies that simply get tossed in the fridge for a later date. Those later dates don't always come, but he just doesn't like to waste anything.

"I think there's something in the back of the freezer," my aunt called from the living room, "in some kind of box or something."

My fingers made their way to the back, to the box. I opened it, and there it was. The mother of all trips. It was green. With hair. And what appeared to be fingers. Who would be stupid enough to ingest this oddity with teeth simply for a few hours of laughter?

"Cool, I'll take it," I said, shutting the freezer door. "You sure you don't care?"

"If we wanted it, it would've been gone by now."

Gone by now? How long had it been there? Well, I calculated in my head, they've only lived here for fifteen years. It couldn't possibly be that bad.

"All right," I said, tapping the top of the box. "I'm gonna go home. Rest up for tomorrow."

"What's tomorrow?" my aunt asked.

"April 20. Four twenty. National Get High Day."

"What do you plan to do?"

"My friend Michael and I are partaking of this and then going to see *Fantasia 2000*. It's playing at Disney's Imax."

"Have fun. Take care," as they both hugged me goodbye.

12:43 the Next Afternoon

Michael was late, so we were forced to consume the mushroom on our way to the movie. We dunked its limbs into a jar of peanut butter to kill the horrific aftertaste.

"Do you have any water?" he asked, a mouthful of chewed-up fungi sticking to his lips.

"Yeah, here," I said, handing him the bottle. "Do you want to get high? I always get high right after I take mushrooms. It makes the transition smoother."

"No, thanks. I'll just wait for the 'shrooms to kick in."

Michael was one of those snobby drug users. He will say yes to a mushroom with eyeballs, but turn his nose up at a toke of pot.

"Suit yourself," I said, sitting back in the car. Relaxed from the intake of smoke, I amusingly gazed at Michael while he struggled with traffic. Twenty minutes later and about ten minutes from flying, we pulled up to the theater.

"You get out and get us the tickets. "I'll go park the car."

Approximately twenty-five feet from Disney's greatest adventure, I saw the sign. SOLD OUT! Of course it was sold out. The complete reason for swallowing that poison, and now we have nowhere else to release it. There was no alternative. No Plan B. Heartbeat racing and breath shortening, my eyes scanned the area. Spotting Michael, I headed straight for him.

"The fucking thing is sold out! I am seriously about to be tripping in five fucking minutes, and all that is around me is the fucking airport! I don't want to go trip out on the airport!" An example of major downfall when it comes to ingesting substances: Once they enter your body, there is no turning back.

Eyeing me slyly, Michael exhaled four words. Four words that changed my whole outlook on our four twenty.

"Long Beach Aquarium, baby," said simply and with ease.

"Get the car. We are so there."

1:12 the Same Afternoon

Because we were driving as if we were the Indy 500, the Long Beach Aquarium came into view in no time. Parking the car in the nick of time, we ran to the ticket purchasing line.

"Sadie, are you sure that Snoop Dogg is from Long Beach?"

"Yeah, you know the line, 'Kickin' it in the LBC.'—that's Long Beach Compton. He is totally from here." Looking around at all of the children in sneakers with red balloons tied to their wrists, I reconsider. "Well, I don't think he's from *here* exactly, but yeah," I said, confused as to why Snoop Dogg wrote such harsh lyrics about a community that held the infamous Queen Mary.

"Whatever. Let's get our tickets," Michael exclaimed, jumping up and down while clapping his hands. He himself was turning into a little boy.

Entering the three-story aquarium, it was as if I was four years old again, seeing the Barbie section at FAO Schwarz for the first time. Too much goodness and joy to know where to begin. We decided to hit the bathroom first, since it's easy to forget about normal human functions while under the weight of hallucinogens.

"Where do we go now?" Michael asked, the same small child peering through his eyes.

"I don't even know where we are *now*," I said, as the walls began to blur in with the floor.

"Let's go *there*." We skipped outside. Once we arrived on the grassy knoll, we lost all train of thought as to why we had come. Standing in silence for three minutes, Michael spontaneously shouted, "Let's go touch the sting ray!" Grabbing my hand, he pulled me in their direction. Groping sliminess did not sound appealing in the slightest, but we were kickin' it in the LBC.

The sting ray "meet and greet" lasted approximately two minutes. The skin-to-skin action was less than arousing. Following the signs to the Deep Sea Creatures, we fell further into our journey.

"Ooh, *creatures*," I drooled. "Maybe we'll find something that looks like our mushroom!"

One of the many things that makes the Long Beach Aquarium miraculous is the lengthy hallways made entirely of glass. Walking through them, you are literally surrounded by an underwater extravaganza. And not just household aquatic fish, but deep-sea creatures seen only on the Discovery Channel. We decided to camp in one. For two hours, on the floor, with our noses super-glued to the glass, we became one with them. I entered the mind of a fish. I was neon purple with red polka dots, swimming through reefs, dodging larger fish, and breathing through slices in the sides of my body. We were one species.

"Sadie, How does a fish feel?" Michael asked, as sincere as a child on Christmas.

"Lonely," I said. "But incredibly fulfilled."

We then moved on to the sardine tube. It's a vertical cylinder that stretches the entirety of the wall. It's only large enough for one body to stand in, but under the circumstances, we made do. We stood there while thousands of sardines swim circles around us. About three hours later, Michael and I found ourselves camped on the floor, exclaiming over how incredibly amazing and special each individual fish was.

"Oh, my God," I said, pointing to a single sardine. "Look at his eyes! He loves that one. He stays behind her wherever she goes."

"How can you tell which is the girl and which is the boy?"

"The hips."

For one astonishing afternoon we lost all notion of social order and appropriate behavior.

And I was not even in Congress.

6:17 the Same Day

Spread-eagle against the coral tank, cutting a Jesus-like figure, I said, "I want to join you, you little blue-finned fishy, you. I want to be a part of your world!" Suddenly my body became a two-by-four. I turned around. I saw Michael first. "Okay," I thought, "I can deal with that."

Then a class of second graders came into view. Michael was one with them, sans the sack lunch. He joined their trip and left mine. All jaws had dropped, and their bewildered eyes were stapled—not to the lovely coral, but on me. Seeming to have become the main attraction on Mrs. Johnson's field trip, I took baby steps away from the tank. It was clearly time to go home.

"See, drugs should be legal," I said, shrugging off the entire situation.

6:23 the Same Day

Attempting a walk back to the car, a realization unexpectedly entered my mind: Because we leave the *place* of experience does not mean that the actual *experience* has left us. It was after 6 p.m., and we were about to get on the freeway in Los Angeles. We still had a long trip ahead of us. But, lucky for me, I am not a snobby drug user. I took advantage of this traffic jam to smoke a bowl. Sitting back, I glanced amusingly at Michael while he struggled. Eyes glazing over, I relaxed with the intake of smoke.

Incident at Mar Vista / Michael Simmons

> The visible world is no longer a reality.
> And the unseen world is no longer a dream.
>
> —William Butler Yeats

My close encounter in October of 1999 began with a phone call from an acquaintance I'd met at a seminar by psychedelic philosopher Terence McKenna up at the Esalen Institute in Big Sur. He invited me to a party at a house in Mar Vista near the beach in Los Angeles on the following Saturday night being thrown by, as he described them, "veterans of Burning Man."

My friend informed me that this wing-ding would be "electric" via the ingestion of psilocybin mushroom fudge. Chocolate, I'm told, potentiates the effects of magic mushrooms, as well as making them easier to digest. I was pretty damn excited. As a psychedelic vet of five decades, I'd been desperately in need of some paradigm-shattering travel.

The consensual reality where most of us dwell has been getting grayer, duller, more predictable. More ridden with hype, duplicity, lies. And I've never understood this need of people to excitedly go stand in line for the latest bazillion-dollar Hollywood block-buster when we can be off living our own movies. I had a gut feeling that this '90s variant on the acid tests would be an epic, and I was right.

After thoroughly cannabinoiding myself and downing a couple of shots of Jack Daniels to quell my nerves, I took a cab to prevent interaction with the Los Angeles Porcine Department. When I arrived, I walked though the house and exited into a large back-yard filled with 300 PoMo BoHos. But it was clear that this wasn't merely another Hollywood wrap bash for some glib yuppie sitcom. Naked people hopping in and out of a hot tub is not that uncommon a sight at a show biz social gathering, but here there was a genuine vibe of tribe versus the usual bunch of acquaintances who get thrown together because of a mutual pursuit of a paycheck.

For reasons having to do with the asininity of the drug laws in this country, I'll refrain from being overly descriptive of the physical layout of the backyard. But it was magical ground, over which hovered a huge tree. Multicolored lights accentuated the surreal atmosphere. Some kind of recorded trance music was being transmitted, but I don't remember whether it was of the electronic or traditional variety or the latest combina-tion. Hell, my reportorial skills were severely hindered by the grass, sour mash, and all-consuming awe at the sheer amount of freaks in one spot.

There was, of course, the young girl with long, straight hair down to her ass who seemed to be following me around and staring into my soul, all the while sensuously tooting a recorder affixed to her slightly parted, full-bodied lips like some musical phal-lus. She reminded me of Crazy Alice, who'd sit barefoot in trees blowing a flute for hours with lysergicized faraway eyes when she wasn't blowing me or any of my male hippie brothers back in 1973. I mean, you can't have a legitimate, communal, grilled psyche-delic reality sandwich without some space cadette deep-throating a wind instrument.

Otherwise, the partygoers seemed to be of that unique '90s beat/hippie/punk/hip-hop/grunge/goth/raver/modern-primitive crossbreed. Hairstyles ranged from shaven to long-long-long, dyed or not, maybe partly shaved and partly dyed. Lots of tattoos and body piercings. Some "costumes," I guess, but what differentiates a costume from a lifestyle? People came as any damn variation on any damn thing they wanted, and that's the way it should be.

After asking around for my friend for about twenty minutes (and getting a lot of half-answers from people who'd gotten past that boring language hang-up), I found him and he procured me a thin wedge of the heralded fudge. While chocolate may potentiate 'shrooms, evidently so does reefer and whiskey, because I got off quickly. I passed the lift-off stage where giddy giggling and irrational fear coexisted, and inanimate objects became anthropomorphized, their molecules clearly in flux, motivated by an intelligence.

In fact, in my time I've seen lawn chairs that appeared to have more going for them than some humans. The polyhue of the lights, the sonic whirling dervish of the trance music, the snatches of random conversation, the carefree nudity—all began to meld into a free associating, primal energy force whose sum was mightier than its parts. *Blur. Blue. Green. Red. Bright, Wery red. Is that a trumpet? Its tone is Wery, then slithering. Fiery red. It matches the red light. The red light is reXected in the shiny brass of the trumpet. The red light sounds lovely! As lovely as that girl's red pubic hair! Each strand of her pubic hair is like a living, slithering red snake, curlicuing wet, wet like the puddle of beer I'm standing in.*

At that point I had to sit down. My prosthetic hips and aging corpus couldn't keep up with my born-again, astronautical mind. I found a seat—it was either a tree stump or a beer keg—and stared upwards at the huge tree hovering over us, and I swear it was a flying fucking saucer. Initially the Fudge People on the ground seemed like smallish, gentle creatures in comparison to the glowing, looming spaceship. They didn't look like they could be Homo sapiens who commit drive-by shootings or fly-over bombings or even just emotionally piss on others.

They were fudged and fragile flesh, convened to welcome this flying fucking saucer to earth, and they were all staring up at this clearly Identifiable Flying Object, and then *they* became the Object, and the Object became the Fudge People, and any delineation was no longer recognizable. The Fudge People and the Object were breathing in unison in big, oozing breaths, and all the petty little shit of everyday consensual reality was for that moment in time nonexistent. "Here's the proof, folks," I thought to myself. "There's more to reality than Starbucks!"

I realize that whatever I saw at Mar Vista that night can be taken literally or not. I'm not going to get into a how-does-one-define-reality dialectic. What I know I experienced was the emergence of a group mind with like-minded individuals on the same trip (250 fudge wedges were distributed). I haven't even touched on the live music and dance, group massage, and fire-breathing display that occurred because, quite frankly, I either missed 'em or was too loaded to take more than a casual glance. While specific close-encounter imagery appeared to me, it's not just my subjective analysis of my trip that led me to believe that a transcendent tribal phenomenon occurred. A large portion of the population of this Temporary Autonomous Zone, as writer Hakim Bey would reference this outpost of consciousness rebellion, stayed up all night and attended a ceremony by the Dalai Lama at the Universal amphitheater the next day. Evidently, much of LA's psychedelic community was buzzing, dazzled about the incident at Mar Vista, even if they were so otherwise distracted by their pubic-hair revelry as to miss the descent of the flying saucer entirely.

Weeks later, I spoke with a musician who performed there, and he confirmed city-wide postcelebratory outbreaks of euphoria. A group mind can be a recipe for fascism, but he properly credited the success to the old Tim Leary concept of set-and-setting, pointing out that both the house and the participants brought their own magic to the event. "Normally when you're surrounded by people and you're on drugs, you're forcing yourself to make sense to interact with people," he mused. "In this case, we were allowing ourselves to open."

And he didn't even eat the freakin' fudge that night! But he's an experienced entheogenic voyager and communicated with the Fudge People through his guitar. One needn't "eat the fudge" to understand much of this, but to paraphrase the late Terence McKenna, dying without having done psychedelics is like dying without having gotten laid. McKenna referred to the hyperdimensionality of the psilocybin trance: "All of these places that were thought to be discrete and separate are seen to be part of a single continuum."

Which is just another way of saying God or the Infinite or the Whole Enchilada. I missed out on the Dalai Lama, allowing myself to be kidnapped by some speed-freaked friends of mine, and taking one really weird ride through LA. And life has not been some blissful Nirvana since. I take the demands of the squares personally, and I spend much of my time suffering from acute melancholia. I read some LAPD "expert" on the drug MDMA (Ecstasy) discuss how one of the drawbacks of indulging is that the raver can find ordinary life pleasureless and become easily depressed. Take that logic a few steps further. If you'd spent Saturday night kissing God, wouldn't it be a bit of a downer to have to show up at the box factory Monday morning?

Michael Simmons is working on a book about the Detroit band MC5 and the White Panthers.

Through Rain, Snow, or Hail / Marbles

Salvador Dali once said, "I don't take drugs, I *am* drugs." This was pretty much the philosophy of my college tenure. In fact, for a while I had wanted to major in drugs, but the college didn't allow me.

There was one small problem in my goal: my serious lack of money. I had developed ways to get as much free drugs as possible. I had started doing small favors for some of the on-campus dealers, including taking notes for them in class, and even writing a dissertation or two.

Next, I had formed a band with my dealers, and they would always provide drugs for rehearsals, so this was a plus. For me, this was not enough. I needed more, more, more.

Then I came up with the greatest solution—I'd get a job! I know your reaction—a job? I assure you, I was as aghast as you. But I found myself a great job. I began working in the campus post office. It was a fun job, and I found that I would be able to go to work stoned, and sometimes even get stoned at work.

About a week after I started working there, a friend of mine received a package from Graffix Bong Company. I called to let him know it was there, and he invited me over to celebrate and break it in.

The following week, another friend received a package. He picked it up from the post office, and told me to come by his room when I got off work. I showed up at his room, and he handed me a fat bag of weed. I asked him why the sudden generosity, and he explained that the package was a delivery of his product. He told me that now that there was an inside man, the dealers could get more deliveries through FedEx, UPS, and sometimes even regular parcel post.

He called all the dealers and told them of the situation. They all agreed that if I would keep them posted about package arrivals, and ensure that no one from the post office became suspicious, I'd get a "gratuity."

This was the greatest arrangement since JFK got the Secret Service to sneak his mistresses into the White House. I was on Easy Street. No, make that: I was on Easy High Street. I went for about three months without paying a single cent for drugs. It was great. Then the unthinkable happened. A package arrived, but I didn't get a cut. Here's what happened . . .

It was mid-April when the package arrived, about three feet wide, three feet deep and two feet tall. It weighed about sixty-five pounds, and stunk to high heaven. It was addressed to one of the more prominent dealers on campus, and I immediately called him. He came by the post office and picked up his package.

As the months of the arrangement went by, the agreement was that I would receive my free drugs two days after the shipment arrived. This package came in on a Wednesday, but when Friday came and went, I didn't get worried, though I was a little upset. Saturday came and went, and so did Sunday, yet no delivery.

Monday afternoon, I went straight from work to the dealer's room. He answered the door, and immediately told me the following story.

It turned out the dealer's friend from home had recently moved from Connecticut to rural Pennsylvania. They had discussed many times how much money they could make, if only they could find some 'shrooms in the open. His friend asked where to find them and what they looked like. Once the family was fully settled in, the search began. He mailed everything he found to my friend, the dealer.

The punchline to the story was, they had discussed that 'shrooms grew on cow shit, so he went out in the fields for weeks and gathered all he could find. Unfortunately, he didn't know what 'shrooms looked like, or the proper method of harvesting them, so he sent everything he found. This meant my friend received a sixty-five-pound box full of cow shit covered in toadstools. Wrong type of fungus, not properly harvested. I was offered as much as I wanted!

To add insult to injury, my friend dumped the box out on his bed so he'd be able to sort everything, ruining his $200 silk blanket. Add to that the $115 shipping cost.

I took Dali's advice. I didn't take the "drugs," but in this case I had the option to be totally shit-faced at no cost.

Head Game / Mike McDermitt

D ue to the existing anti-'shroom programs in northeast Florida, I decided to elim- inate the problem of getting busted for trespassing on the fertile local cow pastures, and such. I went and built my own. As the crop multiplied, I set up a little party of sorts by dropping off ounces of silly 'shrooms to my friends, and said I'd be back later and that I was bringing some more party favors.

I had gone out the night before to catch fireflies, and kept them in a big jar, in a nice dark place. I had done this trick to some friends in Michigan, back in the early '70s, and my friend Larry never really recovered from it.

I knew that the people would get together at J. W.'s little woodshop, to have a few drinks and eat the treats, as it had been quite a while for any 'shrooms to be around, due to the continuing drought conditions. So I parked my car about a block away, after waiting about two hours for the "victims" to reach their peaks.

Opening the jar, I poured as many fireflies as I could handle into my mouth, and then put the rest into my shirt and in my hair. I knocked on the door and stepped back. When they opened the door, I said, "Hi, man, wanna party?" The fireflies flew/fell out of my mouth, and as I turned around for effect, one of J. W.'s pals totally freaked and ran into the night. (He returned later.)

This further endeared me into the hearts and minds of another select group. I have to keep up my image, you know. But I have to admit, the first time was in cahoots with an original member of the Mad Trippers Association, circa 1967, and as he's passed on to his much-deserved personal Nirvana, I decided it would be something he would wish me to continue, because life is just too freakin' short to stay wrapped too tightly.

"I'm Fine" / Dave Channon

Eric and I were visiting Mr. Mushroom on the Batsto River in the Pine Barrens of New Jersey. We were canoeing on the serpentine, tea-red stream through an endless wilderness of cypress swamps. No Ahab could have steered us worse. The canoe was floating sideways, backwards, clunking into boggy stumps, yet ever onward with the meandering current.

I was paddling industriously to no practical effect when I saw a great, black, jagged question mark in the sky. The water's surface became a metaphor for the boundary between life above and death below. I asked Eric how he was doing. He answered, "I'm fine."

This is the same interaction we had the time I slipped belladonna into the peyote we ate for Halloween. I mixed one little teaspoon of dried leaves and seeds of my Aunt Cam's ornamental trumpet flowering bush into the mashed peyote-cinnamon bonbons, doubtful it would do much. A lot of friends were coming over for a costume party, and I felt like a clump of lead.

I lay on the floor and couldn't move my arms or legs. My pupils got so dilated I couldn't read the headlines of a newspaper. Every time I closed my eyes, ghoulish faces would start zooming into my eyelids. I was a little worried that Eric would be having the same fun. He said, "I'm fine." Eric has a cast-iron brain. My vision didn't get back to normal for three days.

Anyway, now I said, "We must get off this boat and rest on a sandy shore until things get more under control."

He replied, "What's out of control?"

"Our boat," I said.

"Eyahhh," he muttered, "we're still going downstream. So what's wrong?"

I said, "Let's go ashore there."

We did, but no sooner did we lay down on the bank than we spied a large mound of some unidentified powdery gray substance, no doubt deposited by a renegade Mafia toxic dump truck for which New Jersey is famous.

We got back in the canoe and soon came out on a wide, tranquil, shallow lake, almost at the end of our ride. A powerful roar shattered the peace. It was a bastard jet fighter from a nearby Air Force base dive-bombing us at treetop level. I felt very Vietnamese.

It wasn't always that way. Not on Turkey Hill Lake. Rainbows glittered on every ripple. The mushrooms built a temple out of sunlight on the clouds. We ate blueberries until our tongues turned purple, and laughed and laughed. We swam naked, and the water tickled our skin like puppy tongues. For hours we laughed until I shouted, "Laughing is too much work!"

Son of a Beatle / Sadie Leon

"Hey, great hair," Sean oozed, stumbling over to me at this big Hollywood party. "I'm Sadie," I say, extending my hand. His eyes widen with a wave of Ecstasy. "You know, there's a Beatles' song with your name, 'Sexy Sadie.'"

"Yeah, I know," I say, completely composed. "I was named after it." I had to lie. There was no choice.

"My dad wrote that song. That means I'm like your uncle."

With every word, he takes a step closer to me, as though he is examining every fine detail of my face, like he doesn't believe that I am actually a person. Funny, I'm thinking the same thing.

"Right on," I say.

As I turn to greet another great rock legend's son—after all, I have to work the room—I hear Sean's voice, asking, "Can I buy you another pill?" My turnaway suddenly becomes a turnback.

"Sure, I guess," shrugging my shoulders. Attempting to ignore the voice in my head shrieking, "It's John Lennon's son! It's John Lennon's son," I shyly venture toward the stash.

My friend Bekah is providing the entertainment pills for the evening, so scoring this added fun is no issue.

"They're thirty apiece, but totally worth it." Lie. They're really twenty and worth that, but Bekah has to make the rent.

"Okay, but you have to hang out with me." Which gives me that too-much-cheap vodka-in-my-stomach sensation. I hesitate. But since I'm on a bed filled with my dearest friends, there appears to be no harm. After all, "It's John Lennon's son!"

"Sure," I say, "you can hang out with *all* of us," using a typical girl safety net.

Twenty minutes later, eight of us are piled upon a twin-size bed. I'm sitting there, randomly shaking my head like a wet dog, trying to convince myself, No, I am not in love with Sean Lennon, and no, he is not in love with me. It's just the drugs . . . It's just the drugs . . .

"Sadie," he salivates. "I've never met a Sadie before. I bet your parents were a lot like mine." Somehow I doubt it. "What are you doing tomorrow?"

Oh, no. Don't ask me that. Never make plans with anybody for the next day while you're still on a high. They tend to be overly zealous, and no one is as exciting in daylight as they were the night before.

"I have to work." Oh, shit. Tomorrow is the Fourth of July.

"Oh. You wanna call in sick and go to Paris? We can get tickets on the Concorde and stay at the Ritz." See what I mean by overzealous?

It's now 7:30 a.m., and all I want to do tomorrow—or, rather, today—is take a bath and go to bed. A plane ride is not on my agenda. Even on the Concorde.

"Yeah, but what else are we talking about?"

"I just want a lot of cuddles."

No Concorde trip is worth that. Besides, the voice screaming "It's John Lennon's son" has subsided hours ago.

"I'll see ya later," I say, walking to my car.

"But wait, Goddess of the Night, I don't even have your number!" As he runs after me, I catch a glimpse of that little boy the world had known years prior, but only through photographs. It is almost enough to make me reconsider.

"You don't need it," I reply, shutting the door. I drive home, lock my door behind me, and take a hot bath. It isn't the Ritz, but it is home. In America.

Frisco, Baby, Frisco / David Mark Dannov

Craig was Trent's pledge brother back when Trent was pledging the fraternity. Supposedly, he was a real smart guy: 1300 on his SATs. Anyway, like me, he wasn't much into the fraternity scene. After he had become a brother, he eventually moved to San Francisco and got a job as a waiter. His whole outlook on life suddenly changed. He sort of dropped out of society and became a real rave-goer—at least that's what Trent told me after he spoke to Craig on the phone one day. "He wants to invite us up over the weekend. You interested?" Trent was standing in the living room when he asked me that, facing me with an apple in his hand.

"Sure," I said, sitting on the couch. "I've always wanted to try that Ecstasy stuff."

When the weekend arrived, we packed our bags, hopped in Trent's car, and finally headed up to Frisco. The drive took us only about six and a half hours. We got there around 7 p.m. Craig and I hadn't met before. He lived in a studio hidden in the walls of downtown Frisco. Walking by on the sidewalk, one would've never guessed that someone was actually living in that place. The front of the building had no windows, and its surface was metal with horizontal grooves, like one of those military shacks for storing all kinds of guns and cannons.

"This is it?" I asked Trent as he knocked on the metal wall.

That's when Craig opened a door on the side of the building. He popped his head around the corner and said, "Hey, guys, come on in." We followed him around the corner, then through that door of the building. It led straight into the studio. I was surprised by how large it was. There was enough room in there for a whole platoon. There wasn't much furniture, though, just a couch, a rug and a dining table near the stairway.

"I sleep on the second floor," Craig told us, stopping before the stairs. "I share it with another roommate. Downstairs are two more mattresses on the floor." He pointed his chin to the left side of the studio. We followed his gaze: two mattresses a yard apart, bedded with sheets and blankets. "That's where you guys can sleep. Don't worry. All my roommates are gone for the weekend. We have the place to ourselves. Oh, and there's no kitchen, so I hope you brought money for food."

After putting my backpack down, I walked around the place. Hanging on the left side of the studio wall was this giant oil painting of an alien face. Its neck protruded from a distorted dinosaur body with green skin and yellow scales. It wasn't the most amazing image I had ever seen. Whoever painted it needed to learn more about dimension, particularly shadow effect. But I still appreciated its creative quality. "Who painted this?" I asked.

Craig stepped out of his room from the second floor, leaned against the balcony rail and said, "I did."

"Pretty cool," I nodded. "Funky little alien dude."

Minutes later, Craig stepped down the stairs. "Here's the Ecstasy you guys were asking for." He held out the palm of his hand. There they were, two little white pills that looked as plain as any vitamin from a drugstore down the street. Trent and I smiled, then each grabbed a pill and put it in our pockets. "So what's your plans?" Craig asked. He had to go somewhere. "I won't be back until midnight," he said. "That's when the rave starts."

"Okay, then we'll just walk around, check out some bars, I guess."

"Oh, wait a minute," Craig exclaimed. "I know. There's this show playing down the street. It's called the Jim Rose Circus Freak Show or something like that."

Trent's eyes lit up. "Oh, man, I've heard about that show. It's supposed to be crazy."

It didn't surprise me that Trent had heard about the show. He was into all that piercing-punk crap at the time. He had gotten a tongue ring and loved to show it off, pushing the metal ball out for everyone to see. He also knew this tattoo guy in Newport that set him up with all sorts of crazy tribal designs. He got one tattoo on his stomach, on the lower right side, that was some kind of Aztec monkey god. He was proud of that one, especially since it hurt so much, the needle poking into his abdominal muscles.

A month later, he got his second tattoo, on his left shoulder blade, an Egyptian bird with its wings open and its head turned to the side. But it was his third tattoo he was most proud of. Trent had let his tattoo friend ink in whatever the hell he wanted. I was shocked when I first heard about that. I mean, what if the tattoo sucked? Trent would've had to carry that thing around for the rest of his life. But he had faith in his friend's creative abilities. His friend was flattered, of course, but he did warn Trent, "It's gonna be big and crazy."

"That's okay," Trent had told him, sitting in the tattoo chair. "That's exactly what I want." And that's what he got—smack dab on his right arm just below the shoulder—some kind of fiery sun with yellow and orange flames spiraling into an abyss. When he showed it to me the next day, I had to admit, out of all three tattoos, that one was by far the most dazzling to the eyes.

Anyhow, my point is this: Trent had heard about this whole Jim Rose Circus thing through the rocknik grapevine, and he assured me that the show was great. So, after making a few phone calls for directions, we all stepped out of the studio and walked down the street. About a mile down, we found the club where Jim Rose was playing. There was a crowd already gathered outside. We didn't think we'd get in, but Craig knew the doorman, and he walked up to him and whispered a few words in his ear. The doorman patted Craig on the shoulder, then waved Trent and me up to the front of the line. Modestly, we stepped up to Craig and the doorman.

"I'll see you guys later," Craig said. A half hour later, the doors finally opened. Being at the front of the line, Trent and I stepped inside and found a little balcony to the left of the club. Within fifteen minutes, the place had filled up. Once the doors were closed, the lights turned off and the show began. The stage suddenly lit up from a large spotlight. Jim Rose stepped out onto the stage, wearing a black tank top and jeans. He had very short hair and a chiseled chin. The crowd went wild as he stood there in front of the microphone.

"Hello there, Frisco!" he said, in a husky deep voice. "Are you ready to see a show you'll never forget?" The crowd roared. That's all he said. He just growled to the crowd, "All right," then turned around and disappeared behind a velvet curtain. The first performer who came on stage was bald and skinny, a man named Mr. Lifto, introduced by Jim Rose through the speakers. He wore black leather pants, no shirt, with two large silver rings piercing his nipples. All around him were chains, bricks, and cement blocks. He didn't waste any time. The moment he bowed to the crowd, he hooked two chains onto his nipple rings, clipped the other ends of the chains onto two red bricks, which had some kind of metal loops screwed into their surface, and yes, that's when he did it: He lifted those bricks up by the skin of his nipples.

As he bent his back up higher, the skin stretched farther toward the ground. It was quite a sight. I couldn't help imagining his nipples ripping off his chest and causing him to bleed all over the stage. But they didn't. It was as if his skin was made of Silly Putty. After Mr. Lifto finally laid those bricks down and unhooked the chains from his nipple rings, I looked up at his chest to see if any damage was caused to his nipples. None, of course. He was smooth as a thirteen-year-old boy. Crazy bastard.

After the nipple stretch, Mr. Lifto suddenly pulled down his pants and showed his penis to the crowd. It was a cock, all right, a large one with a metal ring piercing the tip of it. Mother of God, I thought, not this! He hooked a thick chain onto the cock-ring, hooked the other end of the chain onto a large gray brick on the stage, stood on a raised platform, straightened out his knees and raised that block of cement with his long, uncircumcised penis.

I almost passed out, I was so disturbed by the sight. But I couldn't stop looking at the man. I was entranced, his cock stretching all the way to the stage. It looked like a giant rubber tube, the way it hung there like that. He even swung the damn thing from side to side to show you how confident he was. But that just made the image worse, for everyone in the crowd. We couldn't help but think of the worst possible outcome. And for all the men in the audience, that was a nightmare none of us wanted to imagine.

There were other performances worth mentioning, like the tattooed guy with little horns somehow implanted into his skull. For his act, he ate a cup of living worms and maggots. They were real. The man just opened his mouth and showed the crowd those slimy little creatures squirming on his tongue. He seemed to like it, though. He just chewed them up and swallowed them without a trace of disgust on his face.

Even Jim Rose came out and did a little performance for the crowd, his hammer-a-nail-right-up-the-nose routine. He also stuck this humungous needle through the sides of his cheeks. That was impressive. Afterward, he threw himself on a pile of broken glass. Someone from backstage moseyed out and stepped on the side of his head. Jim Rose held a microphone near his face just to capture the sound of crushing glass underneath his cheeks. He was okay, though. He just stood up with a smile and brushed himself off. Not a scratch on him.

But still, out of all this mind-over-matter courage, it was the final act that impressed me most. He was a normal-looking man wearing pants and a T-shirt, but that image soon changed. From his pants pocket, he pulled out a red balloon and stuck it up his right nostril. Within seconds, he was able somehow to blow it out his mouth. That made me laugh. Then he got serious. From a cardboard box, he brought out a bottle of Hershey's chocolate syrup, ketchup, and castor oil, poured all that into a glass, stirred it up and actually drank it down like the best-tasting beer he'd ever had. The crowd laughed and clapped.

He then stuck a long tube up his right nostril and kept pushing it there until it settled in the pit of his stomach. Calmly, he held up the other end of the tube. It was a pump mechanism made of glass with an empty chamber of air in the middle. The man smiled at the crowd and pulled the lever. Green bile suddenly shot out of his stomach, through the tube and into the clear chamber of the pump. The crowd moaned. Disconnecting the tube, he turned the pump upward like a cup, popped off the cap, licked his lips, and lifted the green bile for everyone to see.

Oh, no, I thought, he's not gonna do it! But he did. He lifted the pump up to his mouth and chugged down his own stomach bile. The crowd moaned and coughed and gagged. "Oh, man," I sighed, shaking my head. After chugging half the bile, he brought out three glasses from his cardboard box, placed them on the stage, poured the rest of that bile evenly into the glasses and raised them toward the crowd like a bartender. He actually passed all three glasses out to eager volunteers in the audience. If you can believe it, the front row was screaming for the stuff! I gagged when I saw this one guy with a crew cut chug it down.

I heard someone shout, "My God!" A girl screamed, "Aaaaah!" Coughs and groans. Ooooohs and aaaaahs. I couldn't hold it any longer. The laughter came out of me like a volcano erupting from a thousand years of silence. There was no denying it at this point. Human beings were a deranged lot. Everyone in that room had to agree. Insurance plans, jet airplanes, tuxedos, birthday cards, priests, or religion, or any of that morality bullshit disguised as civilized behavior—all that had suddenly disappeared into the potion of that drink. We were in the thick of it, stuck there, drunk on the filth of our own fears.

When Trent and I arrived back at Craig's studio, we found him sitting on his couch reading a book. We told him all about the show. "Man," he laughed, "I can't believe I missed that." We didn't know what to say. We felt bad for the guy. A half hour passed before we all hopped in Trent's car and drove down the streets of Frisco. We were headed to a club where an all-night rave was taking place. I had never been to a rave before, but I had heard stories. Supposedly it was a club or a party full of people on Ecstasy with techno music blasting through the speakers. I had never been too enthused about techno music, but what the hell, I was always open to new experiences.

In the car, we popped those pills and chugged them down with a bottle of water. Trent and I were excited—our first time trying Ecstasy. We arrived at the club around one in the morning. Walking through the entrance of the club, Trent asked if I was feeling the Ecstasy yet. Just when he said that, the three of us ran into a crowd of people boogying down in the middle of the dance floor. Blue lasers beamed from above while techno music boomed through the speakers. My heart soared with excitement as if I had just jumped off a waterfall. The Ecstasy had kicked in. It was a strange sensation, not like LSD or 'shrooms, but similar in its own trippy way. The intensity of colors was definitely there, magnified to a point of seeing double, but I wasn't confused.

Objects weren't breathing or melting or anything. They merely dazzled like a diamond in the rays of neon light. Then there was the emotion itself—that was the powerful part. I felt like I had just walked into an orgy in the Garden of Eden and experienced sexual desire for the first time in my life. But it wasn't just sex. It was affection for all living souls—the adventurous arrows of Cupid. They were everywhere, invisible and moving like an underwater current. Lips and eyes and arms and breasts, all of it was a pool of touching and pleasure. Like a devil cat, I wanted to lick it all up with a smile. "Yeah," I shouted to Trent. "I'm feeling it! How about you? How do you feel?" He shouted back, "I don't feel a thing!" I laughed. For some reason, Trent always reacted to drugs slower than I did. "Just wait a little while," I shouted. "It'll happen."

Bombarded by the crowd of people, Trent and Craig went off to the bar. I just started dancing away. I couldn't help myself. I was feeling too damn good to just stand around and watch. Everyone seemed to be high on Ecstasy as they moved their bodies to the beat. I had no idea what I was doing, but I didn't care. I was too entranced by the crowd. Maybe it was those beautiful girls in sundresses all around me, grooving without a care on their minds. They weren't teenyboppers in a mall, they were sexual beings, tribal, putting on a wild display of tits and ass.

An hour later, Trent suddenly stepped up to me. "Hey, what's goin' on?"

"Hey," I smiled, still dancing with the crowd. "Where've you been?"

"Walking around. Checking things out." He was tripping, all right. I could tell by the smile on his face.

"You feel it now, don't you?"

"Yeah, but I had to take another one."

"Another one? Jesus, Trent, you're crazy."

"Listen," he exclaimed, staring up at the balcony. People were up there dancing. "I've gotta keep moving."

"Okay, but I'm staying right here. This is the spot!"

"Well, I've got more people to meet! I've been going around, shaking everyone's hands." He took my hand. "Hi! I'm Trent. Nice to meet you." Then he was off, blending into the crowd. People didn't stop dancing until six that morning. We all began to file out of the club. Walking through the exit, Craig put his arm around Trent's and my shoulders and said, "Are you guys ready for another one?"

"Yeah, sure," we laughed, the morning sun glaring into our eyes.

"I'm serious. We're all headed to this other club that starts up in ten minutes." Trent and I looked at each other. We couldn't believe it. Another rave? Craig just stood there, waiting for our reply. After a few minutes, Trent and I shook our heads and looked at him with a smile. What the hell, we figured, the idea was so crazy, we had to go for it. We arrived at the club a half-hour later. Walking toward the entrance, I recognized people from the previous rave. Jesus, I thought, don't these people ever sleep? Then we were inside the place—neon lights, blue furniture, green laser beams, a small crowd talking on the dance floor.

That same techno music was blasting in the background, and it got on my nerves. The rhythm never seemed to change. Plus, the whole not-sleeping thing seemed ludicrous to me. Sure, party it up, but this was out of control. The speed from the Ecstasy kept these people from going home and sleeping in a nice comfortable bed. They wanted the high to last as long as possible. But it was morning now. No matter how far they tried to escape into the oblivion of drugs, the sunlight reminded them of the reality in which they lived. "Like fucking bats," I shouted to Trent.

Exhausted from all that dancing, the three of us went up to the second floor of the club. Craig led us into a little room where all sorts of neon eyes looked at us as we entered its darkened chamber. Once our eyes adjusted, we noticed a group of people sitting on a rug in a semicircle. In front of them, right there on the couch, was a black man with long dreadlocks, holding a helium tank leaning against his lap. We sat down in a corner of the room on yellow beanbags and just absorbed the energy of the scene. Me, I didn't quite know what was going on, but I knew something was up with that black guy and his helium tank. His multicolored clothes glowed in the black light, especially that Dr. Seuss hat he wore. "What's with the tank?" I whispered to Craig.

He looked at me with surprise. "It's a nitrous tank." I didn't say anything. "You mean you guys have never tried nitrous before?"

"Nope. What is it?"

"It's that gas dentists use to knock you out before surgery."

"Ohhhh," I nodded, staring at the group of people on the rug. They were passing a few balloons around and breathing in the gas. One guy took a hit and just laughed, real slow, as if his brain suddenly went backwards, dropping his vocal chords into a dunce-like pitch. "All right," I said, "I'll try it. How much is it?"

"Just give the guy in the hat a few bucks."

Fuck it. I inched my way over to the guy and handed him a $20 bill. "That enough?"

"How many you want?"

"Three."

"Yeah, that's cool." He took the money, stuffed it in his pocket, gave me some change, filled three balloons and handed them to me without a smile. Then I crawled back over to the corner, handing Trent and Craig a balloon. We each had a toke from Craig's pipe before we got started with the nitrous. We wanted to make sure we were nice and high. I know I was. Craig's weed was green and soft, and it fucked me up good. It even kicked the Ecstasy back in. I was all euphoric like before, floating in a dazzling ocean of warmth.

"Are you guys ready?" Craig asked. "Now, remember, it's like smoking pot. Just breathe it in and keep it in your lungs for a few seconds."

We looked at each other, smiled, then put those balloons to our mouths and inhaled. As I closed my eyes, my brain lost all balance and control. It floated around like an underwater bubble. But my ears were still there. They acted as microphones for the music downstairs. Each instrument crashed into a hundred different sounds, triggering an explosion of images—shooting stars, blue sparks across a canvas of dark space. Then I heard voices from those people near the couch—"Look at him, he's fucked up!"—as I opened my eyes and saw faces distorted into a mesh of demons and masks.

So I closed my eyes again. That's when I heard Trent's laughter. It was deep and monstrous, the primitive Trent laughing from all the pleasure of earthly desires. For some reason, that didn't scare me. Fear was non-existent in this world; there was only bliss and the pounding heart in which I lived. This pounding became faster and faster, as if my skull was rippling in and out of existence. It was a wa-wa sound: wa wa wa wa wa wa wa wa wa wa wawawawawawa . . . and then silence.

I opened my eyes and looked at Craig and Trent. They were sitting in front of me, grinning with eyes closed. "Holy shit," I said, "that was amazing!" I looked around the room and saw a few of those people grinning at me from the rug. They knew exactly how I felt. I turned back to Craig and Trent. "I don't know about you guys," I said, "but I'm doing that again."

After an hour of nitrous hits, we finally left the club. At the car, Craig told us to go on ahead; he was off to another rave. We laughed, it was so hard to believe, but off he went, disappearing with a few friends around the corner of the club. Trent and I looked at each other. We were beat—twenty-six hours without sleep was enough for us. We hopped in Trent's car and immediately drove to Craig's studio.

We woke up on those mattresses around five that afternoon. It was time to head home. We just grabbed our things and packed up the car. But Craig was nowhere in sight. We didn't know what to do. At first, we thought of walking around and trying to find him, but that would've been futile. We had to get back. As we were driving down the road toward the freeway, we saw a group of people walking across the street. We recognized a few of them from the club. "Unbelievable," I said. "These people never stop!"

That's when I saw Craig a few yards up ahead. He was standing on a sidewalk talking to some people at a bus stop. "There's Craig," I shouted. "Pull over, Trent, pull over!" He slowed down and stopped at the curb. Craig saw the car and walked up to the open passenger window and asked where we were going. Trent leaned over from the driver's seat. "Sorry, Craig. We had to get going, man. I left the key on the coffee table. We waited around, but . . . We just wanted to say goodbye, and thank you for everything. It was an unbelievable time, man."

"Yeah," I agreed. "Amazing. Thanks a lot."

"You guys take care," Craig said. He let go of the window frame, stepped back a few inches, and waved goodbye. Trent pulled the car in the road and stepped on the gas. I saw Craig's image shrink in the side-door mirror. Adiós, brother, I thought. What a cool fuckin' guy.

Good Vibes from Sharon Tate and Charlie Manson / R. U. Sirius

PART ONE: Fame Damage

The mid-'90s were not a high point in the strange career of my occasional friend and mentor, Dr. Timothy Leary. Sure, the party was going night and day at his house in Beverly Hills, and during a single week-long stay I could hang there with Billy Idol, Mark Mothersbaugh, Helmut Newton, Sheep on Drugs, filmmaker Brett Leonard, and an avant-garde theater director obsessed with Charles Manson. Hell, I could even glimpse Yoko Ono sitting in the back of her limo waiting to take Timmy on a date to go see the LA Symphony.

But Barbara, who had been Leary's wife (not to mention social director) for nearly a decade and a half, had left with a wealthy Brazilian man a few years earlier, and there was still a sadness around Tim. He was the sort of man who didn't really feel complete without a mate and a mission, and at this point he didn't really have either. Nevertheless, at any given moment, Leary could tap into some inner resource that seemed to evoke a kind of instant joie de vivre amongst everyone who happened to be in the vicinity.

I was staying at the Leary home for a couple of weeks, along with Scrappi and Simone, cohorts in a musical crime called *Mondo Vanilli*. We were zipping around LA with our friend, Yvonne, a talkative Chicago girl who was sort of a longtime (ahem) adjunct to the rock music industry. Yvonne always had rock and roll stories to tell—about Keith Richards and Anita Pallenberg, about Al Jourgensen—so many stories, filled with flashes of glory and many many complaints. But most relevant to this particular story, she never hesitated to walk in through the front door. We were in LA for the same reason that any number of twenty-somethings were there (only I happened to be forty-three at the time): we were there to get our demo tape into the hands of people within the music industry who could make us stars.

Between Yvonne's list of friends and the connections I'd made as publisher and editor-in-chief of *Mondo 2000* magazine, we had plenty of major league music industry people who would give our peculiar dog and pony show an hour of their time. In between visits with various labels and power agents, we dropped in on Casey Cannon. She put together lots of the film trailers you saw in theaters throughout the late 1980s and early '90s. Casey was tied into the Industrial Light and Magic crowd up in the Bay Area and James Cameron's gang in LA, but she seemed to know everybody. And she knew where the parties were. She was a bit of a B-list queen. In LA, the social A-list is made up of film producers, directors, and stars, and possibly a few major "old money" rock stars from the '60s and '70s. With the exception of Madonna, post-'70s rockers are strictly B-list. That was where we needed to be.

Sure enough, Casey had a peculiar and resonant B-list suggestion to add to our social calendar. The Nine Inch Nails man, Trent Reznor, was having a party that night at home. Reznor had recently rented the house that Sharon Tate and Roman Polanski were living in when Manson's girls creepy-crawled over the walls and committed their barbaric slaughter. According to Casey, we simply had to get an invitation to this party. She gave us the magic phone number, and I called it right there.

Cold-calling celebrities always makes me feel weird and uncomfortable. They are the presumed gods of our culture, and we, the unknown or lesser known, are their supplicants, bending down on worshipful knee for the favor of their attention. Okay, that's probably a bit of an exaggeration, at least among hipsters like ourselves. Let's just say, as a lesser known, I've got issues that an unknown might not have, because I'm in the game. I'm just way down there in the minor leagues. And there's nothing like a major celebrity asking who the fuck I think I am calling on their private number (Hi, Yoko!) to make me feel like a worm. Luckily, Reznor didn't answer the phone. I got to leave behind a message. Being a well-mannered boy, I didn't try to scam up a party invitation; I simply told Mr. Reznor why we were in town and that we hoped to meet him. And in that message, I got to say that we were staying at the home of Timothy Leary. Aside from being the greatest host in the world, the Leary name was a first-rate calling card.

That evening, we were settling in with low expectations for what seemed like a rare quiet night at the Leary estate, when Tim came out of his office space with phone in hand. He was talking to Pighead Christopherson, who was up at Trent Reznor's house. Trent wanted us all to come to his party that night. What a surprise!

PART TWO: It's too late to have a date with Sharon Tate

As you can tell, my head was all jammed uptight with low-level, nervous-making careerist issues around fame and status as we got dressed for the Trentfest. And when Dr. Tim emerged from his bedroom with a mint dish full of square white Ecstasy tablets for the taking, I rather wished that they were Valiums. Simone said yes to the doctor's kind offer to join him, but Scrappi, Yvonne, and I just said no.

However, being of sound mind but low income, the thought of turning down a free hit of Timothy Leary-quality Ecstasy irked me. I wandered over to the mint dish and pocketed one. Then, just before getting ready to head up the hill to the ol' Tate mansion (not far from Timmy's house), as we dawdled over our last beers, I impulsively wolfed down my Ecstasy hit.

I must have had an empty stomach that night, because it came on quick. There was a cherry red Ferarri tailgating us up the winding path, and when Leary pulled over to let it by, the long-haired fellow inside started gesticulating wildly. Eventually, he stuck his head out the window and shouted that he was following us up to Reznor's place. It was a familiar face, indeed a veritable poster-boy face for bad behavior. It was Gibby Haynes of the Butthole Surfers.

On arrival, the enthusiastic Haynes, excited to meet Leary, jumped out of his car, bragging that the Ferarri he was driving belonged to Johnny Depp. At that moment, with the Ecstasy really coming on, I entered a comfort zone with LA media culture. It's all the same fucking playground; Johnny Depp is just another kid. Even Madonna is just another kid, as within reach as Theresa Bonasia, the little girl I had a crush on in the first grade. The world was a friendly place.

But not friendly enough. We walked past one house with all the lights out. A sign said that the party was in the other house. We headed back toward a large square structure that looked like a glorified garage. Inside, the scene was Grunge Boy meets Barbie Doll. To my stoned brain, it looked like hundreds of clones. The guys all had longish hair, black leather jackets, and puffy beer-abuser faces (just like me, actually), and the girls all looked like perfect blonde babes with inflatable boobs and noses pointed upward toward the sky.

Gloomy Kraut techno blared too loudly for conversation, and the general mood seemed dour. Everyone carried plastic cups with beer. No one was talking to each other. The girls all looked disappointed. There were no rock stars in sight. This was nothing but a college kegger! Where the hell was Trent? Leary looked lost and confused. Nevertheless, he asserted his tribal leadership and brought us all to safety—a place to sit—stone benches around an unlit fireplace. Once settled, Tim and Simone found comfort locked into each other's eyes, while Scrappi, Yvonne, and I continued to search the room with our eyes for a glimmer of glamour.

After a while, I realized that I had a choice. If I sat there any longer, I was going to trance out into the rather boring pink sponge-cake that the inside of my head had turned into, or I was going to have to get up and do something. By now, I was too bored to get paranoid or creeped out. I grabbed Yvonne by the hand and suggested we should explore the grounds for their "creepy crawly possibilities."

As we exited the building, Reznor appeared and greeted us with a sly grin. He followed us out, and around the corner there was Anthony Kiedis of the Red Hot Chile Peppers. Reznor introduced me. Kiedis inquired, "Your name is Are You Serious?"—with just the slightest indication of contempt. I had a split second to locate my psychedelically displaced ego. I found it next to my slightly mangled wit, and together we mustered up a response. I looked up at the towering pop star whose face had filled my TV screen repeatedly over the previous decade or so.

"Yes," I smiled, "and who are you?"

Kiedis deflated. "I'm Anthony," he muttered humbly, and we shook hands.

And so Yvonne and I soldiered on to check the perimeters of the Tate mansion, wondering what walls a creepy crawler would crawl over, what bushes a Squeaky Fromme would creep through. It was all a game to us, and Squeaky Fromme was just a funny name, like Oprah or Uma. Somehow the horrible reality of that day some twenty-five years earlier didn't seem any closer at hand on the grounds of the Tate mansion than it had from any other spot on the planet. If there are ghosts, maybe Ecstasy chases them away.

After a good half hour of wandering and videotaping the arriving party guests (Yvonne kept her Sony video camera with her at all times), we noticed that there was a little bit of light peeking out from behind the curtains of the main house that we'd passed by on our arrival. We slinked up to the door. There was a handwritten sign that said, COME IN HERE TO BE KILLED! I actually cogitated momentarily over whether this was a serious threat.

Let's see. Trent Reznor is a major rock star with money and ambition. He wouldn't want to die right now from a lethal injection, particularly one that doesn't get you off first. Now maybe if he had spent the last year trying to suck up to Terry Melcher and Dennis Wilson, only to have his song lyrics ripped off by the Beach Boys . . . *aaaiiiyyyy,* don't go there. Thankfully, Yvonne put a stop to my internal reverie just before it transformed into full-blown empathy for the devil.

She did the only sensible thing. She pointed her camera in front of her and opened the door. There they were. Seventeen Illuminati figures, including Marilyn Manson, George W. Bush, David Bowie, and the Penguin, in black robes, huddled around a girl who looked like Britney Spears lying in the center of a pentagram, while Reznor raised the blade. Well, okay. None of those people were there, not even Bush. Actually, what we found was a party going on inside. Gibby was berating this absurdly perfect LA babe who wouldn't believe that this greasy long-haired drunkard with a Texas accent was the driver of the red hot Ferrari and that it actually belonged to his buddy Johnny Depp.

"Cunt," he screamed. "Stupid fucking LA cunt!" But somehow the only person there feeling any bad vibes was the girl, who turned on her high heels, stuck her perfect nose in the air and strutted out the door while extending her middle finger behind her.

And that's basically the whole story. Let's see, I did observe Reznor with a plastic baggie full of 'shrooms popping them into his own mouth and those of two apparent girlfriends. And everybody I talked to was in the music business, but they all wanted to talk with me about the Internet and virtual reality. Here I was, finally at an LA B-list party, and it was just like any party in San Francisco. I don't think anyone in that room was entertaining a single thought about Sharon Tate or Charles Manson, or a girl named Squeaky. Well, maybe Gibby was.

The next morning, it occurred to me that the person I was in the 1970s would be very impressed if he learned that I'd taken a psychedelic drug with Dr. Timothy Leary on the site of the Manson murders. But it was nothing, really. And speaking of nothing, I did get to have an interaction with Mr. Reznor over a recording contract with Nothing Records, but Nothing came to nothing, and some day if you care, I'll tell you how my rock career was killed by Bob Dole, Marilyn Manson, and Yoko Ono.

In the meantime, here's your take-home message: Famous people are about as boring or interesting as your friends. If you take Ecstasy or other psychedelics with them, forget about glamour, forget about murder, forget about the major cosmic reverberations you think you're getting that you're the reborn Lizard King of Atlantis, or the reincarnation of Aleister Crowley and *The Flying Nun,* and just give them as much love as you can.

R. U. Sirius is the author of *Counterculture through the Ages: From Abraham to Acid House.*

Rollin' / Pat Mormino

Okay, I can understand how doin' Ecstasy every other day is pretty damn bad for your body and brain, but I have rolled twice (about four months apart), and I think it might even be the best thing that ever happened to my head.

The first time, my friend told he was gonna give me half of an 007, but he ended up giving me one quarter of a hit. That roll didn't really make me look forward to Ecstasy. But my friends were like, "Yo, we can get Ecstasy." Next thing I know, we got the rolls on a Friday along with two twenty-bags.

When we pulled up to my house, we decided to smoke a lot of weed first and save the Ecstasy for after dinner (when my parents wouldn't interfere). We popped the Ecstasy around 5 p.m. I can remember swallowing it. I could feel a stream of some crazy chemicals traveling down my throat. It took about an hour for it to start kicking in.

I accidentally hit my leg, and goddamn, it felt bizarre as hell. So I pounded my leg on purpose as hard as I could, and it hurt for a second. Then I felt a tingling wave float through my body. Music had never sounded better. I could feel my serotonin skyrocketing.

We went down to my basement to just sit and chill. We ended up sitting and chilling from 6:30 to about 11:30, thinking only like forty minutes went by. The two people I was chilling with turned into my two best friends after that experience (now one is an asshole, but I'm still best friends with the other).

I was never happier in my life than during those five hours. I can now say that after that experience, I understand people a lot better, even if they are assholes. They want world peace so damn bad, just put all the world leaders on MDMA, and I guarantee this world will be a better place.

Night Flight / Gregg Rounds

My band, Soviet Corn Bread, was scheduled to play one night in the San Francisco equivalent of a gothic opium den—an ancient and charming bar called Café du Nord on the far slope of the Castro hill. The eerie cloak of the dark venue's spirit shook us immensely the last time we played there, so we were excited about the show that evening. The band consisted of four members, all formerly natives of the Texas hill country, and all recently transplanted into this rocky and wintry mountain land.

At that particular point in our band's early conception, we were experimenting with a post-modern space-rock sound that was apparently already passé. But we still firmly believed in the mind-numbing, string-squealing chaos as a means to express our sexual frustrations from an imaginary deep space. Call us naive, but our fan base was present and acute.

We had several groups of friends in town. Most of them had commuted from various points of this mystic peninsula to show their support, or at least encouragement. An early evening party was arranged near the base of Ashbury Heights, not far from the stone pillars. Wine, cheese, and a halting amount of cocaine was available for the attendees (none for me, though; too early).

However, rumors of Ecstasy floated around the house as twilight pushed the Arctic fog over our heads and whistled icy breaths through the crowded rooms. I decided to set out on a search-and-recover mission. What did I care? Control was for the narcissistic bastards of mainstream rock and roll. Underground artists had no use for such restrained methods of performance.

On my way to the back porch to smoke a cigarette, I scanned this mixed bag of has-been ravers, alcoholic Texans, snotty tech warriors, Vespa hipsters, fever-broke rockers, and stoic natives, but I didn't spot anyone supplying. A couple of steps from the back door, I passed an old friend from college, a tall specter of a man. Brian's hair was as light and translucent as silk; his crystalline eyes were the only vibrant feature of his pale person to hang your gaze on.

For quite some time, he had possessed an overeager appetite for potential opportunity, always pointing forward, never pausing, not ever, and he had an unlimited tolerance for oxidants. There was even a recurring fable about his mythic mortality. He'd apparently been the lone survivor of several apocalyptic car wrecks.

We shared a smoke on a rickety porch that peered directly into the lonely interiors of a hundred claustrophobic apartments, and he handed me a couple of Ecstasy tabs. Brian kindly thanked me for the guest-list pass and swiftly left me alone to deal with the heartbreaking bay winds. I dropped one tab and put the other in my pocket.

As we were leaving the party to go set up at the club, my blood warmed to a dark green color that heated the inner reaches of my soul. It was impossible not to smile as I passed under the arches of wise, rogue Cypresses. My eyes narrowed as the drug's familiar strobing effect invaded my vision. I thought of all the cultures that had walked these paths before, and I felt an intense nostalgia for all those that I'd never known.

The show was spectacular, the Ecstasy had dug in comfortably, and the rare spiky points had only enhanced a rather well-needed cathartic release. The outlines of the crowd members looked like feather-tipped, cardboard cut-outs. We thought the songs sounded top-notch, although later folks would tell us that it was sloppy, but to us their masturbatory feedback had been exactly what we needed to sincerely articulate the appropriate soundtrack for that precise moment in time.

Later that night, I reunited with my old friend Brian, and we left the Transylvanian arches of the Castro and slowly descended into the infernal reaches of San Francisco's skid row to a dance club called 1015 Folsom. The place was hot red and thirsty. Ecstasy was passed around like cigarettes. Beautiful bodies and faces writhed past us in every conceivable direction and manner.

Time became fluid as it always does, and fifteen minutes turned into two hours. Shutter vision, euphoria, and a sense of peace prevailed and transformed the club into a universe of its own—nothing existed outside of the present. Each of the club's different levels represented an alternate slice of reality. We found ourselves in the belly of this beast, a converted basement lined with plush booths.

Brian was engaged in a passionate dialogue with a blond-haired Japanese lad. Curious about their enthusiasm and the subject matter, I snapped out of my meditation and scooted over, only to discover that the Japanese guy didn't speak a single word of English—and Brian doesn't speak Japanese—yet they continued to speak to each other ethusiastically as if they were old friends.

I also discovered that the Japanese guy was handing out tiny Ecstasy capsules, and we each took another one. Time evaded us and passed behind our backs until we found ourselves back on the roof of my apartment building off Van Ness Avenue. A small crowd had gathered up on the roof, and music blared through the open window of someone's apartment. The majestic lights of the surreal city were partially obscured by the relentless nocturnal fog. We drank vodka like thirsty Russians until everyone turned in.

Back in the warmth of my apartment, we mixed another drink and smoked some grass. It wasn't until then that I realized my friend's trip had taken a serious turn. He began circling the room, pretending to speak into a phantom cell phone. He apparently thought he was in the airport.

I asked him, "Who are you talking to?"

"My brother."

"Oh, really? Where is he?" He began frantically searching his pockets, and even went so far as to look under the couch cushions. "What in the hell are you looking for?"

"My brother."

"Oh, fuck."

I found a strong sedative and gave it to him, I turned down the lights and put on some mellow music. After making his bed on the fold-out couch, I pretended to be tired, hoping that the feeling would be contagious. Brian appeared to be relaxing and went into the bathroom to wash up. I told him goodnight through the door and gratefully crawled into my damp, rigid bed.

As I was drifting into the unknown reaches of my drug-induced slumber, I heard soft footsteps run out of the apartment and up the stairs to the roof. I lurched out of bed and followed in my pajamas. Outside, on the roof, I could barely make out Brian's outline as he marched to the far edge of the five-story building's roof. There wasn't any railing along the side, and the fog had rolled in so thick that it practically touched the edge of the roof.

I imagined that through Brian's perspective, the perfectly guttered cream corduroy of the fog appeared to be an extension of the roof that gradually led all the way down to the ocean cliffs. But of course it wasn't. He walked off the side of the building and dropped 100 feet to the grassy courtyard far below.

The only thing that saved him was the nurturing limbs of a massive eucalyptus tree. He somehow slid down its lush branches in a cartoon-like fashion, cracking a couple as he went. I ran down the five flights of stairs and out through the basement door into the courtyard. Prepared for the absolute worst, I approached his motionless body.

I expected a cracked skull, blood pouring out of his mouth and eyes. I imagined what his last words would be, and the phone call to his mom. Tears poured out of my eyes. My face flushed with fever as I turned him from his side to his back. He didn't have a scratch. Perhaps he really was immortal. His eyes opened, and I thought he might laugh. I didn't know if this was really happening. I almost fainted.

But then he spoke. His words came out all jumbled. It took all of my strength to help him up, because his equilibrium had been severely distorted. After getting him to the hospital, they informed me that it was a serious concussion, but he'd be fine in a couple of weeks.

False Alarm / Paul Krassner

It was one of those rare occasions when my wife Nancy and I could take off for a weekend vacation in the desert. I made sure to bring our favorite designer drug, Ecstasy, along with marijuana, snacks, vitamins, and bottled water. In our room at the spa, we smoked a joint to ease us into the Ecstasy, then swallowed our capsules. We hung out, soaking in the hot springs pool with a beautiful view of the mountains as we got higher and higher.

Because taking Ecstasy is such a sensual and loving experience, there is an agonizing irony about its distribution. Just as the Mafia began distributing LSD in the '60s, so organized crime—the pinnacle of mayhem and murder—has been distributing Ecstasy. Thus, Salvatore "Sammy the Bull" Gravano, former hit man and government snitch responsible for the imprisonment of mob boss John Gotti, got a dose of he own medicine when he was arrested.

Although the DEA declared MDMA illegal in 1985, its popularity has been increasing steadily—one out of twelve high school seniors has tried Ecstasy—and it's the drug of choice at rave parties. But, just as there was hysterical media panic in the '60s about brain damage caused by LSD, there is now the same kind of propaganda being spread about Ecstasy.

Recently, *Sixty Minutes* presented a twelve-minute segment on Ecstasy, featuring material intended to scare the living shit out of viewers, including footage of a young man who had gone into a coma and died as a result of taking five hits of Ecstasy.

Not included was footage of Ecstasy pioneers Sasha and Anne Shulgin—despite an extensive interview with them—nor any mention of the therapeutic and medicinal uses of MDMA. Also omitted was the footage of the Dutch government's national drug prosecutor saying that pill testing "saves lives," and the interview with Trinka Poratta, former LA police officer and National Police Consultant on Dance Drugs, who expressed her support for harm reduction and on-site pill testing, specifically by DanceSafe.

However, Emmanuel Sferios of DanceSafe was interviewed for two hours—two minutes of which were shown on the program, depicting him talking about harm reduction and testing pills at a rave, plus the DanceSafe website was shown.

"In short," he says, "they chose to portray us as the lone representative of harm reduction, with no support from police or policy-makers. This is unfortunate and grossly inaccurate, but not entirely unexpected. Prime-time television likes controversy. We are and were aware of that. Our choice to work with *Sixty Minutes* was based on a recognition that, at this point in time, national press coverage on raves and Ecstasy that mentions harm reduction is better than no mention at all.

"Now don't get me wrong. It was a ridiculous, overly alarmist, and totally sensationalistic hit piece on Ecstasy, but this is what made DanceSafe and harm reduction look so reasonable. The undercover Orlando police officer, Mike Stevens, came across as overzealous and ideological, whereas we came across as pragmatic and reasonable. You could hear the emotion in his voice as he spoke—'Ecstasy is no different from crack or heroin'—whereas I sounded calm and collected.

"Middle America is getting fed up with the drug war. They are looking for an alternative. We should consider this *Sixty Minutes* segment a huge victory for harm reduction. If we hadn't interviewed with them, they would have run the same show, just without us at the end, and harm reduction would not even have been mentioned."

Moreover, TV viewers have since been flooding their website.

Meanwhile, someone sent Peter McWilliams a new product that contains concentrated coffee and is promoted as giving the consumer a "lift." He responded: "Are you letting people know that caffeine is an addictive drug to which the body builds up an immunity within two weeks, and after that you're pretty much taking it to ease the pangs of addiction and to get back to 'normal' again? A little warning label such as that, and you'll have a great product, marketed with integrity.

"Caffeine is marketed to children in Coca-Cola and a dozen other sodas. It is a harsh drug, akin to cocaine. It should be used sparingly by adults—once or twice a week at most. Children should never use it. What it does to their developing nervous systems is nothing short of horrific! That tens of millions of kids swill sodas every day is the most serious drug problem in this country. That's why I call caffeine the most dangerous drug in America."

Well, my wife and I hardly ever drink coffee or soda. But that time we took Ecstasy in the desert—or thought we did—we finally realized that we had ingested Vitamin C by mistake. We had been getting high from a combination of THC and the power of suggestion.

Holiday Trip / Robert Anton Wilson

My first experience with a major psychedelic was with peyote in 1962, and that was full of marvelous philosophical revelations, beautiful colors, magnificent visions, and at the height of it—this was New Year's in 1962—I went into the other room and looked at the Christmas tree and the ornaments, and everything was beautiful.

It was the most beautiful Christmas tree I ever saw. And then I realized that the Christmas tree loved me, and I burst into tears. I was running back to tell my wife and my friends, "The Christmas tree loves me!" Even telling that story, tears came to my eyes, I remember the experience so vividly. The Christmas tree that loves me!

Robert Anton Wilson is the author of *TSOG: The Thing That Ate the Constitution.*

Dope Cactus / Lola Granola

In 1964, I was a student at Barnard College, living off campus between Columbia University and Harlem. That's where I found a florist selling a little cactus that I had only seen before in books, *Lophophora williamsii,* also known as "the dope cactus."

"Why is it called the dope cactus?" I asked the florist, feigning naivete.

"Maybe because it looks so dopey," he said.

"Gimme all of 'em," I said, and walked home with seven peyote plants.

Freedom to Misbehave / William Walker

In 1963, I was studying, more or less, at Shibboleth College, a benighted, all-male Presbyterian institution lost in the cornfields about twenty miles north of Charlotte, North Carolina. It was the worst of times. If you were in a fraternity and had a car, the available outlets, sexual and otherwise, were dismal. If not, and you weren't gay, they consisted of masturbation and trips on foot to a beer joint about a mile up the road from the town and campus, both of which were officially and stringently dry.

The college's policy on booze was severe, and if you were caught with it on campus, you were thrown out. As to sex, perhaps there was an explicit policy, never articulated, but the assumption seemed to be that it didn't exist, and so you didn't need to think about it for your four years in the place. What we later came to regard as the '60s hadn't started yet. Well, in Berkeley, where they had always existed, I suppose, but they certainly hadn't trickled down to the wasteland of the Piedmont.

I do not think that in this cultural vacuum the word "drug" had acquired any strong connotations except in combination with "store." It would not have occurred to most of us that alcohol and nicotine, the latter consumed massively in those parts ever since the seventeenth century, were drugs, or that getting high had correct and incorrect applications, depending on the substance being abused. Uppers and downers were somewhere in the future.

The situation was actually, now that I reflect on it, much more wretched than the '50s, that era being dead, and the other apparently powerless to be born. I sometimes hung out with two guys who were studying premed and biology, and maybe these subjects predisposed them to more adventurous experimentation. One of them, Jonas Hunley, was an amateur taxidermist and would skin and stuff mice he caught in the dorm and line the little corpses up on his shelf next to the stale bread and the jars of jam and peanut butter.

I never knew what else the other one, Harris Tripps, did apart from farting around and getting into trouble in a lethargic sort of way. It was Harris, however, who showed up at some point with an ad for peyote cactus buds, which could be ordered from an outfit in Texas called Sunshine Ranches or something similar. I wish I could remember more about the ad, and what if anything it said to suggest that the buds contained psychedelic substances, but Harris claimed to know that they did.

I doubt we had ever heard of Timothy Leary, or the relevant writings of Aldous Huxley and William S. Burroughs, but the notion was conveyed that the buds would somehow open the doors of perception for us. If there was any legislation about growing or possessing or shipping the things, nobody was paying attention to it, and so one day Harris fetched a plain cardboard box, maybe a foot long and four by five inches on the sides, and containing several dozen light green, tough, bulbous, circular objects, with little clumps of spines sticking out here and there, from the old redneck at the post office on Main Street, just as if he had ordered a supply of tulip bulbs.

Another thing I don't recall is what they cost, only that we all kicked in a few bucks. Now came the very practical difficulty of introducing them into our metabolisms. They were so tough that a sharp hunting knife would barely slice them; we had better luck rasping off little strands and chunks with a nail file. Once through the dry outer skin, we found the insides were a pretty emerald green, and somewhat moist, but squeeze and pound them as we would, we could not extract a single drop of liquid.

Maceration was suggested and was equally unsuccessful. Drying them out on windowsills and radiators just made them tougher. But the real problem was the taste, bitter beyond imagining, when we tried to chew the pieces. When we swallowed some of them whole, we promptly puked them back up. Harris felt rather burned by these results and persisted after Jonas and I had lost interest. A good while later, he reported to us that he had kept enough down that he'd had a "vision" while staring at the grillwork of a sports car. I wasn't impressed. Much later, when I did read around in the sacred texts, it struck me that Harris's account was suspiciously literary.

These memories line up with another set from the same time and place: There was always in those days one charismatic, crazy professor at tight-assed, conservative colleges, who was usually in the English department, and who was granted, up to a point, *Narrenfreiheit*, the freedom to misbehave accorded to the fools during Carneval. The obligatory archetype at Shibboleth was Dr. Kornholt, about whom much has been told and written. Dr. K ran the drama program as his personal fiefdom and made extreme demands on the time and emotional stamina of anyone involved in his productions.

It was an open secret that if you were in trouble over sleep-debt, he could fix you up with pills to see you through the worst. It was said that he had a brother in another state who was a doctor or pharmacist who had given him an open prescription for the things, which were actually capsules, one end yellow, the other black. We called them "yellowjackets," and this was the only term I ever knew for them. Obviously, the contents were some sort of speed, another unfamiliar word to me then, outside the everyday contexts. More than once I saw him pop open several of the gelatin capsules and tip the white powder into a mug of rancid, luke-warm black coffee, stir the mess up with a pencil, and swill it down.

A couple of plays—Aeschylus's *Agamemnon* and Maxwell Anderson's *Winterset*—were especially hard on everybody and were fueled from start to finish by yellow-jackets. The story is told that during the rehearsals for *Agamemnon,* Dr. K chased a couple of actors from the chorus, who had mutinied because of his all-night sessions, into the parking lot behind the Fine Arts Building (which everybody called the FARTS) to remonstrate with them.

They whimpered and gibbered that they were flunking out, couldn't take any more, etc. He howled, cursed, slobbered, and blamed them for the decline of civilization. They were still in costume, with raggedy robes and long, ratty paste-on beards. At the climax of his rant he gesticulated with his pipe, flung hot ashes all over the place, and set one of the beards on fire. Perhaps the tale is apocryphal—I didn't witness it—but it fits in perfectly with the atmosphere of the speed, the nervous exhaustion, and the crazed intensity the man could conjure up.

I do not believe that any of us involved in the scenes just described had the slightest thought that we were enacting a rebellion, which is also part of the cultural vacuum of the times. Politicization came later. Our parents and the authorities at the college wouldn't have approved of our chewing cactus buds and popping amphetamines, but then, they didn't approve of any number of things we did, and that was a condition we lived with. There was no special aura to messing with these "drugs," which, as said, was barely a concept and which we would have been surprised and offended to hear applied to what we were doing. Besides, in those days, a hit off a Kool cigarette probably did as much for me as any other substance I had access to.

Buds and Birds / Fran More

In the beautiful fall of '74, I escaped boredom and vexation and baby diapers for several days with my new pal, a world citizen named Jamie Moonbeam, who had mastered the art of hitchhiking in and out of our remote Oregon redneck small town. We went halfway up Mount Shasta where her pal Singing Tree had erected a real tipi and had a big sack of peyote buds.

The ceremony was refreshingly reverent. As everyone began to eventually disperse, later to retire for the night, I became alarmed at an old man I kept seeing everywhere, swooping around in a long black satin cape lined in scarlet. He was accompanied by a four-foot-tall old woman who resembled a carp. No woman I'd ever seen was that horribly ugly, and the Dracula dude was a bit much.

I'd planned on leaving the real Indians alone in the crowded tipi and sleeping alone under the stars, but I decided to sleep in the community cabin with whoever was crashing there, out of undefeatable paranoia. I spread my sleeping bag by the fireplace and cozily zoned out on the beautiful patterns that the crackling fire was throwing on the large bare white walls.

As I finally relaxed, the walls became a pink and baby-blue wild criss-crossing display of interlocking lines of endless geometric thunderbirds, lines of pink tail-to-beak garudas rising from southwest to northeast one way against baby-blue tail-to-beak garudas criss-crossing into infinity for hours from southeast to northwest. I forgot all about Dracula.

Offending the Toilet / Lorenzo Milam

It was 1962, just before I put KRAB on the air. Some of the other radio people and I had been experimenting with uranium power, a highly concentrated fuel called peyote. In those days, it was all quite legal, so I ordered up a hundred buds from Lawson's Cactus Gardens in San Antonio, Texas. The peyote came, along with a refund of $4.11 and a letter from Mr. Lawson explaining in detail how I had paid too much. The whole thing was franked with a Texas Department of Agriculture seal of approval.

My friend Julie—who claimed to have a PhD in Dopeology from Ken Kesey—showed us how to take the buttons, cut off the grey fur, and cook them at 250 degrees in the oven to dry them out. After twenty-four hours, we ground them up, the stinky little nasty things-they looked just like shrivelled monkey cocks—and stuffed them in Double-O gelatin capsules. When take-off time arrived, we swallowed them down with lemon juice to counteract the alkalinity and Pepto-Bismol to make our stomachs stop revolting.

The first time, Julie, my friend Warren, and I sat around for a few hours, waiting for something to happen. After a while, I said that this was pretty dumb, since all it did was make me feel like puking. I looked over at Warren for agreement, but he had turned into Prince Hamlet, which was pretty silly, since there were no dramatic performances called for in the evening's script. I turned back to Julie to complain about this play-acting, and she became the great, pink, warm Gaia mother of us all. She began to intone, "Round and round it goes, and round; where it stops, there it will round in the roundness of knowledge, back into itself."

"Where in God's name did she get that one?" I asked. She was a goddess, and I never knew it before. Not only was she a goddess; she was profound. "Holy moly," I said (by this time I had turned into Captain Marvel). I looked around, shifting my muscles under my cape, overwhelmed by it all, the colors, these colors that had started leaking out of the woodwork, from under the door, down through the skylight, colors turning, twisting, slowly, a fog of glorious dark colors invading the room.

Like pain or religious conversion or love, drug visions are peculiar to the individual. The knotholes in the walls of the house began to speak to me, in my own voice. Captain Marvel flew out the window. An army of marching Chinese came into the living room, shuffling through, on their way to the door, into eternity (for all I know, they are still there, shuffling through). They were followed by a noisy, large herd of baying hounds, the Hounds of the Baskervilles.

I looked down. As I did, my eyes made a great swiveling sound—can't you hear it?—because I had turned into Gargantua. My face was as big as the moon; my eyes were as huge as Jupiter's moons. My hand! What had become of it? Remember that saying, "I know it like the back of my hand." Well, I can now tell you that's a very foolish thing to say, because no one knows the back of their hand. I certainly didn't recognize mine. It had become the hand of the Colossus! Strange that I had never noticed it before. Those fingers, those folds, the bends, the veins, the shape of it—David's hand, Blake's hand, God's hand. I held it up and, like a great snake, it bent and moved and twisted before me.

It was time to make a journey, a great journey, a long journey, and a difficult one—a little different from *The Odyssey.* It was time to go to the bathroom. After a few years, I rose and passed through the great solid door of the bathroom. The floor of the shower, rough concrete, had turned into a mass of miniature volcanoes, puffing up little smoke-rings. As I pissed, the commode began to be filled with hundreds of tiny, red-string snakes. "How beautiful this void," I said to myself. I was afraid I was offending the toilet by what I was doing, but then it turned out that it was a friendly old man—friendly Mr. Toilet, mouth wide, ready to accept anything I chose to give him.

When I looked in the mirror, there was this stranger glowering at me from behind the glass. The more I looked at him, the more ominous he became, but then his face began to melt like an ice-cream cone. I looked down in the sink and there he was, tutti-frutti. As I turned away, he disappeared, completely, into the void. "Wow, I said. "Just . . . wow!"

Well, after a century or so, I managed to find my way back to the other room (not without many alarms and excursions), and I stood there for a long time, watching Hamlet and Gaia motionless on the floor. I opened my mouth, but before I could say anything, this noisy stranger chimed in: "You know, I know, at least I think I know, or know I think I know (pause for a week; they don't notice), I know I've taken this pee before."

It was very queer, that stranger—the one I thought I had left behind in the bathroom—right here, talking just like me, probably thinking he was me. "There's something missing," I thought. I wondered if Hamlet or Gaia noticed the change in my face, the fact that I had aged so much in the last eon between the time I was with them on the floor and the time I had gone to and come back from the bathroom. I looked at my watch on the bed table. It was huge, stuffed with minutes, days, hours. Time was moving so slowly they didn't have time to get out.

Hamlet was no longer there, nor was Julie. The two of them had turned into the Himalayas. It was time for me to go to Tibet, time to make the slow journey up the tortuous mountain passes, to find the master, the perfect master I had been seeking all my life. I lay down next to the mountains to prepare for my great journey, upward, to find the truth, on the snow-capped peaks growing all around me.

Everyone has stories like this, and although the nightmares of some subsequent journeys made me give it up forever, the god of the peyote plant taught me one thing. He (or she) (or it) taught me that what we call Reality is an Agreement, and nothing else. We make a contract with ourselves—and with the world—that says that walls will be walls and people will be people and universes will be universes. Whenever we choose, however—and one can choose through madness, self-analysis, meditation, or peyote (from Lawson's Cactus Gardens)—whenever we choose, we can break this agreement about Reality, turn it away, or upside down.

I know now why peyote, LSD, and all these gentle drugs are the subject of so much propaganda and vilification on television, radio, and in the press by the politicoes. If people were to learn that what we call Reality depends on such a very fragile agreement—made between one's self and the universe—then I suspect that too many of our operating systems (institutionalized fear, human isolation, economic competition, social hostility) would disappear.

Thank God so few people know about it.

MESCALINE

Buzzing to Sweetgrass / Dave Channon

Our eyeballs were all bugged out from driving 700 miles of Rockies on mescaline. Janis Joplin, Jimi Hendrix, Jerry Garcia, and the Rock and Roll Train were stampeding to Calgary, Canada. Us, too. We stonedly played hot potato with a tin cookie box full of tablets, blotters, buds, and bones. I got bored and stuck the tin into driver Nancy's sweatshirt hood.

"Gedditout," she wiggled. So I did.

Many buzzing midnight miles to Sweetgrass (no shit), Montana. Dawn was coming and the border station looked deserted, so we drove quietly through the gate. Flash! Gong! Siren! This Marine crew-cut guard bolted up out of nowhere. "Pull it over." Shit. A raggedy row of VW buses and other hippiemobiles lined the lot. "If you make it to the concert, tell my cousin we got impounded," wailed an unshaven, while the pot patrol pried off our hubcaps and plowed through the oatmeal.

They popped out door panels and got flat on their backs with flashlights peering 'neath the dash. One cop cracked, "Let's look inside the tires," and the other beamed, "That won't be necessary," wagging a little hash pipe that had been collecting greasy dust-bunnies in the spare-tire well, next to an expired can of Gunk Out. Then he showed us a pretty cool display case full of confiscated head gear and told us not to come back to Sweetgrass anymore. So we didn't.

We pulled out of the lot and glanced back at fourteen paisley-clad weepers. Nancy asked me what the fuck I did with the box of drugs anyway. "I just stuck it under the driver's seat," said I, thoughtfully tamping a bong bowl. Then we all made simultaneous eye contact with each other and collectively shared a tingling shiver like that which accompanies a well-earned piss.

And, by the way, Janis was awesome.

My Favorite Sister / Elmore "Buzz" Buzzizyk

Back in 1970, a drifter hitchhiked through our small town. He was a friendly, young, long-haired hippie, so our small group of freaks took him in and found him places to crash and got him stoned. To our surprise and dismay, he was quickly nabbed by the local cops for dealing a few hits of mescaline.

After we bailed him out of jail, he was scared and asked us to please remove and dispose of a big stash of organic mescaline capsules that he had squirreled away in the last house where he'd stayed. Once out of jail, he disappeared, and we never saw him again. His bail hadn't been very much, so there were no hard feelings. As it happened, he had left his host with a gallon jar filled to the brim with capsules of organic mescaline. For five dollars, I bought enough to fill my pocket till it was bulging. The stuff was very potent, but still produced a mellow buzz with no stomach upset or anxiety.

That summer I was eighteen, had no job, and every morning I ate a tab or two for breakfast, for weeks. It was a strange time in my life. I believe it solidified my conversion to the spiritual underpinnings of the freak culture of the time. I experienced a profound empathy for everyone I knew, even those people I had previously disliked.

I felt a very strong connection to all human beings. I became less sarcastic and judgmental. I began to feel sorrow for those people who had previously inspired my hatred. I developed an overwhelming certainty that life was a great blessing and that some unifying force, of terrible beauty, connected every person and every atom of the physical world.

Food tasted better, sunshine felt like a loving caress, colors took on a new vibrance. The patterns in nature were spellbinding. I vividly recall watching a giant spider building a large concentric web for hours one sunny morning. The whole world ceased to exist except for this tiny but miraculous event unfolding before my eyes.

Music became a new concept to me. I listened with a heightened perception. On one occasion, I took an empty paint can and a couple of small sticks into an old storm sewer under a huge highway embankment. The long concrete pipe, eight feet high, had a very satisfying echo. I spent an afternoon experimenting with rhythm on my primitive steel drum. The complexity and intricacy of the beats, compounded by and interwoven with the echo, were absolutely absorbing. I recorded it on a cheap tape recorder and, listening to it, even years later, I was pleased to know that I was capable of producing such imaginative and compelling rhythms.

Many specific wonders remain in my mind from that long-ago summer, seeing every blade of grass individually in a field. Seeing the branch structures of trees so clearly that I could identify every tree by species in a vast forest canopy. Having outrageous and creative bouts of imagination. Experiencing uncontrollable mirth with my friend, and laughing to the point of tears.

But there is a limit to chemically induced consciousness. After a while, my body adjusted, and it took more and more hits to have any significant effect. And sadder still, the overuse of psychedelics starts to dim a person's mind when they are not high. The end of my long strange trip came when my favorite sister came home to visit. She had been away at college, and I had been missing her.

I grabbed my sketch-pad, and we took off for a long hike through the countryside. I thought everything was fine and was really enjoying her company when suddenly she stopped dead in her tracks. She is just one year older than me, and we were very close. Growing up, I don't recall the two of us ever having a single argument. But she looked at me disgustedly and said, "Let's just turn around and go home." When I asked her why, she said, "All you have said this whole time is 'Far out' and 'Wow.'"

Stunned, and without thinking, I looked at her and said, "Wow!" Even as I said it, the realization came over me that I had dimmed my own light. I had spent too many days using an artificial spark. I had overdone it. That day, I gave away the rest of my stash.

After a few days, I could feel a clarity of mind return to me and, strangely, I realized a newfound respect for an unaltered state of mind. I still believe that psychoactive substances are a useful pathway to awareness, but only if used sensibly and in moderation. And I believe that there is a spiritual aspect to the psychoactive chemicals found in nature. There is a sacred quality that should not be abused or ignored.

Four-Way Street / Frederic Berthoff

It looked like a purple aspirin tablet. And they said it was synthetic, not the preferred organic, but that it came from Berkeley and it was real good. The Purple Mescaline. It was already famous on the local scene. They were "four-way tabs," which meant strong enough to split into quarters and still get you off. All the freaks agreed, it was the best around.

Mescaline was supposed to be mellower than LSD but still very heavy if you took enough of it. So with all the hype about going blind from staring at the sun or chromosomal damage or Art Linkletter's daughter jumping out the window on acid, I figured I'd try mescaline for my first trip. The psychedelic experience was obviously not to be missed. I mean, that's all you heard about. In the news, on the street, everywhere. Seems like everybody was tripping, from The Beatles to the Hells Angels, to my best friend Johnny Mills from Lincoln, Massachusetts. Everybody but Elvis and the Russians.

And the coolest place to trip, if you had the balls to do it—if you could handle the crowd and the travel and the general crush of it all—was a big-time rock 'n' roll concert. Where all the freaks from the great megapolitan buzz congregated to see and be seen, first of all, and then, have their gilded egos acid-washed to oblivion and be mystically transported to some esoteric high meadow of universal mind.

Crosby, Stills, and Nash were playing with Neil Young at the Boston Garden. A huge hall above the commuter rail station, of peeling paint and hard edges, it was the kind of steel-girded hockey and basketball venue where arena rock made its first big splash.

We took the train in from the suburbs, and Johnny Mills told me to "Let it dissolve under your tongue." This took about twenty minutes, and by the time the purple tablet was gone, our train was pulling up to the platform, and I already had that weird metallic taste in my mouth. A queasy feeling like I'm a little nervous, a little excited and . . . wow! It was the summer of 1970. I was fifteen.

The crowd was outrageous. Hairy, freaky, tumbled out of the house in old jeans and leather jackets and, oh-my-god, a girl in a day-glo miniskirt all blonde and pink and flashy, walked up ahead like an underworld princess. Moving from the train across the parking lot, everyone was aglow in a coincidentally great mood. The pavement shimmered with microlithic slate and bits of colored glass—crushed 7-Up bottles, the emerald green detritus of a great and rising civilization.

We were early. The crowd milled around, cliqueing and morphing in the parking lot. This girl in day-glo was a friend of somebody we knew and was standing next to me all of a sudden, in a clutch of people gathered around somebody's "magic" ring. A constant buzz of conversation seemed to hold us all together like dancing electrons. I looked at her and she looked at me and I looked at her and blurted out, "Can I touch you?"

Can't believe I ever said that. And the funny thing is that it wasn't a "line" even though it was a good one. It just seemed the most natural thing to say. And she said, "Sure." I held her hand. It was warm. And she giggled, giving me a gentle squeeze before moving off with her friends, a lingering glance cast over her shoulder. I stood in awe, watching her float away, and thought, "Man, this is going to be great."

The parking lot filled quickly with new arrivals. A pimply kid with wild hair handed me a smoldering joint out the window of an idling car. A complete stranger. Sweet-tasting Mexican wrapped in wheat-straw papers that, along with all my childhood conceptions, were coming unglued at the seams. One toke and the city transformed. Splashes of color filled strangely unfinished cartoon panels, cracked at the edges where weeds pushed through the cement with the same urgency of the energy that surged up my spine into the cool twilight.

Inside the station, we gushed through stark cement hallways, like water molecules flowing through a municipal storm drain. Tramping feet, impersonal echos, until emerging exalted into the stalagtite-encrusted middle of this huge man-made cavern, the Boston Garden.

I got off pretty well on the mescaline. My last time to the Garden had been for a Bruins game with some other boys and somebody's dad. But it was Brave New Worldsville now. The freaks from the parking lot moved onto the main floor, spreading out like leaves, climbing to the upper balconies, young and brimming with worldly independence.

Structural borders were breathing, alive, decorated with intricate hallucinatory patterns. Persian rug motifs ran off walls, down through the crowd, pulling us all together into one huge squirming mosaic. I followed Johnny Mills to our seats down front, and the band started, bathed in a soft purple light.

As soon as the house lights went down, it seemed like everybody in the place lit up a joint. Thousands of matches flared in unison, and soon multiple strains of anonymous pot wafted through the crowd. I'm laid back in this folding hockey-watcher's chair, staring up at phantom landscapes in the rafters. The band worked their way through the first set and then stopped.

Lights up. Hard edges all over the place, steel and cement, clumps of wire and equipment. Shouts, whistles, voices murmuring like a gentle surf. Echoes in the great hall. And the lead singer, I think it was Steve Stills, said they had a new song.

" . . . And you've never heard this song before . . . and you may not know what it's about right away . . . but when you hear the chorus, maybe you will . . . and if you do, sing along with us."

The lights went down again, stage receding into patterned purple darkness. Crosby, Stills, Nash, and Young began the new song in a column of yellow light.

Sometimes you find yourself riding a wave through history at a moment when it crests and curls right there underneath you. You may feel it's something special without knowing just yet, before "his-story" has been told and told again, and it's still only the spontaneous experience.

Like earlier that spring, when the helmeted, rifle-toting National Guard came up over the rise during a peace in Vietnam rally at Kent State University in Ohio. And opened fire on the crowd. I always suspected it was a contrived event, as if someone deep in the executive branch had said, "We've got to teach these commie punks a lesson." Four dead in Ohio.

Even now, thirty years past, when I hear those opening chords on the oldies station, when they play the classic *Four Way Street* live album (a play on words to those in the know), I get a chill down the back of my neck, and I remember that summer. It seems only a wink since I looked up through the purple haze and they sang:

> Tin soldiers and Nixon coming,
> we're finally on our own . . .
> This summer I hear the drumming,
> four dead in O-hi-o . . .

It was as if that night, when we walked out the doors of our parents' houses and boarded that train for the big freak exodus, we had finally stepped into the real world. A world of exotic contraband and nubile teenyboppers, of riot police and thundering helicopters; Vietnam itself looming over our generation as an evil genie rising in a cloud of sweet-colored hash smoke. A world of joy and death and consequence. Finally on our own.

The house lights in the Garden came up strong, and suddenly we were all on our feet together. Ten thousand souls in chorus clear as a bell:

> Four dead in O-hi-o . . .
> Four dead in O-hi-o . . .
> Four dead in O-hi-o . . .
> Four dead in O-hi-o . . .

Camping in the Trees / Maximum Traffic

I had a bunch of pals when I was a teen, and we all liked to go camping, canoeing, and swimming in the local rivers, and staying up late around campfires. I spent my whole youth roaming the woods and rivers.

One weekend we were camping at a favorite spot outside of town near some abandoned ponds. It was a warm summer night, long past midnight, with a nice blaze going, when we heard something crunching through the woods toward us. It had our hair standing, but then a voice called out, and we knew it was another of our friends.

To our delight, he had brought along a hit of THC for each of us. We had been getting sleepy, but after taking the small pills, we were soon wide, wide awake. The night took on a new intensity. The stars were brilliant, the woods inky black.

In a sudden flash of energy, it occurred to me to see if I could climb one of the tall thin saplings that were highlighted by our campfire, and do it as I had seen native coconut pickers do it, their bare feet against the trunk and walk up it while holding on with their arms outstretched. I took off my shoes and to my delight I found I could run up the small trunk like a monkey.

I vividly recall looking down twenty-five or thirty feet and seeing the campfire lighting the amazed faces of my friends as they looked up at me. I quickly walked down the tree and said, "You won't believe how easy it is to do that."

In one minute flat they had all pulled their shoes off and were all running up and down the slender trees around our campfire. The night took on a wild hilarity and a dreamlike quality. We were like squirrels. Running up the trees after each other, cackling with mirth, all of us were in the trees at once and laughing so hard we were in danger of falling out. We were awake all night and saw the day break, and, man, life was beautiful.

That's the Way It Is / Paul Krassner

In the late '60s and early '70s, I was enjoying—I mean experimenting with—THC, a white powder featuring the ingredient in marijuana which gets one high, so it was like super-pot.

In New York in 1969, I met Jada Rowland, an actress in the soap opera *Secret Storm*. I fell in love with Jada, but I hated soap operas. But, she maintained a sense of integrity. Once, for example, the script called for her to put down her little daughter by referring sarcastically to her imagination, and Jada refused to say the line.

Richard Avedon had invited me to be included in a book of photographs of countercultural figures, and I accepted on the condition that I could choose the pose with Jada. What we had in mind was a takeoff on the *Two Virgins* album cover, where John Lennon and Yoko Ono stood nude, holding hands. Jada and I would both be naked, smiling, with our arms around each other.

But, she would also be holding a patriotic cup with stars and stripes, and there would be arrows pointing to her breasts and crotch, and I would be holding an American flag. And I would have an erection. If *Two Virgins* was about anatomy, this would be about physiology. And Jada was willing to risk losing her $1,000-a-week job to participate just for the fun of it.

I ingested a capsule of THC for the photo session. We were standing before the camera and the only thing missing was my hard-on. I had heard that THC was actually an elephant tranquilizer, and I would soon find out if that was true.

Avedon asked what music we wanted in the background. I asked for the Beatles' "Hey, Jude," but he didn't have it, so instead we put on Bob Dylan singing "Lay, Lady, Lay." Jada and I began to kiss.

"This is obscene," she whispered.

"No," I whispered back, "it's very pure. But you're right, it is kind of goal-oriented."

We continued kissing. Dylan was now asking the musical question, "Why wait any longer for the world to begin?" My penis rose to the occasion, and the crew cheered us on.

I signed a release, assuming the photo would never be seen, because the publishing of an erection was such a taboo. However, in 1999—three decades later—my bluff was called: Avedon's seventy-five-dollar photography book, *The Sixties,* was published, and Jada and I were in it. A review in the *Los Angeles Times* said that I looked "sheepish" and "sustained" an erection. Little did they know.

In 1974, I was living in San Francisco and investigating conspiracies in general and cults in particular. My roommate was Stewart Brand, founder of the *The Whole Earth Catalog.*

On the night that my favorite improv group, The Committee, was going to have its final performance, and while Walter Cronkite was concluding the news with his customary sign-off, "That's the way it is," I snorted all the THC that remained in my stash, as preparation for my personal pilgrimage to The Committee Theater to celebrate the end of a satirical era.

The last thing I remember was brushing my teeth, talking to Stewart, and being overwhelmed by the drone of his electric saw. Since I was out at the time, here's how he described to me what had happened:

"I had been building a bed while you stood in the hall doorway reporting the latest turns in your hassle with Scientology. After a prolonged peculiar silence, I peeked in the hall to find that you were gone, replaced by a vacant-eyed robot which opened and closed its mouth, made a drifty gesture with a tube of toothpaste and said, 'Nn . . . Gn . . .' Terrifying. All I could think was that the Scientologists must've finally zapped you.

"After a while, the thing (you) toppled like a tree, crashed, and commenced baying into my buffalo rug. I phoned a friendly shrink for consultation. He listened to symptoms-you were by now into a howling slow-motion laugh, 'Haaaaaa haaaaaa haaaaaa haaaaaa'—and the shrink suggested I take you to UC hospital for evaluation. I told the nurse, "He's editor of *The Realist.*' 'Is that so?' she said politely. You spelled your name for her."

It was 11:30 that night when, as they say in comic books, I came to. I tried to fly so I could tell whether I was dreaming, but I couldn't flap my arms because I was attached to the bed by restraining devices. There were canvas straps tying down my wrists and ankles. I was definitely awake, but I had no idea where I was or how I had gotten there.

I would learn later that Stewart had brought me to this hospital with the aid of a couple of students from the Zen center a couple of blocks from our apartment. I did remember a doctor asking me, "Okay, tiger, what'd you take?" I started to answer, "T-H . . ." I was tempted to spell out THE ULTIMATE DRUG, but my motor control was not exactly the answer to a tightrope walker's prayer, and I had to struggle just to utter "T-H-C."

"Affording us bedsiders enormous relief," Stewart recalled. "We didn't know what the hell you were down with. At the THC announcement, the doctor smiled and relaxed.

'Let him enjoy it.' On other subjects you had been equally loquacious. In answer to any question whatever—'How you doing, Paul?'—you would intone, 'My name is Paul Krassner. I am editor of *The Realist*. P-A-U-L-K-uh-A-S-N-R-E.'"

Of course, I had assumed that I was in some secret laboratory, being debriefed by the CIA. A couple of friends were now leaning over my hospital bed. I managed to ask two questions: "Did they inject me with any drug?" And, "Have they been taping what I've been saying?" It was my paranoid way of trying to bring things back into focus. Stewart was gone, but he had left a note for me on the table beside my bed.

9:30 p.m.

Hello Paul—
Since you're merely flipped out (stoned) and not dying, I'm gonna go meet my date. Background: you passed out in the hallway—at 7:30 p.m. I brought you to UC emergency at 8. You started coming around at 8:30 and let us know you'd had some THC (and LSD?). Wavy [Gravy] or others may drop by later. I'll call in from time to time, and I'll check by later.

Stewart

P.S. You promised to tell the American people the truth. You also remarked that "It's okay!" Hope you remember details.

All I could remember was that for a few hours I had been in a space beyond good and evil, yet clinging hard to the paradox of human subjectivity. Birds flew by with the faces of my loved ones. While my body was writhing with ecstasy—which is why they attached me to the hospital bed—my consciousness was in some other place that felt like pure energy, where everything was related to everything else simply because it existed. I'd had my first overdose and missed The Committee's final performance.

At home the next day, Stewart said, "I would've put you to bed, but I thought you were having an epileptic fit."

"Did you stick a *TV Guide* in my mouth like you're supposed to?"

"You were doing fine with the buffalo rug."

OPIUM

Poppies / Lisa Law

In the late '80s, while living in Santa Fe, I was visiting an old friend, Count Carlo, when he asked me to step into his garden. He was a distinguished old gentleman with white hair and a pointed goatee, a straw hat, and a Sherman smoked elegantly. In his time, he had been a jazz entrepreneur, managing several seminal clubs in New York—Downbeat, The Embers, and Basin Street East among them.

He had given Charlie Parker and Dizzy Gillespie their first gigs as headliners, at the Royal Roost, and named Birdland after Bird. In the '30s he hung out at a legendary Harlem tea-pad called Kay's—a big, dark basement room with large couches and a full refrigerator. A dollar at the door got you four joints, which you shared with the room.

On this particular day, we went out to the garden alongside his apartment, and he showed me some nice rows of opium poppies he had planted, which he planned to harvest at the end of summer. The seedlings in the back row were doing fine, although they were all bunched together, but the front row had barely broken ground, and the Count wanted me to transplant some of the back row to the other rows. I, of course, obliged and spent the next two hours transplanting all of his supposed poppies.

I returned to him a few weeks later, and he took me out to his garden to see the growth of his wonderful little flowers. I stood there with my mouth wide open, surprised and amazed at the shape of the plants. I looked up, and towering above this little garden was a giant elm tree which had obviously dropped its seeds everywhere. I had transplanted eighty-five elm seedlings. Not one poppy had sprouted.

Lisa Law is the author of *Interviews with Icons*.

Cookin' and Flyin' / Ted Milikin

My preference has always been marijuana, but Nixon's "Operation Intercept" kept Acapulco Gold and Panama Red from crossing the border. LSD became a regularly used option, but if minds are expanded too often, it could lead to overexpansion and even insanity. Uppers and downers were elevator rides that only led backward. We were locked out from scoring keys, lids, or even matchboxes.

Donovan sang "Mellow Yellow," and someone suggested smoking bananas. We scraped the insides, oven-dried 'em, and got nada. Someone else said they got high on dried sauerkraut. That was even harder to dry and didn't smell too good, either.

Abe, an older and more experienced friend, said he could cop some heroin. I wanted to try everything once, so when all we could find was black tar opium, and Abe said we could cook it up and shoot it, I played along. Spoon, matches, cotton, shared syringe, and Abe were all prescriptions for disaster. Abe shot first and got nothing. He then gave me a shot before he took another.

"You feel anything?"

"No, you?"

So we both went home to dinner. I had the worst headache of my not yet twenty-year-old brain and went to bed. Man, did I ever need pain relief. When Abe came over, I found out he'd also previously tried to get high shooting blond Lebanese hash. What can you expect? They don't put labels on these things.

The best plane ride of my life began in 1978 in Honolulu while standing in line for check-in. A very attractive long-haired blonde was also flying back to San Francisco. I offered to share a reefer of some fine Hawaiian leaf, but she preferred cocktails in the bar. She then showed me some brown tar opium, and we both swallowed a spoonful.

By the time we boarded and took off, we were already in international air space. The plane had few passengers and we sat in the rear, with no one near us. Since neither the crew nor anyone else seemed to care about what we were up to, I lit a fat torpedo. No one said anything to us as sweet smoke filled the fuselage, and tourist became first class. How sweet the buzz.

Smoked Lennon / Paul Krassner

I remember a moment of epiphany at Shea Stadium in 1964 while the Beatles were singing, even though I couldn't hear them above the screaming of the crowd. It had to do with the way that members of the audience could identify with each Beatle in a personal way. This was summed up by a young girl holding aloft a hand-lettered poster that said, It's All Right, John—I Wear Glasses Too!

During the following years, the Beatles took us along on their musical journey from youthful innocence to psychedelic awareness; from "I wanna hold your hand" to "I wanna turn you on." The unofficial credo of the burgeoning counterculture became "Take a sad song and make it better."

I first met John Lennon with Yoko Ono in July 1972. When I asked him a naive question—"Was 'Lucy in the Sky with Diamonds' about LSD?"—he denied it with the wink of a dedicated prankster, just as Peter Yarrow had denied that Peter, Paul, and Mary's song, "Puff the Magic Dragon"—with that line in the lyrics, "Little Jackie Papers"—was about pot smoking.

My friend, comedy writer Dawna Kaufmann, had been "keeper of the marijuana" for George Harrison, and he tried to teach her how to roll a joint with one paper. She preferred the two-paper method, "which George found amusingly amateurish," she told me, "so I would hand the stash to him and he'd roll these single zig-zag bombers. Such a talented man."

John and Yoko spent a weekend at my home in Watsonville, California. They loved being so close to the ocean. In the afternoon I asked them to please smoke their cigarettes outside, but in the evening we smoked a combination of opium and marijuana, sitting on pillows in front of the fireplace, sipping tea and munching cookies.

We talked about conspiracy researcher Mae Brussell's theory that the deaths of leading-edge musicians like Jimi Hendrix, Janis Joplin, Otis Redding, and Jim Morrison were actually political assassinations because they served as role models, surfing on the crest of the youth rebellion.

"No, no," Lennon argued, "they were already headed in a self-destructive direction." A few months later, though, he would remind me of that conversation, adding, "Listen, if anything happens to Yoko and me, it was not an accident." Such was the level of his understandable paranoia.

After all, the Nixon administration had been trying to deport him, ostensibly for an old marijuana bust on another continent, but actually because they were afraid he was planning to perform for protesters at the Republican counter-convention in Miami that summer.

Indeed, in April, J. Edgar Hoover had directed the New York office of the FBI to "locate subject [Lennon] and remain aware of his activities and movements . . . . Careful attention should be given reports that subject is heavy narcotics user."

Ironically, Elvis Presley—who originally had such a profound influence on the Beatles—was totally stoned when he visited the White House, received a Federal Narcotics officer's badge from Richard Nixon himself, and then warned the president about the danger posed by the Beatles.

Anyway, under the mellow cloud of opium, we also discussed the Charles Manson case, which I had been investigating. Lennon was bemused by the way Manson had associated his own dreams of chaos with Beatles music.

"Look," John said, "would you kindly inform Manson that it was Paul [McCartney] who wrote 'Helter Skelter'—not me!"

Yoko interrupted. "No, please don't tell him," she said. "We don't want to have any communication with Manson."

"It's all right," Lennon said, "he doesn't have to know the message came from us."

"It's getting chilly in here," Yoko said to me. "Would you put another cookie in the fireplace?"

Lennon was absentmindedly holding on to the opium doobie. I asked him, "Do the British use that expression—to bogart a joint—or is that only an American term? You know, derived from the image of a cigarette dangling from Humphrey Bogart's lower lip."

"In England," Lennon replied, with that inimitable sly expression on his face, "if you remind somebody else to pass a joint, you lose your own turn."

DMT

Falling in Love / Stephen Gaskin

DMT was a funny kind of dope. It was supposed to be the businessman's lunch of psychedelics and give you a twenty-minute slice out of the middle of an acid trip. I wasn't too impressed with it when I saw it. It was a few cruddy-looking brown crumbs wrapped in a wrinkled piece of tinfoil. When I smoked it, I was impressed. It didn't look as space-age as it was.

I did think it smelled like burning Melmac plastic dinner plates. Later on, I met Stephen Szara (who synthesized DMT) and complained about the smell. He said, "You weren't supposed to smoke it."

I fell in love with Ina May on DMT. We sat down, Ina May on the couch and me on the floor at her feet, and we lit off a pipe each. I looked in Ina May's eyes, and every edge, every line, every detail became electric and alive with threads of color running through it, until the entire environment was neon, psychedelically, pulsingly, crawlingly alive, and lit. She looked into my eyes and smiled as we lit up the environment, and played with our DMT.

As I looked at her, I fell telepathically into her and saw that we matched up to many decimal places and were really as telepathic as we could be. It just blew me away. She was with someone else at the time. I looked at her for a second, and I had to put my eyes down, because I couldn't keep looking at her, or I knew I would get so far in that I'd never get back out. It was too late.

But that kind of thing happens to people. Get stoned with somebody, look at them, fall in love with them, and the whole rest of the material plane doesn't match. And then, suddenly, as fast as it had come on, coming down a perpendicular square-edge drop-off, everything will be perfectly ordinary again. After it was gone and I hit bottom, it took me a second or two to forgive myself for ever coming down from it. As it turned out, over the last thirty years, in many ways, we never did come down from it.

Stephen Gaskin, founder of The Farm commune, is the author of *Cannabis Spirituality.*

Finding God / Irwin Gooen

I call this "How I Got High for the FBI and Found God." Well, I just had to use that title, since I once smoked some cannabinol-dosed cigarettes for the state of New Jersey. The title stems from an old joke poking fun at *Reader's Digest*, and was the working title of a book I was going to do in the '60s.

So, it was for the state of New Jersey and not the FBI that I got high, and it wasn't quite psychedelic (I didn't find God), though I have had a few psychedelic experiences via cannabis. Other times they have been induced by LSD, psilocybin, DMT, magic mushrooms, and, yes, even the act of making love, wherein my lover disappeared. There was no "other"—it was pure oneness with the universe.

As my first LSD experience taught me—just a short bit into the trip, I said, "Hey, this is no drug, this is Truth in a pill"—what gets you off into merging with cosmic unity isn't the important factor. The trigger, which I prefer to label an active sacrament, just allows you entry through a portal to whatever is lying inside of you.

Alan Watts once said that we don't have the language to describe these experiences, because our everyday is concerned with our everyday, comparatively mundane lives. Shall I bother to try?

On my first experience, I ascended to a place where I felt that for the first time I was experiencing the cosmic truth, and as soon as I said, "Oh, now I see," I was elevated to the next level, where I said, "Oh, now I see," which brought me to the next level, which was, "Oh, now I see!" On and on it went, and not being able to accept living in this condition of experiencing infinitude, I repeated a few times, "It's too much!"

My "guide," thinking I was just expressing myself in a hip manner, smilingly said, "Yeah, like too much, man." I wanted to grab him and say, "You don't understand, it really is too much!" But I went on from there, with bells flashing and lights ringing and who knows what else. When I was coming down, I was trying to get in touch with my daily self, but I had no idea where that ego image was. I then saw one of my photographic pieces on the wall and I said, "Oh, that's it, I do graphics" (which I had never called my work before).

It had been the most profound experience of my whole life, and sometime later I did another acid-sacrament trip outdoors, at a beautiful place in Woodstock. As it was a more external trip, I had my camera with me, and I went through a total change in perceiving the objective world and a sea change in my photography which eventually led me to exhibiting in the Psychedelic Showcase and then being published in *Psychedelic Art*.

Nevertheless, DMT was, in some way, my favorite sacrament, although its first message to me was that was not good for my body to be ingesting. It was there, boom, right up front, came on fast, and lasted not even an hour. I recall being at a party in New Jersey where I had brought some grass in order to turn on some local public defenders and one guy from the DA's office. They wanted to experience the stuff so they'd know what they were talking about in court.

At one point, sitting on the floor in a kind of loose circle, I passed a joint to some conservatively dressed man. He said, "Oh, are you still playing that pot-smoking game?" I got defensive and said, "What's wrong with smoking pot?" He took out a nice Kaywoodie briar pipe and a tobacco pouch, passing them to me with, "Here, try some of this." I did. Whoosh! This physician had distilled his cannabis, put it on pipe tobacco and, while it retained its potency, it did not have the odor of pot.

Oh, yes . . . the DMT. Well, I needed to get away from the party for a while and take a break, so I went upstairs to a bedroom and put a small bit of DMT into a hash pipe. Scratched a match. I was off. Eyes closed, I saw these beautiful colors moving around, finding their places on the screen of my mind, settling as some sort of interlocking jigsaw puzzle pieces, each a distinct brilliant color. But the very center was empty and I was disappointed; it was blank, a dull cardboard gray.

And then it came to me: It was not blank, it was gold. The gold intensified, and it was in the figure of the Buddha. And when I recognized that this emptiness, nada, gornisht, zilch, no-thing, was the source of everything and the Buddha itself, the gold began to pour out of the figure in all directions. All over me. And I cried. Tears of gold.

AYAHUASCA

Ram Dass Enjoys Dinner / Stanley Krippner

In 1996, I went to Manaus, Brazil, for a conference on transpersonal psychology. The theme was technologies of the sacred. Many of the participants, including Ram Dass, wanted to try ayahuasca. There are three major Ayahuasca churches in Brazil, all operating with government approval, and one of them, the Santo Diame Church, gave the group permission to hold a session there, but not as an official part of the conference.

I wanted to go because my roommate, Marcus—an adventurous friend on a spiritual path—had never taken ayahuasca and would be very interested. I signed up for both of us. That day, we all fasted as was recommended and showed up at the gates of their hotel where the bus was waiting to take us into the rain forest to this church. But the organizers had miscounted, there weren't enough seats on the bus for everybody, and some people would have to be left behind. I confided in my friend Kumu that I would stay behind, but I felt responsible for Marcus, not wanting him to have such an unusual and intensive experience without my being there to support him.

So I was sort of locked into going. I could go and not drink the ayahuasca, but that's not the point. There's plenty of ayahuasca, there's just not plenty of seats. So, after Kumu made that announcement, Ram Dass, who was preparing to get on the bus, said, "Well, I will give up my seat to somebody else." And Kumu said, "Oh, no, Ram Dass, we want you there more than anybody else. It would be such an honor to have you at the event."

Ram Dass said, "Well, I would like to go, but I have to follow the principles of my teaching, and I am taught to be of service and to give up my place to others when the occasion demands it."

Now he did not say this in front of the whole group—he was not making a show out of this—he said it only to the two of us. Ram Dass said, "I've been fasting all day, I'm going to go down to the restaurant now and have something to eat." So Kumu was almost in tears, he was so disappointed, and I said, "Well, what you have just seen is the mark of a truly spiritual person who will give up this opportunity for somebody that he doesn't even know, and for somebody who, for all we know, might not get anything out of the experience, so this is truly an unselfish act."

People started to get on the bus, when unexpectedly a van showed up out of nowhere. One of the organizers thought they'd better have another vehicle in case there wasn't enough room on the bus. So now there was enough room for everybody. Kumu went running down to the restaurant to get Ram Dass, but he was already eating a delicious Brazilian meal.

"Ram Dass," said Kumu, "there's room for you in the van, you can go."

"No," he replied, "it's too late, I've been eating—I've been really pigging out, I'm so hungry—and it just wouldn't work for me to go, having eaten such a big dinner."

And of course he was right. I think he had come to peace with that decision. And also, of course, it's part of his discipline—these are not events that you enter into frivolously—and so, seeing that the discipline was to fast, once he broke his fast he couldn't really turn around and make another decision. So I said to Kumu, "Well, this is the second spiritual act that you've seen. Having eaten something and broken his fast, it simply would not be the same. It wouldn't have the integrity that he would have wanted the experience to have."

Stanley Krippner is the co-author of *Extraordinary Dreams and How to Work with Them.*

Psychedelic Vision Quest / Rasa

A friend told me about a new book that bridges recent discoveries about DNA-emitting biophotons with an ancient psychoactive beverage that one Amazonian shaman calls "jungle television." Coincidentally, on the day I started reading the book, another friend excitedly told me that he had found a shaman who was conducting traditional ceremonies with the beverage.

When I first tried psychedelics, there was little written about ayahuasca that made one want to travel south for the experience. William Burroughs and Allen Ginsberg in *The*

Yage Letters offered entertaining but thoroughly depressing narratives describing their unsuccessful search for the yage (ayahuasca) experience in a good setting (Burroughs wrote, "Yage may be the final fix").

Dr. Andrew Weil also searched for the brew and the ceremony, and had disappointing and dangerous experiences without finding a vision worth reporting. Countless hippies have wandered some miles off the Pan-American highway and paid drunken shamans for an evening of dizzy puking. Even the first European to write about his experiences, botanist Richard Spruce, mostly describes his nausea in 1853. Since then, the good Dr. Weil has had more success, and Dennis and Terence McKenna have taken the experience to the outer reaches of playful reason. Recently, reading Jeremy Narby's book, *The Cosmic Serpent: DNA and the Origin of Knowledge,* I've come to wonder if Narby is right and DNA can speak to us through the chemical and bioelectrical internet found in a jungle vine.

The ayahuasca ceremony was not what I expected. Yes, in its form—the actions of the shaman, the music, the duration, the jungle pharmacology, the visions, the "purging"— all these things were similar to descriptions I have read, but in the same way the experience of eating a meal shows nothing of the processes of digestion and nourishment, the ayahuasca experience was still, several days later, changing me in ways my conscious mind is only now gradually comprehending.

In preparation, on Friday we ate very lightly, with only liquids in the evening. Saturday we ate only a little watermelon in the morning and water sparingly during the day. We arrived at a friend's yoga studio at about 7:30 in the evening. We were a group of thirty-five women and eight men, including the shaman, Kimah, and his assistant, Carmen. We sat cross-legged on the floor, leaning comfortably against the wall with cushions under us and behind our backs. Women were on one side and men on the other.

Each of us had a small bottle of water and a plastic bucket for purging. Kimah instructed us to only rinse our mouths out with water if we had the need, for any water we swallowed would most likely just come up again. Kimah and Carmen sat at the head of the room on a large flokati carpet, their various tools for the evening spread out in no apparent order—a few old bottles of scents and herbs, a tobacco pouch and pipe, sage in bundles, some other small artifacts, and of course four large Mason jars, each filled with a thick dark red liquid. All of us gave full attention to the jars as they were slowly and reverently lifted from Kimah's shoulder bag.

Kimah is a small-framed man with deep-set eyes, long graying hair and beard. He wore a soft cotton poncho-like robe over his ordinary street clothes. Carmen, like the rest of us, wore simple white clothing. I liked the idea of this tiny congregation all in the white of the initiate, but really we all wore white so that if need be, we could easily be seen in the dark. After the drinking of the "medicine," as Kimah calls it, we would be in total darkness until the sun came up in the morning. Occasionally, Kimah's lighter would shatter the darkness as he lit his tobacco pipe, but we all had our eyes closed for most of the session so as to facilitate our visions.

The shaman not only brews the potion and directs the ceremony, he also enjoys the hallucinogenic properties of a South American strain of tobacco some ten to twenty times stronger than commercial cigarettes. Pharmacologists have determined that in sufficient doses, tobacco is highly psychotropic. Shamans say that the tobacco spirit is their closest ally in their interactions with the spirit of the ayahuasca as well as all the other spirits that manifest during the ceremony. They also claim that minus the chemical additives of commercial tobacco, the plant has profound medicinal qualities. Brain physiologists have found that the human nervous system has unique neural receptors that lock onto tobacco molecules; the tobacco enters the brain like a key fitting into a lock.

As we began, Kimah looked around the room at all of us approvingly, offering a warm smile or kind eyes for each of us. He asked the five of us who were new to ayahuasca what experience we may have had with mind-altering drugs. He especially wanted to know if we had experienced any kind of guided or ceremonial excursions, or if we were only used to drugs in a party setting. He explained that ayahuasca is a very powerful and unpredictable medicine. He suggested that we feel comfortable, let the experience come as it will, and yet we should also protect ourselves by surrounding our bodies with the mental image of shiny armor or white light.

He emphasized the word "shiny" in the helpful practical way an adult might tell a child how to wear a scarf to protect against the wind, and I immediately received this vivid mental image of evil animal spirits frightened off by my shiny suit of armor. I hesitate to call this telepathy, because I know mere suggestion itself is a powerful agent of change, but shamans say ayahuasca is "very telepathic," and years ago, after also experiencing a ceremony, the first scientist to isolate the psychoactive alkaloid in ayahuasca named the chemical "telepathine."

Kimah told us we would invoke many spirits during the ceremony, and he went on for a while naming them—mostly animals: panther, bear, eagle, vulture, various snakes—but he would also call on plant spirits as well as natural phenomena like waterfalls and rivers. He made a point of welcoming all spiritual traditions. He said we may invoke Buddha, or Shiva, or Jesus, and that all helpful energies were welcome. He asked that we not leave during the ceremony unless we needed to use the toilet. He said don't be ashamed if we had to vomit, as purging is a natural process for cleaning the body. He said in particular that ayahuasca looks for evil, negative energy, or toxins, whatever term you prefer, and expels them from the body.

With the lights still on, he shook the four glass jars, mixing the solution, and then opened them all and arranged them in a row in front of himself. Treating each jar as if its contents were alive, he peered in, examined the dark dry brown residue around the rims, and lifted up a jar to examine the underside, perhaps looking to see if it was fully mixed. With no discernible formality, he began to half-whistle/half-sing little melodies to each of the jars. The ceremony had begun. After a while, he loaded his pipe with tobacco and, with more singing and other odd but soothing sounds one might expect from a jungle bird or snake, he blew tobacco smoke into each of the jars.

Soon he began to call our names in order of how we were seated, and he poured a cup of ayahuasca for each of us. Sometimes the cup was three-quarters full, sometimes completely full. He knew about half of us from a previous session, but even though he had asked about our individual psychedelic experiences deliberately, he seemed to determine dose by intuition more than any other criteria I could determine. I was third to be called. He poured me a full cup, and, thanking him, I took the cup with both hands and drank it all in about four or five swallows. The taste was strong, but only a little bitter. It went down easily, and when I tried to compare it to other liquids, I immediately thought of milk, tomato juice, and root beer mixed together. Perhaps it looked more like that than how those three liquids combined would actually taste.

Ayahuasca has been taken by shamans in the Amazon for at least 5,000 years, anthropologists surmise. The drink is actually a mixture of two or more ingredients, depending on what part of the Amazon you're in and what the shaman is investigating. Shamans mix in a wide variety of other plants. The ayahuasca tells the shaman—in visions, they say—how to use the other ingredients for specific cures of all varieties. Modern pharmacologists have not come up with a better explanation of how these "primitive" people could have such a remarkable understanding of so large a number of the more than 80,000 species of Amazonian plants.

Ayahuasca is an amazing example. The brew always includes the vine ayahuasca, which contains the mild psychedelic alkaloid now known as harmaline. The strong psychedelic effect of the drink actually comes from one of several other plants that contain dimethyltryptamine (DMT). The truly strange thing is that DMT is made completely inactive by stomach enzymes when eaten, but a chemical in the ayahuasca vine that specifically blocks that absorption and allows for the DMT to act on the nervous system. Scientists still don't know how Amazonians figured out how to mix these two ingredients that can only work in combination. Chance is always a possibility, but mathematicians say that when you run the numbers, chance is virtually ruled out when native Amazonian pharmacology is considered in its entirety.

In Kimah's Peruvian tradition, ayahuasca is mixed with the leaves from a bush called chacruna. Chacruna is one of several Amazonian plants that contain DMT. He described the long process of preparing the brew, basically requiring many hours of boiling the chacruna leaves together with the thick bark of the ayahuasca vine. When asked why chacruna is added to ayahuasca, shamans often answer, "To make the visions brighter." After all of us drank our cups, Kimah poured a cup of ayahuasca for Carmen and then one for himself. Carmen said that even though we may feel the ceremony going on and on without end, it will end, and by morning all would be back to normal. If we needed help, we should just ask, and she or Kimah would come. Kimah said we should try to stay seated where we were with our eyes closed and not talk or touch any others around us. "Everyone will be very sensitive to all the energies in the room. Keep your attention on yourself. Don't feel responsible for anyone else. Don't try to vibe anyone."

Then the lights were turned off. Kimah and Carmen started to sing a soft and lovely soothing melody. For the next twelve hours they would be singing nearly nonstop. Amazonian shamans sing in a combination of their native language, Spanish, and what appear to be nonsense syllables (I've read that what I took for nonsense is supposedly the language of the ayahuasca spirit). Kimah says these are communications with the visiting spirits but also serve as a focus for our minds as we experience potentially disarming visions. Kima told us that he would also add some words of English from time to time to help us focus.

Soon after Kimah drank his ayahuasca, I began to lose a clear connection to time. A warmth started to radiate from my stomach and spread out through my body. The feeling was very pleasant for quite a while. My first unusual sensation came when Christof, sitting on my left, giggled and then clapped his hands once. The clapping sounded like it had been run through a phase-shifting device. The sound was very bizarre, an otherworldly echo. This seemed very strange to me, as the singing seemed to be extraordinarily normal. I laughed at this thought as I realized that the singing was far from normal; it seemed to be surrounded by an invisible halo of resonant space as if Kimah and Carmen employed a speaker system that was acoustically adjusted to please my personal audio sensitivity. It sounded normal, but felt incredibly warm and supportive.

It may have been an hour later that the first purging began. I heard Oliver sitting on my right try to bring something up out of his stomach, but he just ended up spitting a little saliva into his bucket. Paul, sitting next to Oliver, began throwing up in earnest. I remember thinking that I was glad not to be the first to purge. Then immediately I had this strong impression that I was watching my ego play a pride game. I smiled and relaxed, but some time soon after that I could feel the ayahuasca hunting around in my stomach for evil spirits.

I felt no fear or anxiety when the tingling in my abdomen signaled a purge. There was a pretty quick build up of nausea, accompanied by intense sweating. From sitting in lotus position, I pulled my bucket in front of me and with total abandon emptied the contents of my stomach. It was a little uncomfortable, but fast, and as soon as it ended, I felt remarkably good.

I sat up straight, took a deep breath, and relaxed completely as a field of geometric shapes appeared before my eyes. I tried opening my eyes and saw the same thing—squiggly lines, elongated triangles, and curious textured bumps. The whole image was strikingly three-dimensional and moved rhythmically. After a while, I realized that the patterns were reflecting the singing. I seemed to be watching sound vibrations. I'm sure the songs were all very old and quite familiar to both Kimah and Carmen, but they always allowed for some improvisation based on what Kimah determined necessary in the moment. I didn't notice any signaling between the two of them, but they always seemed to know what the new improvised words would be and they sang them together. Kimah would invoke a long series of animal spirits, for example, and Carmen would sing right along as if she knew what animal he would choose.

If these were random choices on his part, which it seemed, then perhaps there was something like telepathy between them, but perhaps after years of doing this together they had an established pattern. Early in the ceremony, however, they sang a song that included the names of all of us in the ceremony. Carmen easily sang along as Kimah randomly added our names to the verses. After some indeterminable amount of time, my geometric vision faded, and Carmen began a song with a strong staccato rhythm. This melody, like all the songs, was both beautiful and interesting, but something about this song struck me with a tinge of fear. "Oh, no," I said to myself, "this is not a good song." Then, in the beginning of the song's repeating verse, Kimah and Carmen sang the words "body cleaning" in English, and at that point, five or six people in the room simultaneously threw up.

I purged again not long after that. It was a long full evacuation that was again not overly painful, but certainly felt like every atom of my body was folding into my stomach and then pouring like Niagara Falls into my bucket. And then again I soon felt ecstatic relief.

Some four or five hours after we started, all of us were coming down enough that Kimah took us one at a time for personal healing sessions. He would say, "Rasa, how are you? Would you like to come and sit here?" Ayahuasca doesn't seem to trouble the motor skills at all, not that I gave the concept a fair test, spending almost the entire night in one spot. I slowly moved over to the ceremonial center of the room, just in front of Kimah and Carmen.

The two of them began a ritualized healing with perfumed water, fresh sage, tobacco smoke, and of course, more song. The shaman's breath is said to be a great source of healing energy, especially when infused with tobacco smoke. With whooshing breath sounds that could have been mistaken for a large moth flying quickly past my ear, or the whistle of an exotic bid, he blew smoke onto the top of my head, my back, my chest, and into my hands. Carmen sat behind me, tapping my head, shoulders and back lightly with a sprig of sage.

At one point, Kimah crushed some sage under my nose and then pushed a tiny amount into my mouth. He said something about the sweet and the bitter just as the sweet first taste of the sage began to turn into a slightly bitter burning as the full power of the herb hit my senses. All of Kimah's actions were smooth, as if well practiced and thus reassuring, like being in the hands of a sensitive lover. With most of the others in the room, the personal healing included some counseling, either about the person's visions or realizations, or about their personal issues in life—marriage, career, stress. He spent a long time with two members of the group who seemed to have a lot of issues to work out.

I was feeling wonderful, and at that moment couldn't think why my intellect needed to move into a prominent gear. I didn't say anything. Kimah sensed my state of mind, and unlike the pointed, insightful leading questions he asked the others, to me he just said, "Ah, very good."

The personal healing sessions went on for some hours, and gradually the sun began to rise. Kimah began to show signs of his marathon effort. He stretched out and closed his eyes, but still participated in a mellow group conversation largely led by Carmen's questions to everyone about how their experiences unfolded. Several of us had had death visions or realizations. One woman was told in a vision that she should prepare for her death soon. She said this should have been alarming news, but she somehow felt as if the vision was correct, and she seemed reassured by it.

Kimah gently suggested that sometimes death visions are a metaphor for transformation, but the woman was insistent that the meaning seemed to be literal. I had an eerie poignant realization at one point in the night that every breath I released was a little death, until I breathed in again. I didn't have any visuals aside from my geometric patterns, but several people had encounters with a black panther. Oliver had a large boa constrictor fall on him and crush him until he accepted the snake's presence, and then the snake melted into a loving heavy warmth.

Carmen, even though she was singing throughout the entire night, had a disturbing vision in the form of a nasty encounter with her errant brother. At all times, the singing comforted us, and although I don't pretend to understand the mechanism, we all felt as though the shaman's power over (or at least experience with) vision-reality gave us enough protection to explore both fears and dreams with some confidence. I especially remember one song with a pounding fearsome rhythm that I'm sure gave courage to whoever in the room at that moment needed a supportive chorus.

At about nine in the morning we began to circulate and hug farewells. Oliver, Maria, and I drove off in very good spirits. Despite not sleeping for the entire night, we had a lot of energy. We talked a lot during the day on Sunday, and Maria slowly pieced together one of the shaman's songs so that by the end of the day all three of us were singing the haunting melody over and over. Late into the evening Sunday night, we were still without sleep but energized enough to go into Oliver's music studio and record a version of the song. I was just listening again to that tape. It is easy for me to hear the ayahuasca still in our systems as we performed.

Before this experience, my mental picture of an ancient psychedelic vision quest included the pop imagery of pulsing hallucinations and mysterious symbolic riddles. Since my first trips as a teenager, I've gradually turned from gawking in juvenile bliss at the light show to gazing with attentive glee at what might be a corona of enlightenment. I always suspected that I could learn something from going out of my mind.

I have always, at the very least, been annoyed by organized religion. What I realize from this ayahuasca ceremony moderates my distaste for learned elders and their authoritarian mumbo-jumbo. The transcendent experience by definition cannot be contained in ritual, but flexible ritual can serve as a launchpad and telemetry system for inner-stellar flight. But where to go? That's not a bad question, but the first consideration must be "How sturdy is the vehicle?" If I can't steer properly and the windows are fogged over with emotional and psychic debris, perhaps I need to pull the vehicle into the shop. Perhaps I need a healing. A shaman serves as healer. An enlightened shaman allows the patient's belief system to be challenged, but not forcibly replaced by a competing system. The ayahuasca ceremony was not what I expected, because I was just imagining another space ride. I didn't expect a healing. I didn't know I needed one, but I was open to whatever was meant to come, and afterward I felt so clearheaded and energized that I can only describe it as healing. The ceremony left me feeling free of personal fears and limitations, certainly a wonderful state to arrive at after a night of soul travel. Perhaps the healing is the journey.

Glimpsing the Universe / Peter Gorman

A couple of years ago, while visiting my friend Julio Jerena, an ayahuasquero who lives in the Peruvian Amazon, something occurred that seems to me to exemplify the best and worst of the psychedelic experience. It was night, and we were deep into the ayahuasca reverie. The me of me had vanished, and I was experiencing the exhilaration of awareness of spirit in everything. But suddenly my ego came rushing back, and I became acutely aware that I was extremely unimportant in the grand scheme of things.

The feeling magnified, and as it did, I became more and more convinced of my worthlessness. Worse, I imagined that if I knew how small I was, so did the people I was with, and that was a nearly impossible thought to live with. I had a fleeting vision of killing them with my machete, tossing their bodies into the nearby river, and making my way back to Iquitos, where I would explain that Julio and the others had gone night fishing, their canoe had capsized, and the river predators had killed them.

I thought it and saw the movie unfolding as I did. I don't think I would have done it, of course, but just having the thought cross my mind made me feel even smaller and more valueless. In the middle of my horrifying vision and the internal debate it sparked, I suddenly felt someone's hot breath on me and opened my eyes to find Julio blowing smoke into my face. He had my machete in his hand.

"You don't have to act on everything you feel with ayahuasca," he said. "You're just supposed to learn from the spirit and go on. The idea of killing us is just your ego playing tricks because it feels lost. Still, I think I'll put your machete away." With that, the crisis was over. Julio saw it and laughed. "That's better," he said.

I have never forgotten that night. Glimpsing the universe from the mountaintop is always exhilarating. Falling off, or even thinking you might be falling off, isn't.

The Zen Bastard Goes to Ecuador / Paul Krassner

> Some patients decide that only the proper herb can heal, while others put childlike faith in the power of the pill; still others insist that salvation can be achieved by mastering a particular yoga position or by repeating a mantra. Whatever you put your trust in can be the precipitating agent for your cure.
>
> —Irving Oyle, MD

> Laughter is one of the strongest medicines on the planet. If it's strong enough to kill an orgasm, surely it's strong enough to kill cancer.
>
> —Lotus Weinstock

In the summer of 1977, I got a magazine assignment to cover the trial of Roman Polanski. My daughter Holly was then thirteen—the same age as the girl Polanski was accused of seducing—and Holly had decided to come to Santa Monica with me, sit in the front row of the courtroom, and just stare at Polanski. She also planned to write an article about the trial from her point of view. However, Polanski fled the country.

I told Holly, "I'm gonna write about the trial anyway."

"How can you do that?"

"I'll just make it up as if it actually occurred. Roman Polanski's defense will be that the statutory rape laws are unconstitutional because they discriminate against kids."

"How would you feel if the kid was me?"

"Well, I'm a liberal father, but . . . you're right. I'm not gonna write that article."

When she was fourteen, Holly went to Mexico to learn Spanish at a school where no English was spoken. The next year, in the summer of 1979, she served as my translator on a three-week expedition to Ecuador, focusing on shamans and healers. Fellow explorers included six males (two trip leaders, a physician, a harmonica player, and a pair of psychiatrists) and five females (a poet, a cook, a therapist, and a printer studying to be an anthropologist). Holly was the only adolescent among a dozen adults, so this trek would have elements of an archetypal rite of passage for her.

Our journey would climax with a group ingestion of ayahuasca, a hallucinogenic vine similar to yage, used by shamans throughout the Amazon basin to have visions and communicate with jungle spirits during their healing ceremonies. Holly hoped to participate in that experience. Wanting to be a responsible parent, I gave her some literature to read, including an article by Dr. Andrew Weil, author of the *Natural Mind*. "Vomiting is the first stage of the effect of yage," he wrote. "It is not fun, and I say that as someone who likes to vomit in certain circumstances." This did not discourage Holly in the slightest.

Our starting point is Quito, the capital city of Ecuador, known as the Shrine of America. It is 9,000 feet above sea level, and in one day you can go through the weather of all four seasons. In Ecuador, they jest about how the ancient power of the water spirit people was invoked to flood the land when it was seized by the colonists. In more recent years, oil exploration resulted in this bittersweet joke among the Indians: "Maybe we will be like the gringos and have canned sardines flown in from the coast." In fact, one shaman we would visit actually had taped to his wall the wrappers from a can of sardines and a bar of Lux soap.

The unholy trinity in Ecuador consists of the missionaries, the military, and the oil companies. The international oil companies first invaded Ecuador in the late '60s. Within a few years, what had once been a subsistence economy was injected with a strong dose of technological dependence. On September 15, 1972, then-President Guillermo Lara flew to Shell airport with a group of captains and colonels, each the head of a national agency. The flight, which took twenty minutes from Quito, was timed to correspond with sunrise. The plane, *La Cucuracha*, touched down at 6 a.m. Paratroopers wearing red berets, who had been trained in Panama for commando warfare, flaunted their Czech-made automatic rifles at buses and cars. Fixed bayonets lined the route.

The Aucas—there were only an estimated five hundred left of this tribe who survive in unpopulated areas of the jungle—once killed several employees of Texaco. There are crossed wooden swords on any path leading to an Aucan village, a symbolic warning to keep away. We shall not be visiting the Aucas. But gasoline still costs as little as fifteen cents a gallon, and the Shell military camp carries on. While we are there, however, the military government is preparing to transfer power to the newly elected liberal, Jaime Roldos Aguilera. He has beaten one opponent who got a million dollars from the oil people for his campaign, including full-page ads stating: "Vote against Roldos If You're Catholic."

The president-elect announced, "I want to show that democracy can be imposed in an orderly manner and that social justice can be achieved. This might sound utopian and may even be a source of amusement to some, but if we ignore the possibility of achieving social change throughout the institutional framework of the country, it's the same as saying that democracy isn't the most just and perfect form of government."

In Quito, I acquire an advertising poster—they call it propaganda—featuring a man wearing an apron and holding up a bottle of cleansing powder called El Macho. We visit Leaves of Grass, a vegetarian restaurant that has the customary bulletin board. "Free room and board for one female," reads a message. "Dig this experiment in international living." To a poster offering courses in acupuncture, the I Ching, and midwifery, "Hashish for Sale" has been added. In the bathroom, a graffito promises, "Legalize pot and cure the world!" I am told that possession of marijuana could result in six months' imprisonment and $50,000 worth of legalized shakedowns in the form of fines, lawyers' fees, and judges' bribes.

I am also able to verify a few details of one horror case in which an individual was arrested for using cocaine on Christmas, when his wife was seven and a half months pregnant. He has seen her only once and hasn't even met their baby. He has been put in a clinic that charges him $600 a month, plus he has to pay for his own armed guard. He was fingered by a hippie who had been busted in the United States and was then brought to Ecuador to work illegally as an informer for the DEA. There are, of course, legal drugs. Coca-Cola is everywhere. So are cigarettes, coffee, booze, and Ataka, which, claims a TV commercial during the Miss America competition, "eliminates all pain."

The most popular song goes, "Let's just get blasted on tobacco and rum." Number two on the hit parade is "In the Navy" by the Village People. And an automobile horn honks out the first five notes of "Strangers in the Night." Playing in movie theaters are dubbed versions of *Superman, Death on the Nile, Julia,* and *Pretty Baby.* The musical *Grease* was immensely popular, as evidenced by the glut of John Travolta and Olivia Newton-John T-shirts for sale. Westernization has crept in among the authentic Indian goods for sale. On market day, one booth on a side street features a monkey that picks your horoscope from a drawer, and a selection of View-Master cassettes, including *The Flying Nun, Project Apollo, SWAT, Bonanza, Mickey Mouse, Powerful Puss,* and *Lassie.* And, among all the bare feet, an occasional pair of Adidas.

Ibarra, north of Quito, is the territory of the Otovalan Indians, living in the shadow of snowcapped volcanoes. Every Saturday, rows of bland gray beach umbrella–sized cement mushrooms (a gift of the Dutch government) sprouting from an otherwise barren city block, are temporarily reincarnated into a crowded, buzzing marketplace, the sight of colorful tapestries mixing with the aroma of authentic native recipes. The Otovalan Indians are a startlingly attractive tribe—short and squat, with doll-like features—but many seem to be permanently bent forward from carrying heavy loads on their backs. Age and gender are no barriers to that task.

The women's finery always includes choker beads that were originally Czechoslovakian Christmas ornaments. The men wear white pants, bright ponchos, and fedora hats covering long, thick black hair twisted into the traditional single braid. Young boys who don't have braids yet cover their heads with American cowboy bandannas. Their hairstyle are proof that they are members of the indigenous community. If one cuts his hair, he will be ostracized. The Otovalans have had land disputes ever since the Spanish conquest. The Spaniards tried to outlaw anything to do with the Otovalan religion. They even forbade Inca clothing style. Thus the Indians were virtually forced into wearing these brimmed hats.

Even when we get to play six-person volleyball with a bunch of young men in an Otovalan village, the men keep their fedoras on. At one point, the game, for which each side puts up sixty sucres, stops so that an elderly woman can lead a bull through the volleyball court, which is simply a net strung across a dirt road. Athough masculine and feminine roles appear to be clearly defined—men, for example, operate the weaving loom and women do the spinning—there is, nevertheless, an inspiring dignity implicit in a group of well-dressed Otovalan women washing clothes at a dirt road intersection, when they refuse to allow their photos to be taken. In other contexts, they have been eagerly cooperative in posing for our cameras.

Only men can be *brujos* (witch doctors), but some women are permitted to perform abortions by manipulating and crushing the uterus. Two days later, there will be a miscarriage. If the pregnant woman has been touched by a rainbow, she will give birth to a monster. However, that can be avoided if a *brujo* cleanses her. Then she will have a normal baby. Like the Moonies and Scientology and Catholicism—it works. If the universe is infinite, then there is also an infinite variety of paths to connect with the universe.

Our bus stops at a marker signifying the exact dividing line between the northern and southern hemispheres. I absolutely cannot resist the territorial urge to urinate on both sides of the equator in one big bladder splatter merely by adjusting my aim in midstream. Later on, there will be a billboard proclaiming a NASA tracking station, and as a gesture toward the entire space program, I will be urinating on that too. Yet another of my Great Moments in Urinating series will occur in an old-fashioned bullfighting stadium. It is empty, but as I stride to the center of the arena, I can hear a roar, the wild cheering of an invisible crowd of spectators, anticipating my moment of urinary truth.

Between these episodes, there is magnificent scenery, a terrible reminder that there are so many urban Americans who see nature only when it happens to be the setting for a

TV commercial. What a pleasure it is now to observe snowtopped mountains that aren't pushing frozen foods, waterfalls that aren't the background for a can of beer, rainbows that aren't advertising a savings and loan association. The autocarril is a bus that travels on railroad tracks. We take it for an eight-hour jaunt to the little Pacific Coast port town of San Lorenzo. They have electricity there, but not until 10 p.m.

We stay at an extremely funky hotel that costs fifty cents a night. The toilets are seatless, but the beds have mosquito netting. We wake up to a chorus of neighborhood dogs accompanying the raucous sounds of a recorded marching band playing "Stars and Stripes Forever" over a loudspeaker. We never find out whether this is a local daily-morning ritual or just a special welcome for our visit. Where the Sierra Club leaves off, we begin. There are no automobiles in the jungle. There are no roads. We travel along remote tributaries of the Cayapa River in giant canoes, each one dug out from a single sandse or wangaripo tree. The paddles, carved out of the conalom tree, are no longer the tools of mobility for our navigators, though.

A few years ago, Yamaha outboard motors came on the scene, offering the combined enticements of status, speed, and low down-payments. Thus was noise pollution introduced to the natives, along with a significant change in their lifestyle. For they surrendered to the gravitational pull of civilization, forcing themselves into the contemporary version of the Puritan ethic—increasing productivity in order to meet their monthly installments on a five-year payment plan. It is the ultimate energy crisis—working hard to support your electronic appliances—whether you are delivering a boatful of bananas or working in an office trying to transfer all the contents from the in-basket to the out-basket in eight little hours.

It's raining heavily, but we get permission to set up camp inside the Sagrada Familia (Sacred Family) Mission. There is, as an appropriate backdrop to the altar, a mural of the Nativity, apparently drawn by children from this village of blacks who originally migrated from Colombia to escape slavery. The manger has an added local touch. The birth of Jesus is taking place in front of a palm tree with hanging coconuts. We entertain ourselves with early rock 'n' roll. Instead of the usual religious hymns, the strains of "Silhouettes" and "At the Hop" emanate from the church that evening. A commune of pigs is stationed just underneath the floor that our sleeping bags are resting on, and we can hear them snorting through the night.

Next morning, I find a corroded, naked, pink doll—a tarnished angel, to be precise— in a trash bin behind the church. It seems like a perfect souvenir, so I take it. A Christian missionary—whose luxurious house and matching yacht on the river edge of the jungle are in shocking contrast to the simplicity of the native shacks—informs us that, whereas the Indians are into witchcraft, the blacks are into immorality. These, he asserts, are "the besetting sins" of the area. He tells us with obvious disdain that the shamans drink pinde (another name for ayahuasca), and he compares the effects to LSD, which he has never taken. As for blacks, they "can't stand noise or bad news."

The blacks live in small villages. The Indian homes have no walls, but the black homes do have walls—the better, presumably, to hide their immorality. An immoral black teenaged marimba player who has just met Holly asks her to marry him, but she declines his proposal, explaining that she wants to finish high school and everything. Besides, we are on our way to spend a week living with the Cayapa Indians, a primitive tribe. The missionary warns us to watch out for vampire bats.

The Cayapa Indians live in isolated shacks along the river. Our jungle home belonged to a shaman who died a few months previously. The structure sits on stilts and has a sturdy thatched roof, but no side walls. A raised deck is the kitchen area. The lavatory is downstairs, third cluster of bushes to your left. The river is for washing and—if you boil the water for fifteen minutes—drinking. The muddy bank probably discourages such kinky activities as toe-sucking among the natives. This is our medialess environment. No television, radio, stereo, movies, telephone, mail, newspapers, magazines. Instead, we listen to tree frogs imitate the sound of clinking wine glasses.

Every day, three generations of the dead shaman's family arrive early in the morning. They sit serenely, as though posing for an official portrait. The women are bare-breasted. One of them is playing with the penis of her small child. Their social rules are fascinating. Young Cayapas are required to live together for six months before they are permitted to marry. At their wedding ceremony, a couple is given ten lashes each as a sample of the 150 lashes either would receive for marital infidelity.

A bizarre form of role reversal seems to have entered into the process. We are like Martians who have suddenly dropped in on their primitive culture, and we are their live TV show. They see the therapist doing tai chi. They listen to the harmonica player singing "There's a riot goin' on in cell block number nine." With great curiosity, they watch one psychiatrist brushing his teeth and the other one taking notes. So now they have become the anthropologists, and we have become the subjects of their casual observation. "They are still observing us intently," writes the psychiatrist.

As a Zen Bastard exercise, I once trained myself to laugh when I stub my toe. It has become second nature. I didn't realize that I had been searching for an example of how humor could transcend language and culture, but when I stub my toe and automatically laugh out loud in front of this family of primitive anthropologists, they share in the hilarity. I become the first to dispense with my bathing suit, and soon all of us are swimming nude except for our native guides. Gossip about these strange naked whites reaches the missionary who, we learn a couple of weeks later, uses his CB equipment to radio the information back to Quito.

There in the jungle, I began an affair with Dinah, one of the women in our group. On July 23, Holly writes in her journal: "Today's my half birthday! I'm exactly fifteen and a half years old! Oh, yeah, I haven't written anything about the only romance on the trip. Daddy and Dinah! They are sharing a room & Daddy says that if him & Mommy had treated each other as good as he & Dinah are treating each other they'd still be together. I know that's bullshit but it's a sweet thing to say and it's nice to know things are working so well for them. Daddy seems like a kid again, holding hands in the taxi & when we're eating, little kisses on the cheek, and he's so happy. Dinah is 29, really pretty & intelligent. Daddy says she reminds him of Mommy. She lives with her boyfriend. They really make each other laugh. I'm so happy for Daddy! For my 'birth-day' they gave me a rhinoceros beetle's shell that they found." Dinah and I live 3,000 miles apart, and she has a lover at home, so because we both know—and agree in advance—that we will go our separate ways when the expedition ends, our relationship has that much more intensity.

❧

Shamanism goes back 50,000 years. The *curandero* (healer) communicates with those unseen evil spirits responsible for illness. It's also a family business. Built into the over-head costs of our trip was the transfer of enough sucres to insure the privilege of observing and participating in their healing ceremonies. The Christian influence is evi-dent even in the name of one shaman: Jesusito. He is wearing a long silk shirt with short sleeves, resembling a baseball uniform. In front of him is a shrine of hand-carved wooden figures—a soldier, a mama grande (female figure) with white beads, a police-man, a bishop, Atauhalpa (the last Inca king)—bronze eagle-head staffs, polished stones, a prehistoric clay cast of an ox-head, and money.

There is also a pair of perfectly incongruous holy objects: a gray clamshell-like item that opens up to reveal a head of the Virgin Mary that can be lifted out in case you wish to make Jello in the mold, and, the most sacred of all, a sealed-beam headlight from an old Buick which, deep in the jungle, is transformed into some kind of mysterious crys-tal ball. There are 40,000 Cayapa Indians, and hardly one has ever seen a car, much less driven a stick-shift model.

Jesusito chants over each individual that he is healing. He waves a wand of leaves as he makes this sound: *woosha woosha*. He blows cigarette smoke into the patient's face. Would we not think that a medical doctor who did this was being slightly rude and unprofessional? He takes a swig of a perfumey beverage, but doesn't swallow. Instead, he spritzes it out through his teeth in an aerosol mist that helps to cleanse the sickness without making any holes in the ozone layer.

Jesusito notices my tape recorder, and it becomes the subject of an animated discus-sion between him and an assistant. I'm fearful that they might resent this technological intrusion, but instead they request a playback of what has already been recorded. Jesusito listens to himself chanting and going *woosha woosha* with all the attention of Mick Jagger at a recording studio trying avoid overdubbing on a new album. Then, because Jesusito has been ill and is somewhat fatigued, he uses the tape recorder for his next round of healing. Drifting in and out of sleep, we hear Jesusito continue to chant through the night, as crowing roosters attempt unsuccessfully to harmonize with him.

Earlier, he had asked the physician in our group for a second opinion on a couple of liver and spleen cases. Conversely, there is a hospital that has begun to join forces with local healers. And in Canada, the Ontario provincial government has actually granted a hospital $26,000 for a medicine man, because doctors had complained that they couldn't help Indians with emotional problems due to language and other cultural barriers. The medicine man substitutes herbs for medication, and rituals for bedside manner.

We visit a shaman of the Colorado tribe. The back half of his head has been shaved. The remaining hair has been dyed orange-red with the achiote berry, mixed with Vaseline and plastered stiff over his forehead. It lasts for eight days. The shaman does a few sample cleansing ceremonies for us. Cleansing is the first step in the curative process. This shaman has a large magnet—the kind you'd find in a big old '40s Philco living-room console radio—which he hits with a metal cross just above a patient's head, causing a fusion of sound and vibration that will help dispel a disease which was, incidentally, caused by frogs or worms.

There are fifty brujos out of a thousand Colorados, and the profession is generally passed on to sons. Our brujo has a twenty-two-year-old son who is also a shaman, but his hair is modish and his clothes Western. He has his own peer group. But who's to say what's really indigenous? There is a theory that the Colorados' hairstyle was originally an imitation of the Spanish conquistadores, whose metal helmets had similarly shaped peaks. More recently, young Indians adopted the custom of hanging a bath towel around the neck, but they were actually copying an idiosyncracy of oil workers.

We visit another shaman who puts on an Indian headdress and displays an outdoor table full of herbs, leaves, and roots that are used to heal everything from headaches to rheumatism to severe burns. This is an esoteric counterpoint to the narc-squad representative who used to visit junior high schools for compulsory hygiene classes with his display of dangerous drugs. But this display promotes not fear, but healing. The milk of a cactus, pitajaya, soaked into a piece of cloth, serves as a cure for gangrene. Chanco piedra is an herb that reduces and expels kidney stones. The leaves of the juanto bush cure fractures, while the stems act as an aphrodisiac—so in case you hurt your leg while pursuing a potential mate, use both bush and stems. The sap of the incira tree will extract—that is, crumble—a decayed tooth, painlessly. Take shavings from the bark of a large shrub called hipocuru, mix with aguardiente (the poor person's rum) and steep for a week, then add honey, and you have an effective medicine that has cured arthritis. A skeptical Harvard physiologist visiting the area got converted when the profuse bleeding of a machete gash in her arm was halted by drinking the sap of a tree, a Euphorbiaceae, the *Croton salutaris*.

Magical powers are attributed to various species of the cypress vine, used to cure such diverse ailments as eye infections and diarrhea, as well as to prevent pregnancy. Two doses, each at the end of consecutive menstrual periods, will render a woman infertile for approximately six years. An herb that causes sterility for only three years is known as amor seco (dry love). It boggles the mind to imagine by what means these methods of birth control were originally discovered. In the late '50s, American pharmaceutical companies combined racism, sexism and imperialism by experimenting with oral contraceptives on Puerto Rican women. Ultimately, the properties of contraceptive herbs used by South American Indians were ripped off by North American drug monopolies. As early as 1920, the Canelos Indians of Ecuador were ingesting a medicine prepared from the piripiri plant by crushing the roots and soaking them in water. Many tribes also rub such a liquid on their bows to improve marksmanship. The specific methods of preparing this plant—whether for birth control or better aim—still remain among the secrets of the jungle.

But wait! What kind of mirage is this? A beautiful hotel in the middle of the jungle? It was constructed from material brought in via the river. Adorable monkeys roam around and mingle with the guests. A ten-minute walk into the wilderness, and there is an incredibly lush area with a large swimming hole and a place from which to dive. It is the group's consensus fantasy that this is what paradise must be like. For one brief moment, I even entertain the notion of staying forever. On the way back to a gourmet dinner, while I'm groping my way precariously across a huge log that serves as a bridge, somebody behind me starts jumping up and down on the log, trying to make me fall into the water. It turns out to be the playful hotel owner himself. The absurdity of this situation overwhelms me as I attempt to focus total attention on keeping my balance. *Up and down. Up and down.* The Zen Bastard rides again!

The time has come at last for us to take ayahuasca. It will be this evening. Dr. Andrew Weil had suggested fasting after breakfast, but our group eats lunch anyway, rationalizing that as long as we're all going to vomit anyway, we might as well put something into our stomachs now to throw up later. In the afternoon, we travel by truck and ferry, then hike for an hour deep into the jungle. There are butterflies with a foot-wide wingspread. A steady stream of bright green leaves is crossing our path with the aid of unseen ants. When we reach our destination, we are offered plates of boiled manioc, a potato-like root, and bowls of chicha (fermented manioc) ground up and pulverized in water, which tastes like sour buttermilk. We have been told that it would be considered impolite to refuse such hospitality.

Ayahuasca means "soul vine." It is innocent looking enough, an inch or two thick, curving into and beyond a complete circle. There are some twenty varieties of ayahuasca. Who can imagine how its psychoactive use was originally discovered? First it is chopped vertically, then horizontally, and then boiled. In *Wizard of the Upper Amazon*, F. Bruce Lamb wrote: "Drinking a carelessly prepared extract would only cause violent vomiting, acute intestinal cramps and diarrhea, he [Manuel Cordova, an old Peruvian healer] said, and he went on to tell me that ayahuasca must be handled with care and reverence, simmered slowly in a special earthenware pot over a low fire under constant, proper attention." However, ours is being boiled in an aluminum pot by a young Canelos Indian couple in the midst of a lovers' quarrel. But we can't very well tell them that they're preparing it the wrong way. A leaf, datura (similar to belladonna), is added to the potion, which is an unappetizing, rust-colored, muddy liquid that tastes so putrid a bottle of rum must be held in your other hand for an instant chaser. We sit in a circle and pass the bowl around so each individual can drink from it.

After around twenty minutes, the first psychiatrist says, "My thoughts are beginning to become disassociated."

"Oh, really?" says the second psychiatrist. "Mine are always that way."

Inevitably, the sounds of violent retching echo through the jungle. One by one, the members of our group go outside and vomit as though we were wet towels being wrung out by invisible demons. That old wizard of the Amazon was righ—they should have used a clay pot. He had warned that if the ayahuasca was boiled in aluminum rather than earthenware, it would make you more sick than visionary. I pass around the roll of butter rum Life Savers I had brought especially for this occasion. When Holly's insides declare that it's her turn to throw up, I accompany her outside and stand there watching as a volcanic regurgitation takes over her body. Oh, God, I think, I hope I've done the right thing. When she finishes, I begin. The power of peristalsis possesses me so thoroughly that I vomit and fart simultaneously. Holly's tears turn to laughter at my involuntary duet, which in turn makes me laugh. There I am in the middle of the jungle with my daughter—vomiting, farting, and laughing.

"I think this is known as quality time," I finally manage to say.

As we walk back to the shack with our arms around each other and feeling weak, Holly says, "It's nice to be near someone you love when you're in misery."

Under the influence of ayahuasca, the local people traditionally have visions of jaguars and anacondas (water snakes), but instead we Americans see elephants and mice; spider webs of memory; a woman, wearing an 1890 gown and large brimmed hat, eating a loaf of French bread. The corrugated metal ceiling is undulating like the surface of an ocean. Looney Tunes cartoon characters are dancing inside my brain. "Something's got a hold of my leg," someone shouts. "Oh, it's my boot." During their healing ceremony, two shamans keep sucking the poisons out of a patient's head, and then, although they don't actually vomit, they keep making these awful sounds of vomiting, in order to get rid of those poisons. All through the night, we are forced to divert our psychic energy away from exquisite visionary flights simply in order not to throw up again. What was it that Tim Leary said about set and setting? How preferable soothing music would be over the continuous sounds of fake retching that punctuate the shamans' chant:

> Spirit of the mountain lake,
> Come, come, come, where are you?
> Help cure this sick person,
> Old spirit man of the forest
> Up at the mountain lake.

A flash of paranoia convinces me for a moment that there is some kind of sorcerer's trick being played on us, for these shamans are laughing at us whenever anyone succumbs to vomiting. They almost seem to be displaying a playful pride in their catalytic function. Each member of our group experiences a certain type of auditory hallucination—perceiving spoken English as the shamans chat in Quechua during the healings. This phenomenon is comparable to when you've fallen asleep while watching TV, but the voices from the program keep slithering their way into your dream, developing a logic all their own.

In the morning, we're awakened by one of the kids' battery-operated radios, not with Bruce Springsteen singing "Jungle Land," but rather someone else doing a schmaltzy rendition of an old song, "Beware, My Foolish Heart." We are all thoroughly wasted, but the shamans are up and lively, one playing the harmonica, both looking like Ecuador's primitive version of the Blues Brothers. Before we leave, one of the shamans asks our medical doctor for Lomotil, to be used for diarrhea, and the cultural exchange is completed. Our return hike through the rain forest is accompanied by a tremendous rainstorm. While getting thoroughly soaked, Holly and I keep singing "Singing in the Rain" over and over and over again, as loudly as we can. Back in Quito, the exact likeness of that corroded, naked, pink tarnished-angel doll appears on the shelf of a fancy boutique.

"Hey," Holly stage-whispers to a companion, "remember that tarnished angel my dad stole from the church in the jungle?"

I interject, "Why don't you say it loud for everyone to hear?"

But it's a mistake to attempt such light sarcasm on an adolescent who has seen one too many situation comedies.

"Hey," Holly says out loud for everyone to hear (including the clerk, who speaks English), "remember that tarnished angel my dad stole from the church in the jungle?"

Well, of course, we all laugh nervously at that. But Holly and I have really grown closer on this expedition. The family that pukes together has visions together.

There's a current theory that cannibalism among South American Indians is a myth spread by anthropologists who need to feel superior to those they study. Nonetheless, thirty-two skeletons of children showing evidence of having been devoured were discovered in a Colombian jungle. Arms and legs had been almost completely eaten. Authorities confirm that this was not the first time members of various tribes have eaten their youngsters. It is estimated that about 500 nomadic Indians in that area suffer from extreme malnutrition and occasionally eat the corpses of relatives or neighbors, sometimes killing them specifically for that purpose.

It is with this awareness that I return to civilization. We are of the same species as those cannibals. We merely eat our children in more sophisticated ways. A poster at the airport in Los Angeles advises, "A Few Extra Minutes Clearing Customs Saves Others from [in threatening red letters] NARCOTICS!" I have no problem getting through customs. I certainly haven't brought back any ayahuasca. I do have in my suitcase a tarnished angel, but its mate still reclines on a shelf in a boutique on the other side of the equator.

Holly will attend high school in Hollywood and work at a Baskin-Robbins ice-cream parlor off Sunset Boulevard. She will come to know her hooker customers by their favorite flavors, and as we walk along the street, she will point them out to me. "There's Rocky Road . . . . That's Pralines 'n' Cream . . . . That's Strawberry Shortcake . . . ."

And now I'm home again in San Francisco. TV commercials are trying to program viewers with fear of their own bodies, elevators are getting stuck in skyscrapers without thirteenth floors, and MX missiles are enjoying underground amusement-park rides in order to fool the Russians. How can I explain any of this uncivilized behavior to that primitive Indian family that I have smuggled into America, hiding them between the left and right lobes of my brain? They continue to visit me each day. Their image vividly remains as a buffer to my culture shock. They look over my shoulder every moment, never judging, just observing. And so my own neighborhood has become the site of a new expedition, as I begin to see everything through the innocent eyes of my primitive witnesses from the tropical rain forest. In the jungle, canned dog food is unknown. But here, we actually encounter a man walking down the street and holding a leash with a four-legged mechanical pet robot.

Safari, so good.

COCAINE

Spoons / Dana Snow

Back when paraphernalia was legal, I worked on a coke-spoon assembly line in Hollywood. Four of us would take turns in the position: taking little strips of metal, hitting each one with a hammer to dent if so that it became a spoon, attaching it to a chain, and attaching the other end of the chain to the cap of a vial. But I felt so guilty about it, I'd hit the hammer too hard and create a hole instead of a dent, so I ended up manufacturing dribble coke spoons for rich practical jokers.

Outside Looking In / Frederic Berthoff

I called her Moolah after the lady wrestler, who was a pretty good-looking broad herself, though she was black and my own personal Moolah was blonde. A genuine Swedish blonde, or at least a genuine Swede, she might have given her locks a little peroxide push with a monthly treatment she really didn't need. Moolah was naturally very beautiful. She could have been Thor's girlfriend, with that big-boned Viking look, and I pictured her sometimes wearing a horned and studded helmet, stirring a pot of ox-brain stew at some Labrador war camp back in the old days. The skeptics asked if I really loved this Roller Derby Queen, and I said, "Yes, I do." She was all that, and a barrel of fun.

We were both coke fiends. Call it an '80s thing; there we were. When Friday night rolled around, I'd break out the stash, chopping and sniffing until we succumbed to our separate but equal madnesses. After a ten-year habit, I was getting freaked out by this drug, but she was worse than me, hallucinating everything from snakes on her back to other strange delusions like, "Rick, Rick, I'm on fire!"

Then there was "Harry," her imaginary demon, Harry, who was always lurking somewhere, and she'd sink her claws into my arm and holler, "He's under the bed! Arrrrgh!" I'd kiss her on the cheek and hold her close to me.

"Take it easy, Moolah. There's nobody there."

"No, look! Look now!" And on and on.

My own demons were garden variety—you know, the cops are here (or the robbers) and all that bullshit. Now and again, jealousy, that old green monster, would rear his insidious head, and I'd start to read too much into a glance or a gesture. Paranoid? Maybe, but I have had some chicks who drove me to a jealous rage, then told me I was crazy, though I found out later they were guilty as charged. Your friends always give you up in the end, believe me.

But Moolah just wanted to get high. She was cool like that. And when we finally ran out of coke, or I told her we ran out, she'd snivel and pout a little, then, with a resigned sigh, say, "Well, let's go to bed, then." In other words, "You can fuck me now." She used those exact words at least once. I was crazy about her. And when the demons were gone, we made love like mad.

But the demons! Burglars and cops were my twin bugaboos, and I spent way too many hours of a squandered youth spying out windows or the peepholes in doors, looking for the raid that never happened. We lived in the woods with no neighbors, thank God, so my next weirdo move went largely unnoticed. A neighbor would have called the cops for real, bringing my paranoid fantasies to a perversely appropriate conclusion. Maybe we see in fantasy what we want to come true. Or else our neural circuitry goes berserk when too many subliminal wires get overloaded. In any case, neighbors would have probably ended one nightmare, only to start another. But we had no neighbors, and the cops never came.

After several months of this chemically induced intrigue, with our Friday nights now falling as often on a Tuesday, I finally got bored with peeking out the windows, so I went outside and peeked in. That was a major weirdo move. Just a little switcheroo to keep things interesting, I thought, but I'm sure I looked like the psychotic prowler that I was.

My jealous streak, I usually kept a lid on, and never broke weak with that "I know you're fucking the paperboy" kind of shit. Like I said, Moolah never gave me much to go on in that regard. I'd look in the window, and she's just sitting there, sipping a frozen

Margarita in the middle of January until I came down off my trip enough to realize, "Hey, it's fucking cold out here," and came back inside.

Then she'd ask, "Whatta you doin'?"

And I'd say, teeth still chattering, "Uh, just out there looking around."

And she'd say, "Rick . . . come over here."

And so, for what is now considered an era, we passed the time.

Honeymoon Junkyard / Terri Scott

It was my wedding day, September 12, 1981. I poured myself a shot of Jack Daniels around 9 a.m. I needed that, as my mother had arrived and was in charge of decorations. After the ceremony and the opening of gifts and drinking and dancing, I went back to my dressing room. I remembered that someone had given me a vial of cocaine earlier, and I indulged. I was trying to decide if I should change clothes for the after-wedding barbecue, and decided to wear my wedding dress to it. Probably a mistake, as I spilled barbecue sauce down the front, and the stain never did come out.

The next day, we drove off in our 1969 Datsun station wagon on our honeymoon. It threw a rod in Ukiah. We checked into the LuAnn motel. It was conveniently located within walking distance of the used auto parts junkyard and an all-you-can-eat restaurant. The first night and the first day, we just indulged. Cocaine, wine, and sex. We achieved our personal best sex record: six times in one day. I'm sure others have done better, but that was our personal best. We went to dinner that evening, could barely eat, and jogged back to the motel.

The next day, my new husband began in earnest making treks to the junkyard, while I sunbathed by the pool. One kind elderly man came to sit with me. I told him our story and almost made him cry. He mixed me a vodka tonic. When he and his wife drove off to dinner, he still looked like he was going to cry. ("That poor girl," I could hear him say. "Her car broke down on her honeymoon.") No luck at the junkyard, and we had to be towed back from our honeymoon.

We just celebrated our twentieth anniversary. We didn't snort coke, we didn't have sex, and our vehicles are running smoothly. You just can't have everything.

Psychosis in the Park / Preston Peet

Spending nearly every penny on cocaine, trying to kill all feelings of being human, along with all the guilt and loneliness, took a toll on Thomas in ways he never expected. He has been living in Central Park, getting high with a number of really fucked-up people who, when they shoot their drugs, instantly begin to act nuts, doing things like stripping off all their clothes, ripping them from their bodies, or if they are indoors, they might lock the door, then shove all the furniture in the room over in front of the door to keep out the monsters or the devil or whatever it is they fear.

Each time this happens, Thomas just takes it in his stride, realizing that this is not right, but never considering that he will one day have to face the same kinds of demons himself. He has ingested every kind of hallucinatory drug he could get his hands on at one time or another over his getting-high career—acid, mushrooms, mescaline—and thinks he knows what tripping and hallucinating are all about. But he has no idea until he experiences his first time of what becomes normal operating procedure: cocaine psychosis.

He takes his drugs one beautiful, bright, sunny day to the old, dead, dry fountain not too far from Strawberry Field and Sheep's Meadow, but still enough out of the way of traffic to feel "safe," where he goes off by himself to get high. Taking a seat on the far side of the fountain, at the bottom of a kudzu-covered hill, he takes out his paraphernalia, all the tools he needs to get off, and sets to work doing just that.

He is a professional at this and is able to get everything done very quickly and surreptitiously, loving nothing more than to get high right out in the open so blatantly that no one ever notices. At least so far. He continuously looks around, scoping out the area, noticing two or three people sitting on the grass off to the right under a small tree, but spots no one else at all.

Just as he has the needle in his arm, right as he is shoving in the plunger, pushing the drug into his vein, he distinctly hears from the top of the hill behind him, behind the bushes at the top, a voice that says, "Okay, boys, let's get 'im!"—then the sounds of many running feet as though a squad of the undercover cops who patrol the park are coming to arrest him.

"Holy shit!" Thomas exclaims out loud as he panics. The drugs are causing his senses to go completely haywire, combined with the terror he's experiencing. His hearing is gone now, the sound of his pounding heart is so loud, his ears filling with the sound of how he imagines a strobe light would sound if it made sound rather than light. Leaping to his feet, Thomas chucks the works, and the drugs still in hand, back behind him into the kudzu, then turns and walks steadily away toward the fountain, forcing himself to keep a slow pace, not wanting the cops to have any excuse to tackle him or think he knows they are coming for him at all. The old "Don't look at them and maybe they will go away" trick actually works, much to his consternation.

Reaching the edge of the dry fountain, he glances behind him to see how close they are to him, but is staggered to find no one there. No running cops, no sounds of cops, and when he looks to see if others are noticing anything strange, not even the people he'd seen under the little tree out in the grass are there now. Maybe they'd seen him leap to his feet, and decided that they wanted nothing to do with him and split, or maybe they weren't even there to begin with, but that can't be. He heard them before he shot up.

As he is still dealing with the initial rush of the shot, thinking is difficult, but he has trouble believing that he hallucinated that voice or those footsteps. Looking around wildly, he thinks he spots one of the picnickers from before, apparently hiding from him behind another skinny little tree like the first one they were under. Coke really screws up his vision, making everything blurry and hard to focus, and the sun helps keep the figure hidden in shadow. But whoever it is, Thomas can tell that they are watching him, and he can hear laughter. Are they laughing at me? he wonders. He has to find out.

Before he can get to the tree, the person is no longer there, having managed to make it over to a large clump of bushes without Thomas seeing, where he begins catching glimpses of two or three different people, though again only as silhouettes and shadows. Thinking perhaps that they are trying to get him close to the bushes so they can grab him and beat him up, he begins to address the bushes. "Who's there?" he asks, but gets no answer other than quiet rustling and that weird laughter he keeps hearing.

He tries again, in a firmer voice. "Quit playing games with me, and come on out!" There's still no answer, so Thomas looks around for help. He tries to stop one man walking by on the footpath, but the guy keeps moving, giving him a wide berth. Then along comes a young couple up the path. Thomas stops them by stepping out in front of them, asking, "Excuse me, can you tell me if you see anyone in these bushes?" As he says it, he can hear himself and how bizarre he sounds, so he instantly tries to come up with a rational explanation for his question, to try to ease their obvious anxiety.

"See, I was smoking a big joint with some friends, for the first time in a long time, and they've run off, and now they're fucking with me, and I . . ." They run off before he can finish babbling at them. Thomas looks down at his arm, which the girl had been staring at, and finds that in his blind panic he's forgotten to clean off the blood that has since run freely down his arm in long, red rivulets, from his elbow to his wrist. Pulling down his sleeve, he is overcome with paranoia, thinking maybe that nice young couple will run to find a cop, and that the police must now for sure be moving in on him at this moment.

After finally gathering the nerve to run past the clump of bushes where the snickering shadows may or may not be hunkered, waiting to pounce, Thomas heads toward Sheep's Meadow, seeing police literally everywhere, circling, talking into their collars on their secret radios, making special police hand signals to one another, getting ready to snatch and arrest him.

He wanders for a few more minutes, in sheer terror, until he runs into Jay, one of the two guys who first brought him into Strawberry Field, who recognizes what's happening as soon as Thomas starts pointing out joggers all the way on the other side of Sheep's Meadow, saying, "Look, there, cops!" Trying not to laugh, Jay stays with Thomas, reassuring him every time he begins to lose control and wants to run in fear, walking him out of the park to Fifth Avenue, which runs along the east side of Central Park.

Jay then sits with him until the fear passes and the craziness goes away. Thomas had been completely, unabashedly terrified like never before in his entire life. If Jay had not come along when he did, there is no telling what would have happened to him. Everything had seemed 100 percent real to him, and though he could tell he was hallucinating, he hadn't been able to stop or deal with it as if it were only a trippy vision.

Needled / John Shirley

I had given up using psychedelics, mostly, because I tended to dissolve into my environment when I took them. It didn't take much. (And even now, when I look at a blank wall closely, it swims a little, looking miscible, shifting with subtle patterns . . . . Never had a flashback, though.)

But I was living in New York and was making money writing, and my wife was doing other, er, things for moolah, and we tended to blow it on cocaine. Sometimes heroin and cocaine, but mostly coke. Sometimes I mainlined it.

I tell this story with reluctance. I don't like to think about it. I've been off cocaine, off drugs (well, I'd take a little mild mescaline or MDMA if someone offered it, and have, but mostly I steer clear of drugs now), and coke was the only one hard to get away from.

I'm convinced that, at least relative to man, Good and Evil are quite real, and that there are Good drugs and Evil drugs. Good drugs can become bad drugs if they're misused—I learned a great deal from psychedelics, but one mustn't take them too often or under the wrong circumstances, and you shouldn't use them at all if you can't handle a car that drives the mental freeways at top speed, pressing its own accelerator to the floor. But Evil drugs are always Evil drugs. Cocaine, heroin, and PCP, especially. The TV commercial that shows the rat dosing itself to death on cocaine is no bullshit.

Some people have more resistance to coke addiction than others—but anyone will duplicate the fate of that white rat if they have enough coke. Cocaine will rewire your brain. It will push your pleasure buttons, will use reward-conditioning to make you its Pavlovian lab rat.

It pretty much ate through the bonds with my wife, and the marriage fell apart. I remained faithful to cocaine and got deeper into shooting up. One day I went rabid with it. I had two good grams and a fresh needle, and I got feverishly into sticking myself. The needle became as important as the drug. I associated the needle with the indescribably powerful rush of cocaine pleasure, so the needle was lasciviously desirable. I was queer for the needle. I was like a queen wanting cock in me—but I wanted the needle, the hard needle, shoved in a new orifice, one of the many sex-change cuts I was making on my arms and legs, my thighs.

I was babbling, gasping, buzzing, beyond searching for a vein. I had a heavy dose of the shit in me and I was hallucinating from it (oh yes, you hallucinate from heavy coke use), so I couldn't see a vein anyway. Just a writhing nest on my arm. I shoved the needle in at random. And I couldn't feel the pain of the clumsy jabbings because cocaine is an anaesthetic. I was freaking out.

I wasn't getting off as good now, and I was suddenly deep down bone-marrow scared because I knew that the cocaine crash was on the way. A bad cocaine crash, especially the sort you can get from mainlining, is the worst thing I have ever experienced. It makes other drug bummers paradisial by comparison. It makes you wish you were dogshit so you could be something higher than you are. It is the profoundest depression combined with unendurable weakness and pain in every individual nerve ending, every single one, like a short-circuiting socket, shaking and sparking and turning black. It is exactly as I imagine hell would have to be for Adolf Hitler, or someone worse. I am using no hyperboles here. No need for exaggeration. The crash is a welcome mat for suicide.

I was terrified of it, and the only way to put it off, since I didn't have any downers, was to try to stay up. Keep shooting. It wasn't just my fear, though. I couldn't have stopped even then if there was no crash. I was in the programmed cycle the white rat was in. I was trapped in pushing the button. Pushing the button made me push the button made me push the button. . . .

But the cocaine ran out. My heart was beating so fast it was all blurred into one beat. The distortion in my sight was so thick I couldn't see past an arm's length—beyond that it was a sort of hurricane of color and shape. I was blowing up, only it was taking forever. Exploding as if I'd swallowed a hand grenade, but in slow motion. I felt like the guy in *Scanners* whose head gradually explodes from psychic attack. But I kept jabbing, trying to glean some coke from the floor, from my bedspread, from the foil it had come in; I added water, trying to get the last little bit . . . shooting up dust from the floor . . . a miracle I didn't get an embolism or aneurysm or something.

My roommate came home and called an ambulance and they took me overdosing to the hospital (the needles kept stabbing me all the way) and they had to put a tube in my lungs because they were filling with fluid—I almost preceded Belushi—and then the crash hit me when I was in the hospital with the nasty tube down my throat and the sheets were made of sandpaper and I had a third-degree sunburn on my body or that's how it felt and I could not rest but I was so exhausted I wept from it.

It went on for a day or two. Afterward my whole body below the neck—including my dick—was puffed up from needle jabs and coke damage to the tissues . . . looked like I had a terminal skin disease . . . took weeks to go away . . . nightmares about the needles.

It was worse than that. I can't talk about it any more than this, though. I can't think about it any more.

I lived through it, and I stopped using cocaine.

John Shirley is the author of *Black Butterflies*.

BELLADONNA

Buried Spiders / Ivan Stang

I t happened to me when I was four years old—absolutely vivid hallucinations totally indistinguishable from reality, like in a *Nightmare on Elm Street* movie. Yes, some druggist there in Fort Worth filled a prescription wrong, and for the flu I got a double adult dose of belladonna.

I woke up in the morning watching a parade of animals of every kind wandering peacefully around the house, just like Noah's ark. I chased monkeys that kept disappearing. I recall all of this as if it happened yesterday—although I can't recall what happened yesterday, come to think of it.

What I don't remember is the spiders. My mom said she realized that I wasn't pretending, but that I was crazed, when I huddled in the corner and screamed about the spiders. Brrrrr, scary to think that's buried in my subconscious somewhere.

Ivan Stang is the author of *The Book of the SubGenius.*

Paranoid in Punjab / David Macaray

This is an account of a belladonna-datura-opium trip taken in a galaxy far, far away. While it's not a marijuana story, its provenance is marijuana. For just as all roads used to lead to Rome (as, today, all Internet links lead to pornography), you can't do justice to a psychedelic work-up without referring to marijuana, anymore than you can write a history of torture without mentioning organized religion.

In 1968, I was a Peace Corps volunteer in India, working for the Punjab Irrigation Department. Before India, my drug experience consisted of smoking grass fifteen or twenty times (back when a "lid" sold for five dollars and there was no such thing as "commercial"); taking LSD twice in Seal Beach, California, (when it was still sold in little glass vials); doing a tiny pipeful of what was called DMT crystals (billed as "the 45-minute acid trip"); and smoking, perhaps, a dozen cigarettes dipped in paregoric or Romilar cough syrup (that's right).

When we arrived in the northern state of Punjab, we were astonished to find marijuana plants growing everywhere—in open fields, ditches along the road, people's yards, even in the big clearing across the street from the Malerkotla city courthouse. While most of us had heard the stories of marijuana growing plentifully, no one—not even the most optimistic stoner—expected it to be so . . . explicit.

The universal availability was more than a just welcome surprise; in a way, it was crazy. As strange as this sounds (especially from someone who'd had to scrounge for it), seeing marijuana bushes sprouting up all over the place was, somehow, unnerving. It was like a drunken, horny sailor finding naked women everywhere, or a little kid being told that he now owned Disneyland. Exciting, but also vaguely disturbing. Also, it was way too sudden.

On Thursday morning, we were the happy-go-lucky citizens of a country where college students received prison terms for possession of half an ounce, and on Friday night—barely thirty-six hours later—we were residents of a sub-Himalayan kingdom where four-foot plants grew right across the street from the police station.

The contrast in police cultures was another jolt. In faraway Punjab, where there was still no such thing as a narcotic officer (in 1968 the Asian drug industry was minuscule), the "constables" wore little short pants, traveled on foot, and carried no radios, handcuffs, or firearms. When agitated, they beat you with bamboo staffs. Because rigid caste and class distinctions determined how one was treated in India, the police were exceedingly—almost ludicrously—deferential toward Americans.

The cops regarded Peace Corps volunteers as some sort of government celebrities—men who could pull the necessary strings to have them sacked—and, as a consequence, wouldn't so much as come near us. We could be dry-humping a marijuana bush in the middle of Main Street and the police wouldn't dare interfere. Forty million Punjabis and not one narc. It was a stoner's dream.

In truth, while most Indians were vaguely familiar with the properties of marijuana (they knew it could make you "drunk"), no one really paid attention to it, not even with some of the best grass in the world growing in their front yards. During our two years in India, the only people we knew who smoked it were foreigners like ourselves and the Ashraf brothers, a couple of degenerate Muslim barbers in Malerkotla. Getting high on "ganja" was considered low-class and ignorant, something the underclass—the sweepers, cobblers, and rickshaw drivers—might do, but not something an educated "pukka sahib" would even consider, at least not in 1968. In the United States, it would be like expecting a Wall Street banker to sniff airplane glue out of a gunnysack.

Of course, the moment my roommate, Richard, and I discovered the motherlode, there was no turning back. With the hounds from hell unleashed, we began smoking it every day—not just because we wanted to, but because we had to. The logistics simply made it irresistible: there was too much of it, the quality was outrageous, the cops were afraid of us. It gives me no pleasure to report, therefore, that as employees of the U.S. State Department and drawing our pay from American tax dollars, we basically stayed high for two years.

Marijuana was sold legally in New Delhi, in the form of a food known as "bhong." Bhong was a mixture of pulverized leaves, buds, and stems which had been soaked in water, wrung out and pressed into highly-condensed balls. It was supposed to be eaten in small bites, served with pelletized sugar. One ball of this concentrated material, eight inches in circumference and weighing approximately one-half pound, sold for about eighty cents. Government-owned bhong shops—little cubby-holes the size of a newspaper kiosk—were found all over New Delhi.

There was once a story in the Punjab *Tribune* reporting that a decorated Sikh army veteran, who'd had his legs blown off in the 1965 Indo-Pakistan War, was going to be set up by the Indian government with his own bhong shop in Delhi, in recognition of his heroism. I remember discussing the story with Richard over our breakfast reefer, agreeing that if we ever lost our legs and could pick our own business, a bhong shop would be our choice, too.

Whenever we endured the punishing ten-hour train trip to New Delhi, we made a point of visiting a local bhong shop. Smoking was good, but eating it was a nice change of pace. Nature's perfect food, was how we saw it. You can imagine our indignation when, years later, we heard American tokers referring to the pipe used to smoke grass (properly called a "chillum," in India) as a bong. Hey, you dumb shit, we wanted to say, a bong ain't a pipe, it's the stuff that goes inside it. Imagine an Indian citizen visiting Santa Cruz, California, and referring to a marijuana bush as a "roach." Even the peace-and-love flower children would want to kick their ass.

Anyway, in January 1968, to celebrate the winter festival of Diwali, Richard and I decided to do something special for the people of our village of Jomeshpur. Despite a living allowance of only fifty-five dollars per month, Peace Corps volunteers were considerably richer than the average Indian, and many times richer than the farmers of Jomeshpur. Already slightly stoned from smoking grass, we bicycled to the town of Malerkotla, six miles away, and purchased about fifty rupees worth of fireworks and low-grade explosives. In those days, before devaluation, fifty rupees converted to about seven dollars, but in comparable purchasing power, it would be like going to a fireworks stand in Los Angeles and buying $500 dollars worth of goodies.

I can't overemphasize how huge this deal was to the village, how eagerly it was antic-ipated. After we announced the plan, no one in the village could concentrate on anything else. The circus was coming. As corny as this sounds, our little fireworks show was probably the biggest event to occur in Jomeshpur's history. Simply having a couple of American "government men" living among them was thrilling enough, but putting on a fireworks show was almost more exotic than they could bear. Certain city folks may have been familiar with fireworks, but it was unlikely that the farmers of Jomeshpur had ever seen a sparkler up close.

Unfortunately however, their unrestrained excitement had a downside. It was close to 4:30 p.m. when we returned from town, still light, and too early to start the show. But when the villagers got a look at the array of ordnance tied to our bike racks and grasped the significance of what was about to happen, they went totally ape-shit. Anthropologists would tell us that the act of waiting—the notion of putting off until later something you'd prefer to do immediately—is a fairly complex cultural trait and without having had anything comparable to wait for, I'm not sure Punjabi farmers even knew how to wait for a fireworks show. We probably should have seen it coming.

Excited by the bright, gaudy wrappings and, doubtless, inflamed by the material's destructive potential, a group of some of the more aggressive young men in the village tried to overpower us. They insisted we set everything off, right then and there—liter-ally, right next to our front door—where we'd parked the bicycles. We couldn't believe it. These guys were frantic. Before we could stop them, they began clutching and tear-ing at the merchandise, recklessly pulling stuff out of the boxes, way out of control.

It should have been comical in a way—grown men thrashing about and arguing over a bunch of firecrackers—but it wasn't. While there was good-natured laughter during the tug-of-war, with everyone keeping up the pretense that we were just horsing around, there was also an undercurrent of danger. Richard and I were sobered by the knowledge that even though we'd undergone extensive cultural and technical training and could speak the language, we didn't really understand these people. While they'd always been hospitable hosts, we didn't know what made them tick, not really. It got a little hairy.

The only thing that saved the ranch was that none of these guys, thank God, had thought to bring along matches. In their aroused state, had they been packing matches it would have been Adiós, muchachos. Our bicycles would have blown up. But after ten minutes of animated discussion (including some half-hearted pushing and shoving) and with the help of our neighbor, Rajinder Singh, who generously sided with us, we succeeded in getting the young bucks to back off. We told them we were going to put on a variety show—one they'd never forget—but that we couldn't do it until it was good and dark, which meant that we had a couple hours to wait. Reluctantly, they finally agreed.

The moment they left, Richard and I hustled into the house and gobbled down the drugs we'd set aside for the occasion. That was another reason we didn't want the show to start prematurely—we intended to be hallucinating for it. We each ate a small handful of crushed datura and belladonna seeds (the plants were indigenous to north India) and an olive-size ball of opium, which we'd bought from a rickshaw driver in Ludhiana. We'd never taken any of this stuff before. All we knew was that opium was more or less a dreamy sedative and that belladonna and datura were reliable hallucinogens, but we didn't know how they came on or how they reacted together.

Because Richard had a science background and had read somewhere that belladonna and datura were officially classified as "poisons," he was afraid to try them without a test. Therefore, a couple of weeks earlier, we'd experimented with both hallucinogens on Ricky, our pet dog. We ground up the seeds scientifically, into powder form, and spiked his dog food with an amount substantially larger than we intended taking. Ricky wobbled around for a while, appearing disoriented and worried, and then slept for something like twenty hours—which was unlike him—but he didn't die. That meant we had the green light.

At 6 p.m., we came out of the house, lugging three cardboard boxes of explosives. We were already a little high. Most of the fireworks were items you could no longer buy legally in the States—rockets, mortars, small bombs. Say what you will about the government, but one doesn't appreciate the role of regulatory agencies until he lives in a country that doesn't have them. Adulteration (e.g., adding gypsum to flour, chaff to wheat, water to kerosene), false weights and measures, misleading labels, toxins, spoilage, vermin—they were all part of the commercial landscape of India, which made everyday shopping more or less a crap-shoot.

We hauled the material to an open field, fifty yards from the nearest house. A group of thirty or forty men and teenage boys followed us into the clearing, with the rest of the village gathered on the perimeter. Every resident of the village—approximately 300 people—had assembled to watch the show. It was no exaggeration to say that every last man, woman, and child in Jomeshpur was accounted for. Had there been a terminal patient on his death bed, they would have strapped the son-of-a-bitch to a dolly and wheeled him outside to watch. It was like the bicentennial, moon landing, and Y2K all rolled into one.

It was now dark. Richard and I were starting to hallucinate; while not a lavish high, it showed definite possibilities. We felt some dizziness and warping, and a lack of coordination. People and objects appeared to be in hyper-three-dimension, stark relief. The back of my neck was becoming warm and prickly, and, oddly, I was beginning to tire, which alarmed me. Though the walk took only five or six minutes, over flat, well-trodden ground, by the time we reached the field I was exhausted—as if I'd hiked five miles—and mildly nauseous, as well. For guys who were mainly used to the nimble mind-trips of marijuana, it was clear that this mixture had a powerful and unexpected physical kick to it, and I could tell instantly that a physical trip was going to be high maintenance.

One of the problems with eating (rather than smoking) is that once it's in your tummy it's already too late. You're stuck with that whole rhythm section until it's played out. If it's a great, heroic high, then you've got it made, but if it's a harrowing descent into melancholia or madness, you're fucked. Accordingly, as I marched into that field, the first subversive thought of the evening entered my mind. It was the realization that while the moon and sky looked exactly as they did in good ol' Southern California, I was in a place 12,000 miles from home with a shitload of poisonous seeds in my system.

Neither the opium nor the novelty seeds were supposed to make you paranoid—at least that's what we'd heard (I knew a guy in Redondo Beach who grew his own datura, belladonna, and goldenrod, and he raved about the stuff); but ninety minutes after taking it, I began fretting about everything. I agonized over the amount we'd eaten, and what the book had meant by "poisonous." What would the Indians think if they saw us suddenly begin vomiting? Would they try to find a doctor? Would they enter our house and steal our stuff? Every thought I had was slightly irrational and quickened.

I also wondered what would happen if our senses decayed to the point where we just basically crapped out. Would these farmers know how to help, or would they try to overpower us? In our sorry state we'd be as vulnerable as children, and they could do as they pleased with us. It's amazing how obsessed a seminormal person can become with just a little chemical prodding. And then I considered the sixty-four dollar question: What would happen if Richard and I became too sick to continue? How would this audience react if we had to call off the show?

These weren't folks to whom you gave rainchecks; we'd already crossed that bridge back at the house. Clearly, they would not accept a postponement. In my rapidly developing paranoid state, I envisioned the audience killing us. The execution ritual would be swift. The men would gather their farm implements—the mattocks and scythes they used in the fields—and the boys would collect their little hatchets. Together, they would bludgeon us to death, reduce us to something resembling the mango chutney served at Ram Gupta's tea stall in Malerkotla. It was a preposterous notion, but the poison seeds had put my mind on this plane, and it would not budge. Now I knew what people meant when they talked about toxic paranoia.

Richard was getting ready to start the show. In his hand he had what appeared to be a gargantuan cherry bomb, a gaudy thing wrapped in gold foil, like some hideous, oversized Christmas ornament. As he fiddled with his American-made Ronson lighter, I fearfully studied the farmers and their sons standing behind him. In the throes of chemical psychosis, everyone now appeared hostile (even Richard's face looked a little funny). As the men jostled and squirmed for position, I saw them in slow motion, a conga line of rabid animals, writhing and undulating in the moonlight. An Edgar Allen Poe story come to life.

Though we'd just arrived, I was already overcome by the urge to leave this dirt field and return to my room. I was in woefully bad shape and knew it. I required decompression and a sponge bath, and rest. At the bottom of a canal somewhere in my body was a handful of ambitious, hallucinogenic seeds which had long since released their debilitating payload. Remarkably, Richard and I had managed to poison ourselves.

Still, while one part of me—the rational part—wanted to flee, the professional part realized it was vital that we maintain our dignity. Poisonous spores or not, physically ill or not, this was an intercultural event. It was our party; we were the ones who raised public expectations. And as American pukka sahibs, it was critical that Richard and I not come off as candy-asses or freaks.

But the extravagant demands of the paranoia were not to be denied. I was tormented by the notion that this whole deal was impossibly volatile—that unless Richard and I behaved carefully and paid attention, we could be one foolish move away from doing blood penance. I did not want to die—not at the age of twenty-two, not in some faraway sugarcane field, and not by vivisection at the hands of aroused peasants. Whoever said that paranoia was the absolute worst mind-trip wasn't lying.

Richard's little bomb didn't explode for six or eight seconds, long enough for us to suspect that it was a dud, but not quite long enough, thank Jesus, to cause us to investigate. Then, suddenly, it went off like nothing we'd ever heard. The noise was so shattering, so concussive, it was as if an artillery shell had landed on the field—300 people jumped in the air, scared shitless; then the same 300 people laughed and cheered wildly. I was standing five feet away when it went off and felt the air pressure change around me. Numbly, I stretched open my mouth and tilted my head from side to side, believing I could feel material inside it, moving.

The blast was so disorienting that, comically, for one instant (because I'd felt wind on my scrotum) I believed that my pants had somehow fallen down and that I wasn't wearing any underwear—like in those self-recriminating dreams where you're standing bare-assed in your math class. For one moment, embarrassment and humiliation supplanted toxic fear as my dominant emotions. I actually had to inspect myself, look down and rub my legs, to confirm I was still wearing pants. I can laugh now, but it was ugly.

Then Richard grabbed a rocket. When he pulled it out of the box, the Indians cheered enthusiastically. None of these villagers had ever seen a rocket, but they obviously understood the potential of the aerodynamic symmetry Richard was holding in his hand—or at least they could imagine what a giant bullet might look like. Here we were, with the reverberations of that humongous cherry bomb still ringing in our ears, and the crowd was already cheering for the rocket. This was crazy, and I was getting higher, still coming on to the seeds.

Richard stuck the rocket's pointed launcher into the dirt, aimed it away from the crowd and lit it. But before he could remove his hand from the fuse, the little missile blasted off. Though the fuse appeared to be the same length as the one on the cherry bomb, it burned down in a fraction of the time. So much for Indian quality control. Igniting that quickly, it naturally scared the hell out of Richard. Seeing him stagger backwards, wide-eyed and shaken, the audience nearly doubled over in laughter, helpless with delight. What a show we were giving them!

As the crowd howled appreciatively, Richard was fearfully calculating how unstable the rest of these Indian-made explosives might be; and I was thinking how fortunate he was. Had it been one of those bombs instead of the rocket, it would have blown his hand off. My extremities were now turning cold; I was almost paralyzed by a combination of nausea and fear. When you're that messed up, you begin wondering what your face looks like.

Meanwhile, instead of going straight up, the rocket tore off sideways and skittered along the dirt for twenty or thirty feet, crackling and burning. Again, good-natured laughter and cheers from the crowd. One of the farmers standing behind Richard pointed to me and shouted something in Hindustani. Normally, my language skills were pretty decent, but I couldn't make sense of a word he was saying. He shouted another sentence at me, but I still couldn't follow. In my state, the fellow appeared crazed, like a lunatic from a monkey temple, all blazing dark eyes and crooked, disfigured cultivator's hands. I remember thinking that he was warning us, telling me to get ready because they were preparing to kill us. It was dark, we were in a field, and I no longer had traction.

The show could have easily lasted two hours; and, if we'd gotten with the program, we could have milked it for three. We must have had an assortment of fifty or sixty items. But a mere ten minutes into the show, after setting off another rocket and a couple of fire-ball mortars—both with a slow, deliberate fuses—Richard entered a mild fugue like state. Obviously, these little seeds had not produced the trippy mind-dance we'd anticipated. Too much spaghetti, not enough meatballs. The neuropharmacological adventure in heightened perception we'd hoped for (the perfect groove for a fireworks show) had turned into a cheerless skin-trip. Instead of getting all wobbly and disoriented, like our dog Ricky, we'd become hypochondriacs.

Peering carefully into the box, Richard turned grim and apprehensive, as if he dreaded his next move. Like me, his body had started burning, and he was holding the back of his neck, straining against it and scrunching up his shoulders. We were now staring at him, all of us—the men in the circle, the crowd, me—wondering what was going to happen next. Richard didn't make a move for a moment or two. The area smelled terrible, an effluvium of saltpeter, sulfur, and foul gases having settled over the launching pad. Amazingly, while making the two of us nauseous and watery-eyed, the dreadful cloud appeared to energize rather than sicken the Indian farmers.

Then, without warning, he abdicated. Assuming I would take over, he walked the few paces to where I was standing and, without so much as a word, handed me the Ronson lighter, indicating that I was now in charge. With the crowd watching intently, he then walked to the perimeter and stood there. While I was flabbergasted, none of the villagers seemed particularly concerned. No one panicked, there was no screaming, no stampede. After all, why would they be alarmed? They weren't familiar with our routine. For all they knew, passing the Ronson was part of the bit, like an American relay race, and at any moment Richard could be expected to flamboyantly re-enter the circle, doing cart-wheels.

Ever since college, friends had cautioned me that I was too serious and introspective to do acid, that I should stick with grass or, even better (and this was demoralizing to hear in the Age of Aquarius), that I stick with beer and stay away from the mind-alterers—leave the psychedelic stuff to the grown-ups. There was probably some wisdom in that advice.

Anyway, if Richard hadn't walked away—had he stayed in the circle after deputizing me—I might have been able to pull it off. But seeing him standing on the sideline, stupefied but safe, made me think, longingly, of sanctuary. Thus, without a word, and disregarding my fears of what might happen if we stopped the show, I boldly joined him on the perimeter, some ten or fifteen yards away, walking as stiffly and deliberately as a zombie. When I reached him, I solemnly handed back his talismanic Ronson. Totally spaced out, neither of us speaking, there we stood: the two young Americans, side by side, clutching our necks.

Of course, no one in Jomeshpur dreamed we were high. Because our house was located on the outskirts of the village (it had been a storage area, converted into quarters specifically for us), and we'd always been extremely cautious when we lit up, it was unlikely anybody even knew we smoked grass. Plentiful or not, marijuana use was expressly forbidden by the State Department. The understanding was, if they caught you smoking they sent you home; and while it hadn't happened to anyone yet, nobody wanted to be the first.

No, the notion of hallucinogens would never have entered their minds. The only thing the villagers observed that night was that their two young American guests had acted strangely, had suddenly and without explanation abandoned their fireworks show and then, oddly, staggered to the perimeter clutching their thick American necks. What else could have registered? As little as we knew about them, they knew even less about us. They knew we came from a country that was currently bombing Vietnam and that we'd just spent a small fortune on fireworks. Naturally, they were going to assume we rejoiced in explosives. As to why we suddenly stopped, they wouldn't have a clue.

In any event, none of this mattered. Within minutes it was all over. How no one was killed or blown apart that night still amazes me. Moments after Richard and I withdrew, it must have dawned on the farmers that we'd somehow capitulated, that the show was now in their hands and, it was up to them to get us home. Suddenly, as if someone had fired a starter's pistol to begin the one hundred–yard dash, thirty Indian men with waxed matches burst into action, simultaneously igniting every explosive they could get their hands on. It was like that scene in *Lawrence of Arabia* when the mercenaries tear apart everything in the compound, looking for the gold, except this was happening on a farm, with everything on fire.

There was not a hint of discipline or reserve in their methodology and, of course, not the barest trace of fear. There were rockets going off everywhere—sideways, straight up, and straight down nosing into the ground like incendiary burrowing ferrets—those terrible cherry bombs exploding; mortars sending fire balls into the sky; hand-held Roman candlelike contraptions being handled by teenage boys; pinwheels being hurled like Frisbees; people lighting stuff two-at-a-time, throwing them, twirling, running, sprinting with them. Fiery arcs, projectiles, and yellowish smoke filled the air.

Understandably, the unenlightened audience (to say nothing of the participants) had no idea of the magnitude of the odds-defying performance it was witnessing. They continued cheering and laughing, keeping up a steady commentary on the sidelines, as their sugarcane field was transformed into Pearl Harbor. Even Richard and I—as loaded and ill as we were and dimly aware that every guideline associated with a "Safe and Sane Fourth of July" was being desecrated—were overwhelmed by the spectacle.

Then, as abruptly as it began, it was over. Dead silence. In three minutes, with two dozen guys staying busy, all the fireworks had been set off. It was like one of those Ripley's Believe-It-Or-Not gigs, where a man enters a blast furnace and walks out the other side, unscathed. No one was burned, no one was dead; everyone was breathing noxious smoke and laughing. Then everybody went home. Indian farmers weren't used to staying up late. They usually retired shortly after dusk and arose well before dawn to start their chores. With the show over, Richard and I went home, too.

The seeds caused me to sleep late the next day; not twenty hours, like our pet dog, Ricky, but late. It was almost 10:30 a.m. when Richard roused me. Even though he'd woken with a monumental headache and had vomited in our backyard, he was fully dressed and had already gone outside to inspect the launching pad. He asked if I remembered everything that happened the previous night. Unfortunately, I did. He said the field was ruined, covered with scorch marks and debris and yellow chemical stains, like some experimental firing range in New Mexico. Taking stock of my own condition, I told him that I, too, had a headache but still felt drugged and a little buggy.

Brooding over the episode, we drank sweet tea and ate biscuits and sucked on mangoes until we felt better. We stayed indoors with the shades drawn, shared a joint and played two-handed canasta, promising ourselves to go out to the field at dusk, when it was cooler, to clean up the mess. What a pleasure it was, after all that throbbing, heavy-duty physiological punishment, to partake of the virtues of old-fashioned maryjane! Actually, considering how bad we felt when we first woke up, and what we'd been through the night before, we wound up getting pretty high. After a while, we began playing War.

Years later, people who professed to know what they were talking about told me that datura will always give you a headache unless you take it with wine or brandy, and that opium is something to nod off with, not something you want to party on. Others said the problem was that we'd taken too much datura—that you want no more than a level teaspoon of the crushed seeds; otherwise, you're just asking for trouble. Richard said someone told him the exact opposite: that we hadn't taken enough. As for the crippling paranoia, no one had ever heard of such a symptom, the implication being that, somehow, it was our fault.

When we finally got to the field, we saw that it had already been raked clean by the boys. Rajinder Singh told us that the rocket hulks, boxes, wadding, and other corrugated material had been gathered up and set aside, to be used as fuel in the wood stoves. Punjabis saved everything. A piece of string, a Coke bottle, a jar with a lid—nothing got thrown away. "Thank you very much for the demonstration," Rajinder said, choosing his English words carefully. Indians were extremely courteous, frequently shaming us casual, inconsiderate Americans with their old-world decorum.

And that's how he summed up the pyrotechnic free-for-all of the previous night, where unauthorized peasant farmers ignited a carload of dangerous explosives—a "demonstration." Richard was always the consummate good-will ambassador, cheerful and generous no matter what the circumstances. Once again, he rose to the occasion. "Well, Rajinder," he said, without a trace of irony, "we're glad you enjoyed it."

Playwright David Macaray is the author of *Borneo Bob*.

Become a Flower / Gerri Willinger

A friend and I were talking about strange trips. I was interested in deadly nightshade (belladonna), and he told me about his experience one exceptionally crisp night in the Wisconsin woods.

He took belladonna and was walking, fully enjoying his altered state and the indescribable beauty of the woods. As he walked, he happened upon a group of flowers, and he conversed with them for a while. They asked him if he would like to be a flower.

"Yes," he said, "of course."

They showed him a can of magic paint and said, "Brush yourself with this from head to toe and you will become a flower."

He did so, thanked them, and continued walking. He then happened upon an enchanted cabin, where he lay down and slept. A few hours later, he was awakened by an old farmer and some policemen. They were taking him to the hoosegow for breaking and entering the old man's barn and drenching himself in crankcase oil.

He barely escaped the booby hatch, and I never did take belladonna.

La Belle Dame sans Merci / Robert Anton Wilson

The four weirdest and scariest drug stories I know all involve belladonna, a chemical for which I now have the same sincere respect as I have for hungry tigers, earthquakes, floods, wildfires, the IRS, and Dr. Hannibal Lecter.

The first story I'll tell comes from a young friend, then a 1960s dropout hippie freak, but now a PhD in sociology. He tried belladonna around 1965 under the impression that it had much the same effects as LSD. When he immediately went into toxic convulsions, friends rushed him to a hospital where the ER staff pumped out his stomach—probably saving his life, but a bit too late to save him from delirium, since the belladonna had already entered his bloodstream.

When he returned to what seemed normal consciousness, he found himself in a hospital bed, surrounded by people in other beds with different ailments. Then a beautiful blonde nurse with great big hooters entered the ward, accompanied by an olde style New Orleans jazz band.

As my friend watched entranced, the nurse proceeded to perform a classic striptease dance with plenty of tantalizing tease, but eventual total nudity, followed by even more bumps and grinds. The music seemed louder and raunchier than any jazz he had ever heard, and came to a wild Dionysian climax when the naked nurse crawled into bed with a delighted patient and proceeded to make love to him, loudly and frequently and in more ways than a dozen porn stars.

My friend never once suspected that this might be a hallucination. Nor did it seem an unusually innovative medical procedure. You don't ask philosophic or ontological questions during a belladonna journey the way you usually do on real psychedelics. He only began to wonder the next morning if any of that sex stuff really happened.

And that's this whole story. Belladonna erases a great deal of your memory of what you saw during the trip. He might have had dozens of other visions that night, but all he ever remembered was the nurse from Mitchell Brothers Clinic for the Horrendously Horny. I guess I would have remembered her too.

The second, more perplexing yarn, comes from another 1960s veteran, but I lost touch with him and have no idea how his life worked out. He told me he took the belladonna in his dorm room at the college he attended, and then waited for psychedelic fireworks and transcendental experiences.

Nothing happened for a while.

Then his friend Joe entered the room and asked what he was doing. He told Joe about the belladonna and said he was waiting to feel an effect. Joe asked him something, but he didn't quite hear it.

Then his friend Joe entered the room and asked what he was doing. He told Joe about the belladonna and said he was waiting to feel an effect. Joe asked him something, but he got distracted by having two Joes in the room. He tried to explain about the two Joes, but then one of them vanished. He tried to tell Joe, "Hey, you came in before you came in," but his tongue seemed unable to function, and he thought he was merely grunting like a hog.

Then his friend Joe entered the room, and this time he got The Fear. He fled the room and the dorm and hopped on his motorcycle to get away, speeding across the campus and down the nearest highway as fast as he could gun her.

He didn't even own a motorcycle. I often wonder what the other people on campus and on the highway thought they saw when he went racing past them on his phantom bike.

Medieval witches used belladonna in their brews, and some scholars think that's why they believed they could fly through the sky on broomsticks. Modern witches—at least the ones I've known—prudently substitute the kinder, gentler cannabis.

The next morning, my friend returned to "consensus reality" and found himself in a ditch several miles from campus. He had no bumps or bruises—and nobody else's motorcycle, either—but his right shoe and right sock had disappeared. He never did find them and never remembered any more of that night.

My longest yarn involves my own experience with belladonna in 1962. What can I say about why I did it? I hadn't heard the above stories yet, I was young, I was a damned eejit, and the guy who gave it to me said it was "just like peyote."

Let me explain that this happened on a farm in the deep woods.

A few minutes after I took the stuff—drank it as a tea, actually—my wife Arlen developed a severe case of fangs and quickly turned into a beautiful, sexy, red-headed vampire with malice in her eyes. I immediately rushed to the kitchen sink, stuck a finger down my throat and forced several painful fits of vomiting. When I could vomit no more, I told her (she looked normal again for a moment: beautiful, sexy, red-headed, but friendly, not vampirish), "This is a bad trip, but I'll find my way back to you, I promise."

Those were the last sane words I spoke for the next twelve hours.

I remember taking a long walk through a forest of magic green jewels with the Tin Woodsman of Oz. Later, the next day, it became clear that this was Jeff, a friend Arlen had phoned to help me through the emergency. He was walking me around our cabin, thinking that fresh air might help.

I remember some dwarfs in Nazi uniforms trying to shove me into a furnace literally "as hot as hell." I have never felt more terror in my life.

Blank space: memory loss.

I remember thinking the worst was over and trying to tell Arlen and Jeff that some parts of it were quite good, really. I was lighting one cigarette after another, chain-smoking, I thought. Jeff and Arlen saw me striking the lighter repeatedly, but I never did have a cigarette in my mouth.

I remember trying to explain something I had discovered Out There. Arlen wrote it down. The note said, "The literary critics will all have to be shot because of the Kennedy Administration in Outer Space of the Nuremberg pickle that exploded."

Not quite good as the last words of Dutch Schultz, I'd say, but a bit better than what William James brought back from his nitrous oxide adventure: "Over all, there is a smell of fried onions."

Around dawn, I had to go to the outhouse, and Jeff accompanied me to make sure I didn't wander off into the Pink Dimension or get lost amid the buzzing and whistling things in the Realm of Thud.

I opened the outhouse door and found Jeff already in there. I closed the door and told him, "I can't go in. You're already in there."

He persuaded me reasonably that he wasn't in there, but outside with me, so I opened the door again, found nobody inside and took a healthy crap.

I felt even closer to "normal" when I came out, but then I noticed King Kong peeking at me over the top of the trees. He seemed whimsical and unthreatening, and when I looked again, he turned into just another tree.

The next day, I moved slowly back into the ordinary world, and by evening I felt well enough to go to a movie, Kurosawa's *The Seven Samurai*. I enjoyed the first half, especially the innovative technique of alternating between black-and-white and color, but in the second half Toshiro Mifune's nose started growing like Pinocchio's and I knew I was hallucinating again, which vexed me a bit.

No more flashbacks occurred for about a month, and then one day all the people in the supermarket turned into iguanas. That only lasted a few seconds, and it was the last of the trip. I never tried this nefarious chemical again, and I hope to gawd you won't either.

My last story I heard from novelist William S. Burroughs, who bought some "morphine" once that some wiseacre had cut with belladonna. Burroughs never remembered anything of the experience, but a friend did. He said that at one point, Burroughs walked to the window, opened it and stuck a leg out.

"What are you doing?" the friend asked.

"Going down for some cigarettes," Burroughs replied. The friend grabbed him and dragged him back into the room, which was on the third floor.

Bella donna, by the way, means *beautiful lady* in Italian. Go figure.

UFO Sighting / Bill Krupinski

A friend had an apartment on Milwaukee's east side back in the early '70s. His roommate Phil was an amiable guy who worked in a hardware store by day and partied by night. This particular evening I was at their place while going into my second day of an STP trip. STP was like an acid trip for two or three days! Phil had a beer and a joint after work, and somebody suggested going "trucking" (as in R. Crumb's "Keep on Truckin'") to the lakefront, several blocks away.

The two of us, joints in hand, strolled on down to Lake Michigan, past the huge piles of dead, reeking alewives (small silver lake fish dying by the millions back then) and on to the breakwater, the sea wall jutting out into the lake at the marina. The breakwater has a great view both ways—you're out in the lake like a boat, but on solid land with east-side and downtown buildings looming up behind the park. Also a lonely place. I think we scared off some gay winos as we neared the end, almost a mile from shore.

Anyway, we've got the spot to ourselves, so it's time to fire up one of those doobies. We're enjoying our smoke as I notice a light up high over the lake to the east. Figuring it's a jet circling to land at Mitchell Field to the south, I ignore it. We're digging the wave action and stars, but this light's coming closer and lower. And slower. And there's no noise. A jet coming in 300 feet and a mile out would make a huge racket. And those lights had a hue I'd never seen before, an eerie yellowish green.

As it comes toward us, I swear I can see cockpit windows and figures in there. I start to see its form, and damn if it ain't some kind of disc with a flat back end and low fins at the sides. At this point, Phil drops the joint and yells, "Let's get the fuck out of here!" Ever quick-witted (and on STP), I grab Phil's belt and bark out, "You're staying here—I need a witness!"

The UFO (I think at this point we can call it that) slowly comes in and hovers directly above us at about 100–150 feet. The bottom has a huge, round, fan-like, finned section. As it hovers, a harsh light is shone down upon us, and I feel for a fraction of a second that everything I have ever known or felt or have been is taken out and then put back into me.

The "vehicle" slowly, very slowly, turns about to the southeast, and the back section looks very much like the lit-up taillights of a road-boat-era Ford Thunderbird. It slowly moves off and suddenly, in a flash, it is gone over the lake horizon.

We were stunned. We were dazed and confused. I somehow felt violated. We ran back to the apartment. They all laughed at us, especially because of my STP buzz. "But," I said, "what about Phil? He saw it too!" A veteran pothead not prone to great visions had seen it too! Phil was my back-up, my credibility. Six months later, Phil was dead. Fell asleep at the wheel and dove off a cliff near LaCrosse—an unfortunate accident.

Or was it?

Test Case / John Shirley

I guess it's really because you're, you know, sort of a weirdo."

"Who says?" I demanded, knowing full well who.

"All my friends. My mom and dad. You wear that top hat to school. You talk about Aleister Crowley when everyone else is trying to decide if they want to go to homecoming dance. You go crazy at rock concerts. Really embarrassing. God, you dance like . . . like somebody electrocuting a wasp. Everybody sees that. You got on a table and recited from *Trout Mask Replica* in the school cafeteria. You told Mrs. Bellows that she had a face inside her face. You're a weirdo, John. I do care about you but I can't stand the way you act anymore. I don't want to see you anymore."

We were sixteen. It was about 1969 or '70 and it was Salem, Oregon. There are no straighter towns. It's the state capital. I was one of maybe six weirdos in the whole city. I was disemboweled by her rejection of me. My first real girlfriend—first one I had sex with—and I was blown away by social meteorology like a straw in a hurricane. So I did something dramatic. Martyred myelf. (I was prone to doing that sort of thing when rejected.)

A few years later, I joined the Coast Guard when another girl left me for a guru. I took three big hits of STP. This stuff was essentially LSD with a wicked molecular tail added, like the tail of a scorpion, that was, basically, speed. Or anyway this is what I heard. I also heard it was developed by the U.S. Army as a weapon to disorient and render helpless the enemy. So naturally I took some. Was I not the enemy of the U.S. Army? Yes, indeed.

I would prove that their paltry weapons were nothing before my righteous martyrdom. I didn't want to destroy myself. I wanted to go interestingly wild. I wanted to get mentally lost for a while. She thought I was weird? I'd crucify myself on weirdness.

"Don't take it when you're, like, not feeling good about your life, man, you know?" That's what they said about psychedelics. "Don't take it when you're, like, mad about something." I was mad at her. At women. Woman Herself had rejected me.

"Don't take it when you're upset" is a sound rule. I ignored it. Maybe that's why the thing quickly came to resemble a *Reefer Madness* sort of scenario, or a movie they show you in health and hygiene class, in which some guy who takes LSD babbles, "I can fly," and leaps off a roof. Or picks up a knife.

Some of it I remember, some I was told about later. I came into my house boiling over with fury translated into hot electric sensation and curled off me in a sort of psychic steam, the steam becoming idetic imagery that infused the walls with a wallpaper pattern of devils riding dragons into Judy Chicago caverns.

The drug had lit a fire in my groin. I wanted sex. And it was an angry wanting. I tore off my clothes—they kept the lava—outpour of heightened sensation close to my skin, threatened to boil me in my own psychic oils. I remember thrashing about on the bed, which became a giant breast for me, like in the Woody Allen movie, but it wasn't enough.

I experienced a sort of apotheosis of the rapist's anger-against-women violence, I'm afraid. At least, so I assume, because my mother says I chased her around the house with a large kitchen knife, trying to get her to put out. My erection wagging. At some point I threw some nameless kitchen appliance through a window. I remember that: the slow-motion fascination of the breaking glass (shattering of some glassine hymen), the whirling, glittering shards blossoming in the air where there had been annoying brittleness, the sound of it heard more clearly than ever before, a Harry Partch experiment in tonality that seemed to go on forever. It impressed me enormously. At some point I wrote a short story about all this called "Breaking Glass," which was later lost. In the story the protag hallucinated the glass breaking overtop of everything, over and over, like a tape loop, which was almost what it was like.

And all the time I was watching myself. I saw all this happening from an entirely detached viewpoint, as if floating above myself on some idiotic Shirley MacLaineish psychic tether, one part of my mind—the back-brain, presumably—had simply taken over, and the part that's usually conscious was in the backseat, watching as the primitive consciousness drove. Helpless to interfere.

My mother got away, thank God, and called the cops. I was babbling in utter incoherence, literally foaming at the mouth, smashing things, and waving a knife and my dick in the air . . . .

I don't blame her at all.

I don't remember the cops' arrival, but I remember the bite of the cuffs on my wrists and ankles—yes, both—the way it felt, the cold metal like an electric shock, like it was gnawing at me. They hauled me to their cruiser—and I bit one of them on the ankle. Savaged him with my teeth. They tossed me in the back, just sort of threw me in, and I promptly threw up on the vinyl seat. I remember the smell of the vinyl, the smell of the vomit, the feel of the seat. The vinyl bit me too.

My sensations were murderously sharp, and everything was an assault. Broken glass ground into my nerve ends. The whole world humming with a monstrous energy that fried me in my own juices. Everything seemed absolutely inevitable, and like it was part of all there was in the world. I had experienced nothing before the bed, the knife, the broken glass, the cuffs, the cops, the vomit, the backseat. That chain of events was the universe, it was the whole thing, the big bang and all its consequences, nothing had come before or after and nothing existed except me and my mom and the cops, and it was going to be that way indefinitely, neither bad nor good, just a fierce condition.

Next thing I remember is a light bulb. I was staring up at it, and I couldn't get away from it. A naked bulb in a white fly-specked ceiling. And the tape loop, going over and over. The bed, the knife, the pursuit, the broken glass, the cops, the cuffs, the car, the light bulb. The bed, the knife, the pursuit, the broken glass, the cops, the cuffs, the car, the light bulb. That was my hallucination, that was what I saw, not just in my imagination. I relived it over and over and over and over, ending up with the light bulb on the ceiling of a security room in the state hospital for the insane. Starting over again. It must have repeated dozens, hundreds, thousands of times in my head. I accepted it. Even though it turned me on a spit and basted me in horror. I accepted it because this was the universe.

The universe began in the bed (as it does, in a way, with conception) and ended in a cop car (as it does, in a way—the final authority that is entropy, that is mortality, taking you away into death), the whole nightmare cycle repeating with all its Van Gogh colors, its hideously piquant smells. All the sounds that went with it repeating in my brain, too, my own babbling, my mother's tearful attempts to reach me, the breaking glass, like one of those Roger Waters tape loops of sounds that, repeated, are the rhythm section for a song . . . and the smell of vomit and vinyl . . . not unpleasant or pleasant, just color in my nose, a place in my proscribed consciousness, a world . . . reliving it over and over and over. Not just remembering—literally reliving. Again and endlessly again . . . until they shot me up with Thorazine.

I came out of it and found I was locked in leather restraints. On my back, strapped to a table in a cell with padded walls. The bulb burning overhead. "Hey! I'm okay now! Let me go, okay?" But they didn't, not for many hours, though sometimes they'd look at me through the little window in the door. Finally they brought me out and made me shower and put on hospital clothes and then they shaved off all my hair. Pig-shaved me.

I was in hell. It was the security ward of the state hospital, and it was the very place they filmed *One Flew Over the Cuckoo's Nest*. I mean, this was the actual ward they used, later, in the movie. I was surrounded by dangerous lunatics. The psych aides made me take Thorazine in orange juice twice a day, which made it difficult to control my muscles so my mouth sagged open and I tended to drool. My mother came to visit and I begged her to get me out. Promised to stay away from drugs forever. I'll be good! She was dubious, but she got me out. I went back to school pig-shaved. Now I was beyond a weirdo. The other students regarded me with a mingling of shivery respect and revulsion.

The cops used me as a test case. They'd found no drugs on me or in my room and didn't have a blood test for it then, but there was a new law in Oregon which said that if a person acted as if he's on drugs, you can bust him even if he's not holding. We got a lawyer, and he and the judge snickered over it and threw it out. The law was overturned. Violated various rights. So I was the test case which blew that one off the books. The cops had confiscated my diary, which described drug trips, but this wasn't regarded as sufficiently hard evidence since the diary was so weirdly impenetrable, anyway. I never got it back.

I was as good as my word. I didn't do drugs anymore . . . till I left home, maybe a year later. I moved to Portland.

KETAMINE

Rabbit Brains / David Jay Brown

When I was in graduate school studying behavioral neuroscience, the research that I was involved in required that I surgically implant cold-probes into the brains of rabbits. The drug that we used to anesthetize the furry creatures prior to surgery was an anesthetic called Ketamine.

I knew from having read John Lilly's books that Ketamine was also a powerful hallucinogen. I had read about how Dr. Lilly had used Ketamine to travel out of his body, and make contact with extraterrestrials. I wanted to try this stuff, so I took a bottle of it home with me one night, along with a few syringes.

When I got home, I settled onto my bed and injected 90 mg of Ketamine into my right thigh. Five minutes later, I suddenly "realized" that my doctoral advisors were really extraterrestrial scientists who had been videotaping me in the lab while I wasn't aware of it. In fact, they had actually left the bottle of Ketamine for me to take.

I also "realized" that they weren't really interested in the neural mechanics of rabbit brains; rather, they were experimenting on me. I was the real subject. I found myself naked, in a cage, with cold-probes stuck in my head. Giant rabbits were all around me. They knew everything going on in my mind. They were watching and measuring me right at that moment. I felt totally helpless and at their mercy.

Even though the trip lasted for only around forty-five minutes, after that experience I was never able to see the neuroscience lab the same way again. Needless to say, I didn't last very much longer in that graduate program.

David Jay Brown is co-author of *Mavericks of the Mind: Conversations for the New Millennium.*

Tanks for the Memories / Todd McCormick

When the mail arrived today, I learned that someone I had admired for years recently passed away—Dr. John Lilly. Anyone who has seen the movie *Altered States* has had some insight into some of the work he did with psychedelics and his invention, the isolation tank. In the film, the psychonautic doctor goes to Mexico to do mushrooms with aboriginal people in a sacred ceremony. This experience leads him to bring the drug back to the university so that he can trip in the tank and monitor the effects.

While the movie gets a bit ridiculous, as Hollywood tends to do, it did however turn me on to his work. I began to read about him and became interested in finding where one of these tanks was, so that I could at least try it out, straight or stoned. I really wanted to do what he did in the film—trip!—but realized I'd probably never get the chance.

I'll describe an isolation tank. Picture a rectangular box, four feet wide and eight feet long, standing four feet high. They're usually made of ABS plastic and lined with a thick waterbed-type liner to hold the ten inches of water. The back is squared off and has an air box that blows a soft breeze into the tank, and two tubes for a jacuzzi water filter that is turned on only when no one is in the tank. The front is angled off and has a large door where you get in.

The water temperature is kept constant by a water heater under the liner at around 95.5 degrees, which is around the same temperature as your skin, so once you're floating in the tank, completely in the dark with the door closed, your skin and the water become one. It's as if you can't feel where the water begins and your body ends.

How you float effortlessly is salt, and a lot of it, almost 900 pounds. Which means I would have to huff eighteen fifty-pound bags up to my bedroom every time I move and then to set it up again. Anyhow, once you're done mixing the salt into the warm water and smoking your now medical marijuana for your aching back, you'll be blown away once you crawl into the tank.

How my dream ended up coming true came to mind when I heard that John Lilly died. I had just moved back to the states from Amsterdam and landed in Los Angeles. One of my new friends, Russ, called me up from his psychedelic head shop and asked if I wanted to head over to Malibu and try out an isolation tank. I was thrilled and jumped at the opportunity.

On the way, Russ told me that we were on our way to John Lilly's house and would be going in his personal tank. I thought I was dreaming. When we arrived, we were greeted by Dr. Lilly and his assistant, Russ's friend Craig. I was so moved just to meet the amazing man and felt so fortunate to meet him in the casual setting of his own home.

After talking for a while and smoking awesome bud—actually, we smoked the bud, Lilly seemed content to chain-smoke cigarettes—Craig asked who wanted to go first. I couldn't contain my excitement, and Russ, being the gentleman he can sometimes be, acquiesced quickly.

I had no idea what the hell I was stepping into, but hey, naivete often leads to some amazing experiences. I was told that everybody had to shower before getting in the tank, which I did. Then, as I was standing there naked in Lilly's bedroom, Craig was giving me my last instructions before my innerpsyche flight. I had to know how to rest my arms once afloat, and how to squeegee the salt water off my body when I got out.

It was then that Craig said, "Usually, when we go in, we use about 1cc of Ketamine; would you like some?"

At that moment, my body separated. I heard reason think, "No drugs this time, thanks, I'll just experience the tank itself." But instantly I heard my mouth utter, "Sure, I'd love to try some."

As Craig went off to get the special ingredient, I stood and observed my subconscious side explain to my conscious side of reason that I had made it this far to Dr. Lilly's personal tank, and there was no way I wasn't going to go all the way. My normally lin-control side scoffed at the thought that it would have no say in the matter.

When Craig walked back in the room, my mind was still in cross talk. Then I heard him say, "I hope you don't mind that it's intermuscular injection." Both sides of my psyche jumped—"No needles!"—then to my utter amazement, I heard my mouth say, "That's no problem at all, thank you very much for offering." I then heard my conscious self scream in defeat as the sharp point of the needle pierced my skin and fluid flooded my muscle tissue.

I was going all the way, all right, which was much further than I had ever gone before. After the injection, I thanked Craig again and stepped into the tank. As the door closed behind me and I lay down into the water, I remember thinking, "What a peaceful place to trip." In the tank it's so warm and comfortable; the water covers your ears, so sound is muted.

I thought all was bliss, but then the Ketamine hit me like a tornado. I was instantly hurling through space, I could no longer feel my body's boundaries, sound was weird, and it was completely black in the tank, although I was seeing flashes of light come and go.

After the experience, I remembered feeling like molten lava must feel, being pushed up through a volcano from the core of the earth, where the pressure is so great that flashes of combustion happen spontaneously. Shortly after, I thought that I was going to die—or had already died, as I wasn't at all sure of where the fuck I was heading—when John Lilly entered my cosmic journey.

I couldn't see him, but I could hear him. He told me to calm down, to relax, to breathe slower, that I was all right, simply floating in my cellular being and realizing exactly what it was like. He guided me to amazing areas of, dare I say, my reality. With the drug, he was able to take me to a mental frequency where it seemed like we could communicate by just thinking. It was amazing. After a while, our conversation went full circle, and my trip was coming to an end.

I remember feeling completely in sync with myself and my surroundings. Then it ended. I was back in my body. I sat up, found the door and pushed it open. The light was so bright I thought that I would be blinded for life. Then I leaned out and puked onto the plastic pan that is used to step on when one gets out of the tank.

As I lay there heaving, Craig came into the bedroom to check on me. I recall thanking him very much in between getting sick. He then helped me to the shower where I completely forgot that water was supposed to come out and spray over me. So I stood there for a while, still high as heaven, until Craig came in again.

"It might be easier to shower with the water on, Todd," he said, as I felt the water hit me.

After the hot water ran out, I was pretty much done with the wonder of indoor plumbing. I got dressed (what a project!) and went to go smoke a joint with Craig and Russ. While we were getting high, Lilly came out of the bedroom, and we spoke for a while about how I felt. I told him with great excitement that he was in my trip and guided me through it. He smiled and told me he knew.

On the ride home, Russ asked me what had happened. I told him about Lilly coming into my trip and making everything all right. Russ was surprised. He told me that after I went in the tank, Craig walked out and the three of them began to talk and smoke. It was around that first few minutes that I started splashing around and screaming.

At first Russ was quite concerned about my flipping out, but he was not quick to question the calmness of both Dr. Lilly and Craig. So he just sat and listened to me flail about as if this was a normal part of floating in isolation. Listening to me go crazy made him quite happy that I went first.

In the middle of their conversation, Lilly looked at Craig and asked, "Is he on Ketamine?" Russ was surprised; he didn't see that part of the equation. So Lilly's next question really blew him away when Craig answered, "Yes." Lilly asked, "Would you get me some too?"

That was not what Russ expected to hear. Then, even more so, Russ didn't expect to see Craig come out with a syringe and have Lilly take it from Craig and stick it in his leg and shoot up. All this while I'm still panic background noise being ignored by both Lilly and Craig.

After taking the Ketamine, Lilly stood up, said goodnight, and went into the bedroom with the tank where I was freaking out. All of a sudden, Russ told me, I quieted down. I stopped screaming and splashing, and all became quiet. Russ and Craig continued to talk about the type of tree bark that contains DMT, and other interesting subjects.

I was amazed to hear all this. I totally remember Lilly entering into my dreamlike state and chilling me out. Could it have happened just when he entered the room? Had he stepped into both the room and my mind?

The next day my best friend Brett came over to hang out. I had told him what happened, and he told me his brother had taken it and reported the same effect, that Ketamine can be a telepathic experience and that I should talk to his brother.

So when his brother called later that day, I told him all about my experience. He told me that something similar had happened to him when he did it, and that when he got back to town we would do some together and check it out.

The next week, Craig came over and told me that Lilly was moving all his belongings to Maui. When they were wondering what to do with the tank, my name had come up. He was wondering if I wanted the tank. I couldn't believe it. What a total dream—my own tank, and John Lilly's personal tank at that.

So arrangements were made, and Craig brought over not only the tank, but also John's plastic shoes that he used to wear after each float. That to me was the absolute frosting on the cake, to be able literally to walk in his shoes. Awesome.

After carrying the half-ton of salt up to my bedroom and a few hours of smoking pot and assembling the tank, I couldn't wait to get in. Craig told me I should wait at least twentyfour hours, but in the middle of the night I awoke with the need to go float. I slipped away slowly from my warm and naked girlfriend, Tiffany, to go get in the tank. I blew off the shower because hours earlier we had been in the hot tub.

I became so comfortable in the tank that I fell back to sleep. I awoke when still-nude Tiffany opened the door and looked down at me. Then she stepped inside and cuddled with me in the salty water. We quickly learned that it wasn't built for two and that getting the salt water in your eyes really stings. So we both got out and showered. We never tried to get freaky in the isolation tank again.

Since getting the tank, I've spent many hours in it. I've tried floating with cannabis, both eaten and smoked. I ate mushrooms and giggled my way through hours of thinking I had the world completely figured out. My favorite time to float was when I was half asleep in the early morning hours. I would wake up and just go from my bed to the tank—to the dismay of Tiffany, who often awoke alone—and dream boundless dreams.

I look forward to the day I can combine LSD and a tank experience. For research purposes only, of course. So, John Lilly, as you float through the minds of many, still as alive as an idea can be, I want to thank you. As I walk from the isolation tank to shower in your shoes, I feel your vibes. In our hearts and minds, you'll live immortally.

Remembering John Lilly / Paul Krassner

In 1967, while tripping on LSD at the Seaquarium in Miami, I had a delightful non-verbal encounter with one particular dolphin. I would run to my left, and the dolphin would swim in the same direction. Then I would run to my right, stop short, run to my left again, then back to my right, and the dolphin would swim in perfect synchronization. We resembled that scene in the Marx Brothers movie, *Duck Soup*, when Harpo mimicked Groucho's motions in a nonexistent mirror.

"By the way," I asked "what are you always smirking about?"

The dolphin replied—and I'm willing to concede that this might have been my own acid projection—"If God is evolution, then how do you know He's finished?" Obviously, it was a male chauvinist dolphin.

In 1970, I attended a weekend workshop conducted by John Lilly at the Esalen Institute in Big Sur, California. It was about exploring mysticism with the scientific method. We weren't allowed to use words like "imagined" or "fantasized" or "projected." Whatever we experienced had to be accepted as reality. As an excercise, for example, Dr. Lilly played a tape loop of one word being repeated continuously, but after a while you'd begin to hear other words. "When faced with repetition" he explained, "your human biocomputer automatically programs in novelty."

Lilly had worked with dolphins for so long that he had begun to look like one. And even sound like one, interspersing his own speech pattern with dolphinlike staccato clicks and squeaks. He always wore a jumpsuit, and his license plate said DOLFIN. He had done pioneering research on both psychedelics and interspecies communication, so naturally I told him of my acid-trip encounter with that dolphin in Florida, the one who said, "If God is evolution, then how do you know He's finished?"

"No," Lilly corrected me. "How do you know you're finished?"

It was a simple yet profound revelation. And so conscious evolution became the name of my game.

Lilly considered dolphins to be smarter and more benevolent than humans. His work inspired a movie, *The Day of the Dolphin* (1973), in which the Navy trains dolphins to be underwater weapon carriers. Lilly was dismayed. "They've turned dolphins into little grey niggers of the sea," he told me.

Lilly and his artist wife, Toni, later founded the Human Dolphin Foundation, and in 1980, with computer scientists, he designed a computer system, Janus, to formulate a human-dolphin computer-synthesized language.

In 1981, I introduced Lilly to freelance reporter Sandra Katzman, and she became his "invaluable friend." She kept a journal. Sample entry: "The rooms have mirrors. Above a bathroom sink, a concave mirror stretches. Walls completely framed with mirrors. Light bounces back and forth between mirrors. I ask, 'How much light is lost in each reflection?' 'One-eighth,' replies the scientist."

Back in 1954, Lilly was pondering what effects would occur in the brain if deprived of external stimulation, and he invented the isolation tank where a person could lie suspended, perhaps for hours, in a dark coffin-like enclosure filled with warm salt-water. In the '60s, he added the ingestion of LSD to the mix. And, a decade later, he began experimenting with Ketamine—essentially an anesthetic—to enhance the out-of-body experience.

(Paddy Chayefsky wrote a novel, *Altered States*, based on Lilly's isolation-tank research, and he also wrote the screenplay, but was so disappointed in director Ken Russell's film version, released in 1980, that he insisted on a pseudonym for his writer's credit.)

Lilly adored Ketamine. His standard greeting to friends became, "Got any K?" Whenever he said that to David Jay Brown, the response would be, "I love you too, John."

Brown recalls, "John was one of the most brilliant people I've ever known; he was also one of the funniest. He had an extremely unusual perspective on the world, and with it, a sense of supreme confidence. He just really didn't seem to care what other people thought about him. Even though he appeared grumpy and cranky a lot of the time, everyone agreed how totally lovable he was. He just couldn't take himself seriously, and he always made people laugh."

Once, as a consequence of his experimentation with Ketamine, Lilly was hospitalized. Toni called and asked me to speak with him, which I did for about an hour. He kept repeating a mysterious sentence, "Joe took father's shoe bench out—and she was waiting at my lawn." I thought that he had gone totally crazy, but he later clarified his utterance, which was a test sentence used by the telephone company to test transmissions. It was his way of communicating that he was okay.

Another time, while carrying out his torrid affair with Ketamine, Lilly almost drowned in the hot tub at his Malibu home. This near-death experience confirmed for him that his life "was guarded by higher powers in the extraterrestrial reality, a hierarchy of entities operating through the control of coincidence on a global scale."

Lilly had propounded that concept—calling it the Earth Coincidence Control Office—which struck me as a witty metaphor until I realized that he actually meant it literally. I decided to act as if I believed in the existence of such a process, and as a result I began to lose my perspective. I had bought into John Lilly's cosmic conspiracy. I had gone over the edge, from a universe that didn't know I existed, to one that did. From false humility to false pride.

A couple of decades later, Lilly would dismiss his own concept. "Tooth problems," he explained. "I was trying to get in touch with my teeth."

A close friend of Lilly, known only as Brummbaer, told me: "For over ten years, we were fellow Ketamaniacs. The last time we shot up was a couple of years ago in Hawaii, and already then it took quite a toll on my body and even more on John's. Taking Ketamine isn't just a flirt with death—it's a tantric fuck with death—all nine holes of your body participating—and it's not free!

"I observed John as somebody who was interested in sexual identity, and I once jokingly suggested how it would be if we all had a sex change in the middle of our lives and so would experience both genders. When I heard he wanted breast implants, I was hoping for the protective sanity of his friends, but he wouldn't have been John Lilly, genius, if he couldn't find somebody to do him the favor. John also wore make-up in those days. The boobs were awful! Square and hard.

"Then one day they found John minus most of his blood on the bedroom floor—the wound from the implant hadn't healed—ants were marching around in a wound that John had tried to close with paper clips in the best sense of a pioneer who uses the materials at hand. When I told Tim [Leary] about this, he cracked up: 'My god, Brummbaer, look what a bunch of bores we are—trying desperately to pitch ideas to a software company while John is walking around with boobs.'

"I think the breast-implant story says what John always proclaimed: that you don't know it if you haven't experienced it yourself. And since he regarded his body as some kind of a laboratory/measuring device, to get boobs or any other implant wasn't such a big thing for him."

In the early '90s, Lilly visited Australia. According to his hosts, "All that was on his mind was scoring, no matter what it was. Also he was quite sick and feverish. His breast implants had gotten infected somehow, probably because his liver was none too clean. We rushed him to the local hospital, where they took the things out, and the next day he was fine and delivered a fantastic talk in the local surf club about dolphins."

About ten years ago, Lilly moved to Maui, where he not only collaborated with the Kahua Institute on their project, Dolphin and Whale Adventures in Consciousness, but he also became a rap artist, for better or worse, with such songs as "I Know Nothing" and "The Journey."

On September 30, 2001, John Lilly's journey was over. He died of heart failure at the age of eighty-six. His legacy includes nineteen books, from *Center of the Cyclone* to *Simulations of God.* A week before his death, he greeted Brummbaer with the ritualistic, "Got some K?"

At a memorial, Brummbaer described how Lilly had "refused to work for the government because, when he mapped the brain of the mammals to measure brain activity, he lost access to his own experiments by not having the secrecy clearing of the Pentagon.

"Interestingly, the experiment he wasn't privy to was to remote-control a mule loaded with explosives into enemy territory, using John's electrodes and his brain maps. How odd this sounds today when we have a whole new idea about mules and how to deliver explosives. I think because of this event he became the maverick and never changed until the end."

Postscript: Following the January 26, 2003 bombing in Jerusalem, in which a live donkey laden with explosives was intentionally blown up—shocking people of all nationalities around the world—PETA (People for the Ethical Treatment of Animals) wrote to Palestinian National Authority President Yasser Arafat asking that he urge those who listen to him to keep animals out of the conflict.

Bits of Dragon / Bill Krupinski

I was driving a VW Beetle lent to me by the girlfriend of the drummer in my brother's band. My buddy—a Vietnam vet who had just returned to "the real world" after being on the deck of an aircraft carrier and, while tripping on acid, had a jet fighter crash and explode in front of him—and I were traveling west on I-94 out of Milwaukee, a good straight stretch once you get past Oconomowoc. So he had a pipe but no dope, while I had what we used to call angel dust—parsley soaked with PCP. We fired up a bowl, and I was enjoying what felt like a mild buzz with a slightly ominous overtone.

As designs and patterns started flying past the side windows, I noticed the road was starting to undulate in front of us. Soon the road had turned into a giant serpent's body, and we were in danger of falling off the rounded edge. The evil bugger's head raised up and its tongue rolled out to meet us. We were headed straight into the mouth of the beast! I had a decision to make: Crank the wheel hard to the right and fly off into the patterned ether, or drive so fast I'd break through the serpent's head.

I stomped the gas and took her in at 90 mph (the speed limit those days was already 75 mph). Faster, closer—this was it, baby! We passed into a moment of darkness and kablooie! Bits of dragon went flying in all directions and dissolved as we came flying through the other side. The flying bits of dissolving dragon settled back down into the everyday world we normally live in, and I was going 95 mph on the freeway. No mean feat for a Beetle, I might add.

Luckily, traffic was light, and when I excitedly asked my buddy if he had seen all that had just happened, he hadn't seen a thing.

Bad Cop / Zelda

I smoked some pot with some friends in the drainage pipes under the city. It had PCP in it, and I freaked out and ran around the tunnels with one of those spelunking flashlights on. I must've run outside and not noticed it because I was running from the slime monster down Safeway aisles instead of drainage tunnels.

They arrested me, and curiously enough, the policeman admitted, pig that he was, to spray-painting Satanic symbols on the side of a K-Mart building and inside corporate bathrooms. I told him I didn't believe in God either, but he got brutal because he was Jewish.

They took me back to the drainage tunnels, where I fell asleep, and when I woke up, I was alone. I sat there waiting for the monster, but he didn't come so I went home.

Yoo-Hoo / Jack Walker

Always a glutton for punishment, I've been known to choose jobs that tax the psyche. It's not a condition to always take lightly, however. Such gluttony can also lead one to do things such as abandon a prosperous career for the slightest chance of getting laid in Chicago. But, what now? Yep, that's me rushing off to the streets for community service.

Getting my hands dirty has never been a foreign experience. This time, I found myself in Ohio, tutoring high school crack addicts and recovering convicts. Did I mention the word "glutton" yet? I had the usual clichés to report early on: not really bad kids . . . misunderstood . . . despise being patronized . . . just need a chance . . . cycle of self-fulfilling prophecy.

After a month of work, I was starting to feel some real connection. Not only did we get along, but they were on their way toward that dreaded proof of intelligence— getting their diplomas. Perhaps it was out of gratitude, then, that my students decided to help me loosen up . . .

I had just finished my usual brown-bag meal of microwave chicken, and mashed potatoes, and a bottle of Yoo-hoo. What transpired from that point (around two p.m.)

to midnight is largely a blur. As my prior experiences of mental impairment were limited to the effects of alcohol, I took everything that followed as a series of fever dreams, visions that I either accepted at face value or shrugged off with amusement.

What I remember first is the bat. While attempting to drive myself home in the middle of a stupor, I found a very frisky bat nestled against the ignition. Every time I tried to start the car, this creature would fly around in my face, effectively granting me a case of the heebie-jeebies. So, the car was a lost cause, and my suspicious condition had yet to draw any attention to itself.

It's funny how you lose touch with people. See, I had no idea that so many of my friends owned motor homes. For the next few hours, best buddies spanning this wonderful globe pulled up to the portion of the curb that I had laid claim to and updated me on the currents of their lives. The lack of parking space eventually became a problem, though. Soon, one side of the street was one solid wall of Winnebago as far as the eye could see.

By midnight, a local police officer found my pathetic pile of limbs lying unconscious near the street. With a burst of unparalleled sensitivity, the officer woke me with the following words: "What the hell are you doing?" A quick check into my eyes with his threatening flashlight provided the only answer he needed to this question.

(Now that I've been handcuffed, can I call them The Man?)

My last vision of the night came during an ambulance ride to the detox unit. Lights everywhere. While a paramedic humored my passionate claims that there were fireworks going off outside the vehicle, my "trip" was entering its final stages. The next twenty-four hours would bring drug charges, dropped drug charges, and an odd little theory: My customary bottle of artificially flavored chocolate beverage, known to the learned as Yoo-hoo, had been spiked with some friendly neighborhood PCP.

I checked the nutrition label. It only mentioned vitamins.

Cop Killer—Not! / Volcano Dave

Whenever my friend Charlie invited me to consume some THC or PVC* or PCB or some other acronym in a pill, I would always say yes. Well, this time it wasn't THC. It was probably PCP or what's sometimes called angel dust. We were zooming at a good clip toward Epcot Center in Florida in our rented

---

*PVC is the ubiquitous plastic polymer Poly Vinyl Chloride which I had intended as a techno-acronym joke, but have come to find out that the stuff actually confounds your hormone receptors and endocrine system. Yeah, it's a drug too.

convertible. We had it timed perfectly. We were minutes from the gate. Drop now, fly later. But doggone it, the dust immediately curled my mind, and I zoomed right past the entrance. It was thirty-five miles to the next U-turn. I jammed my foot on the accelerator and felt the floorboards warp like they were made of rubber. The road was empty, flat, and wide. The speedometer was rocking side to side. Alligators glared at us from the shoulders. The world made a U-turn at which time I really hit the gas. Epcot ahoy!

Siren! Flashing lights! There was a tiny cop car in the rearview mirror where objects are closer than they appear to be. Then a cop appeared life-size outside the window. Then as we stood on the saw-grass median and I dug in my pocket for a license, I stared down at the grass and noticed that it was wiggling like millions of worms in the hot sun. Swaying. Not good. I looked at the glinty, shiny cop shoes. The neat cop trousers. The leather holster.

From somewhere else I heard, "You were doing seventy-eight. I'm going to give you a ticket."

I stared at the pistol. I will kill this cop. My mind squirted out and pulled on the bulging pistol grip. Telescopic vision revealed the nicked and notched brown old wood pistol grip in marvelous detail. My mind saw the gory bloody hole and dead cop on the divider.

"This will not go on your record if you pay it right away. Don't speed around here again."

"Yessss, officer."

My lips felt funny. I tried to act normal as we got back into the car.

We finally got to Epcot and rushed into the first exhibit we could find, eager to salvage the waning trippy bubble. There we stood, in a switchback line awaiting some evil-empire corporation's idea of what the future should be like. The family next to us in line had tuberculosis. All of them were coughing up lungs. Man, woman, children, and infants. We were stuck there breathing their unholy bacteria for a long, terrible time. The PCP had all worn away, but we lived to trip another day.

TOAD SLIME

Warning

Description of a workshop, excerpted from a brochure for a conference sponsored by the Hawaii Traffic Safety Forum:

TODAY'S DRUGS: DRIVING UNDER THE INFLUENCE

This session will focus on the substances that people have been using recently that impair driving ability. This includes prescription drugs, herbs and other natural substances, and some exotic practices such as toad licking.

Otto and Maude / Anonymous Yahoo

Every generation has had a drug of choice that exemplifies their lifestyle, whether it was '70s Quaaludes or '80s Yuppie cocaine. Toad juice appears to be at the forefront of the latest drug wave raging across American college campuses. The greenish-brown toads that produce the secretion, Bofu-Alvaris, are found in the Sonoran

Desert in the southwestern United States. They produce the liquid as part of an evolved defense mechanism against predators. Contrary to popular belief, the toad is not licked or the juice drank. These practices have sometimes proven to be toxic.

Stephen, a twenty-four-year old freshman from Narberth, Pennsylania, explained the process for extracting the juice and ingesting its power: "I squeeze my toads, named Otto and Maude, at the juice glands with all my might. I squeeze the juice onto flat glass, then immediately put it into an airtight container to retain freshness. When it dries, we put it in a pipe and smoke it." The glands, located behind the eyes, legs, and forearms, fill up about every six weeks, producing enough for about five or six trips. Only about one match tip's worth of dried juice is good for an intense twenty-minute trip.

"Sometimes we do two match tips, just to be safe," Stephen added.

The intense trip is more powerful than LSD or mushrooms, but not quite as hallu-cinogenic as folklore would have it. It is more similar to a marijuana high, but in exponential proportions. It is also said to be a powerful aphrodisiac.

Kierstan, a premed major from McLean, Virginia, describes her first toading: "It tasted like model-airplane glue. I took a few really deep breaths and got it into my lungs. I felt it immediately creeping down my spine. Within a minute, I was on the ground, thrash-ing around. I had no control of my coordination and a total loss of muscle control. I couldn't speak or anything. It was great."

The trip doesn't last long, and there is about a one-hour recovery period, when you slowly gain control of your appendages and speech. After recovery, the side effects are minimal.

"I always get big-time munchies," Stephen said, "but that could be because I always smoke a little dope to help me come down."

"My face hurts from smiling so much during the trip," said Kierstan. "My dad told me that it's a lot like DMT."

The male toads are about the size of a baby's fist, and the female about twice that. Their diet consists mainly of common field crickets, which makes upkeep inexpensive.

"I think it's great that not only do you get really spliffed, but they make great pets," Stephen said. "I've really grown attached to them, to the point that I don't like squeez-ing them dry, even though they don't seem to mind. Sometimes I just sneak up behind them and yell. That makes them secrete enough for a good time."

While possession of toads is not illegal, local ordinances should be consulted before toading is attempted. Furthermore, the toads are a protected species, which makes it unlawful to remove them from their habitat. Almost all sales are made on the toad black market, where they can cost as much as *twenty-five dollars* each. Toaders think that the trip is well worth all the shady dealings.

"I consider the experience to be deeply religious," Kierstan added. "I mean you're com-pletely in sync with nature. A toad is a gift from God. It's warm and velvety."

Homage to the Visionary Toad / Ralph Metzner

I found myself with three friends in a town in Arizona during the rainy season to harvest some of the hallucinogenic exudate of the Colorado River toad. This magnificent amphibian now actually lives mostly in the Sonoran Desert, spending nine months of the year buried up to two feet down in the moist underground of Mother Earth. They emerge after the rains, which are often very sparse, for an orgy of feeding and copulation, hanging out in grassy terrain near waterways, and hopping under street lights at night to catch flying insects, which is where we found them. Unlike their long-legged cousins, the frogs, toads can't really jump—they just sort of hop around and are easy to catch. Some of the larger specimens barely fit onto a grown man's hand, measuring maybe six inches from head to rear and four inches in width; plus they seem to be able to expand their girth, puffing up to make themselves even fatter. The weight and feel of them is like that of a smallish plucked chicken; but the body is very soft and yielding—you don't really feel any bones. The skin is olive-green in hue with little bumpy warts; two large raised parotid glands, one half inch in length, at the neck; and smaller glands at the crook of the elbows and groins.

We worked in pairs: One of us would pick up a toad, holding it gently but firmly from the top with one hand, and then squeeze the gland with thumb and forefinger of the other hand so that the milky white slime would squirt or ooze out onto a sheet of plastic or glass held by the other man. We would leave the exudate stuck to the glass to dry overnight. We then scraped it off with a razor blade, in the form of little flakes and crumbs, and then put it in a pipe and smoked it.

A shattering annihilation, a feeling of being inside a nuclear explosion, being fragmented into countless tiny shards. I felt as though I was being turned inside out, like my innards were extruding through my mouth. My body was rolling on the ground, coiled into a ball, like the urobouros serpent circle. I opened my eyes momentarily and could see that I was protected by my friends from bumping into things or rolling into the Wreplace. Instant reality check.

Eyes closed, I was immersed again into the swirling, seething maelstrom of synesthetic sensations, in which all distinctions between inner and outer, self and other, even directions like above and below, were obliterated. Animal sounds appeared to be coming from my mouth. There were no feelings of fear, indeed no feelings at all, other than a kind of impersonal ecstasy. No sense of body, no sense of self, no "I."

Images of decapitation, dismemberment, disembowelment flashed by, in rapid succession, including an image of being run through the chest with a sword—yet there was no fear or horror associated with these images. The following thoughts occurred: "Death comes to all, now it's your turn, this is it, the termination. Resistance is impossible and pointless besides— it's too late, the annihilation has already happened." As I gradually came back into my body, after ten minutes in real time, I felt bathed in pure joy and completely at peace with myself, the world and my death.

My personal attitude toward toads, carried over from childhood ignorance and rumor, had been a mixture of aversion and fear. I had somehow acquired the mistaken belief that they could squirt poison at you. But by the time of this expedition, my attitude had changed to admiration, even reverence. I had already had the opportunity to experience the effects of the psychoactive ingredient of the venom of this particular toad, which is also present in several South American entheogenic snuff preparations.

My experiences with this substance, a chemical relative of DMT, have been among the most profound, transcendent, and healing experiences of my life, although they have also included challenging and frightening times. It is no surprise that DMT, which some call the "spirit molecule," as well as other tryptamines, is naturally produced in the human pineal gland, and is related to the mood-modulating neurotransmitter serotonin and the sleep hormone melatonin.

I had the sense of being at an exact balancing edge between an internalizing and externalizing movement. I could let go deep within, sinking, falling, opening to an inner vast spaciousness, or I could let the energy come out and be expressed through body movement and voice. When I let go within, I had feelings of great peacefulness, a soft breathing in the heart, gently approaching knots of contraction or pain.

Out of a hard nugget of pain, in the groin, a serenely exploding flare of light energy spread throughout my body. The softly ascending light flare sparkled like jewels and precious stones, as if the pain had been a locked up treasure chest that suddenly opened. Multicolored lines of light formed a kind of dome covered in a faceted geometric network of jewels; the whole dome spun silently clockwise. The jewelled dome seemed to become a kind of lens, through which I could see into worlds beyond, where the points of light were stars and galaxies.

I was prepared to worship the toad deity that could produce such magic. We approached the lovely creatures with admiration and respect. When I lifted one up I would talk to it softly. I remember being amazed at their soft, weighty body, with skin not slimy at all and the most beautiful jet-black round eyes shining like black pearls. We murmured prayers of gratitude and assurances that we would not hurt them. We told them how the medicine they produced would help us humans understand the nature of reality and give us cosmic healing, visions. After milking the exudate, we replaced them gently on the ground. We had been informed that the toad can replenish its store of venom in about two weeks and is otherwise not harmed.

The first effects were tiny scintillating sparks of light against a velvety blackness, which merged to become a brilliantly colored, weaving, flowing tapestry of geometric forms, extending infinitely in all directions. Then this kaleidoscopic field of patterns dissolved my body into it, so that I didn't see it anymore—I became part of it. Something like a mask or blind over the right side of my face appeared to be coming loose. I could feel my cheek muscles rippling under the skin, and facial nerves twitching, a sense of energy currents inside my body being aligned and balanced.

I recognized certain knots of pain in the body as residues of self-inflicted punishment over some early guilt feelings. A voice-thought appeared, saying: "Stop trying to become enlightened." This cracked me up with laughter, literally breaking up abdominal armoring. The trying ego let go. There was a kind of zipping sound and sensation going up and down my central energy axis, and the sense of a sword-like energy-beam cutting attachments, as it moved rapidly up and down.

Then the energy channel became a vibrating string, as on a bass; then three strings, vibrating, resonating together. I was shown that if I could make certain sounds, the vibrations would actually disintegrate the crystallized nuggets of pain or tension. I continued perceiving ascending and descending glissandos, as on a harp, but soundless, kinaesthetic, synaesthetic, soothing, healing.

The venom serves the toad as defense: a dog or coyote attempting to bite it will get a shot of the hallucinogenic slime in the mouth or eyes, which will not kill but definitely will distract the predator from its purpose. We talked to a woman in Tucson who had dogs, and lots of the toads hanging around her pool. One of her dogs had evidently assaulted a toad, and she found him lolling around on the ground on his back, tongue hanging out and drooling, eyes rolling wildly. After twenty minutes he got up and walked away, toad forgotten. There are other ingredients in the toad slime besides the hallucinogenic DMT-relative, such as bufotenine, which may be more toxic. Some say the toxins are active when absorbed directly through mucous membranes (of the mouth, nostrils, or eyes), but are inactivated by the heat of smoking. It's probably best for humans not to try the experiment, although the pure crystalline substance has been snorted without ill effects.

Again, the weaving, waving field of geometric shapes and lines folded and fell over me, or I fell into it. I could see small spherical globules of white light, like pearls, that are glistening, shining, moist, and perfectly aligned and interconnected in complex three-dimensional webs, reminiscent of Buckminster Fuller's dymaxion structures, always changing, unfolding, and enfolding. These webs constituted my body, clustering in certain areas to make organs like my eyeballs. They also constituted all other bodies and forms around me. Each individual was a kind of cluster in this infinite ever-changing molecular web. Each thought or feeling or experience was also a local cluster in this holographic matrix of all possibilities. A sun of pure white light radiated out from the center of the swirling, pearl-studded crystalline grid. Too intensely bright for me to maintain the focus of attention, gradually I lost awareness of it and emerged back out of the infinite oneness into my body-form.

I've come to think that the three-dimensional geometrical web, extending infinitely in all directions, that you first "see" and then become part of, is the molecular level of consciousness and reality. Molecules of carbon, nitrogen, oxygen, and various elements and compounds do not "care" whether they are inside or outside of your body, or any object or form in the external world. There are no objects or bodies or boundaries at this level—only the ever-changing network or web, the crystalline lattices of replicating patterns.

Further, more detailed observations by me and others reveal that sometimes one sees a web that is crystalline-geometric, with straight lines between nodes and at other times more of a fibrous, organic net, with multiple branchings. Grandmother Spider's web of creation. Nerve nets. Perhaps in those experiences we're right at the interface of neuronal nets and molecular grids, seeing now one, now the other. Nerve impulses travel along axons as sodium and potassium ions are pumped in and out of the nerve-cell membrane; transmission across the synaptic cleft is by release of neurotransmitter molecules.

There are ten billion nerve cells in the brain; one hundred million photosensitive rods and cones in the retina. So when you're "seeing" the grid-web, sparkling with jeweled luminescence, you're registering the activation of millions of the light-sensors in your retina; when you're sensing yourself embedded in the web, without distinction of self or other, you're simply sensing being part of the cellular-molecular web of all life, extending infinitely in all directions.

But you can zero in on a particular localized region of your body (or perhaps another body, with sufficient practice), and "see" obstructions to energy flow causing sickness or pain—and remove them. Ayahuasqueros and other shamanic or psychic or yogic healers can sometimes do this.

The pure substance is active in the dose range of 10–15 mg. Each exudate of an adult toad may contain as much as 80–100 mg. That means each toad is loaded with enough energetic force to launch six to eight adult human beings potentially into cosmic hyperconsciousness, to the heart of creation, and return them safely to their human form. This is the mystery, then: Why does the toad do that, or have that power? Why is its defense survival mechanism such that humans, who don't really even prey on toads, can experience mystical transcendence from it? At the least, it is evidence for the inter-connected web of all life at the molecular level. All life does use the same DNA molecule as the code of creation.

Again, there was the feeling of being in the nucleus of the psyche. Awareness of all and every-thing, simultaneously. "This is IT." The Vedantists say at the highest level of consciousness there is only being (sat), consciousness (chit) and blissful joy (ananda). There is no self, no body, no time or space, but there is being. There is also consciousness: I can remember everything afterward, even although "I" wasn't there; there was audio-video record-ing going on. And there was certainly bliss, joy, ecstasy unimaginable. I found myself on my knees, my body was being moved in incredibly smooth, Xuid dancing motions, not by me, but by a spiritual Presence within me that felt totally other, unknown, not-me.

Yet I didn't feel any fear or resistance, just awe, as I willingly gave over my form to be used by what seemed like a deity. I looked at my arm moving, and I wasn't moving it. The Presence felt now male, now female, now androgynous, now serpentine. Shiva, Shakti, Kundalini. The attitude emanating from this Shakti-being is all-embracing, all-encompassing of all of me, my body, and the environment. I remember recognizing what it felt like to be the floor that my body was resting on, the land that the house is on, the planet Earth that the land is on. . . .

A passage from Shakespeare's *As You Like It* expresses this all-embracing consciousness, a vision of mystical oneness with nature, linking this vision of ecological consciousness ("tongues in trees, books in running brooks") to the ancient tradition of a toad with jewels in its head. This image seems strangely significant, in view of the multitudes of glittering jewels one can see when ingesting the venom of this particular toad.

> Sweet are the uses of adversity,
> Which, like the toad, ugly and venomous,
> Wears yet a precious jewel in his head;
> And this our life, exempt from public haunt,
> Finds tongues in trees, books in running brooks,
> Sermons in stones and good in everything.

Ralph Metzner is the author of *Green Psychology.*

The Animal-Free Alternative / Brian Briggs

Norfolk, Virginia—On the heels of their "Got Beer?" program, which discouraged the use of dairy products, PETA announced today their new "Got Acid?" campaign. PETA hopes to slow the resurgent popularity of licking toads for their hallucinogenic properties.

A PETA spokesperson went on to explain that toad licking is often traumatic, harmful, and sometimes fatal—for the toads. "Instead, we find LSD is a much better, animal-free alternative. We know that the toad-licking lobby is powerful, but the message needs to be heard."

PETA has been setting up booths on college campuses nationwide, from which they distribute informational pamphlets and samples of acid. "We put the LSD on these little toady stickers," said PETA volunteer Yolanda Wright. "Now you can lick the toad without harming an animal. Isn't that just adorable?" The pamphlets encourage people to find out the position of both local and national candidates on toad licking before casting their ballot in November.

From the swamps of south Florida, toad-licker Francis Franklin warned, "PETA is spreading more lies. Toad licking lets people commune with nature and, when done properly, doesn't harm the toad. LSD just doesn't give as intense hallucinations as toad licking. PETA can take my toad away when they tear it from my cold dead lips."

Franklin proposes more education on the proper techniques of toad licking, instead of an outright ban. "We must get to children early," he said, "because bad habits are hard to break."

AND OTHERS

Hash Oil / Paul Krassner

The Mad Scientist was neither mad nor scientific. Actually, he had been active in theater. However, when he took LSD for the first time in a lighting booth where he watched a production of *Cyrano* that he had directed, he decided to leave the theater for the streets.

In May 1968, he was in Paris with a suitcase full of hashish. He had been tangentially political before, but now he found himself in the middle of a citizens' revolt. Barricades were being erected with the same cobblestones that had been dug up in the original French revolution. The physical experience of being there served to radicalize him.

None of his friends was a chemist, but somehow they had learned to make hash oil. Meanwhile, he was feeling a cultural force from America's Yippies (Youth International Party)—the Yippie myth had crossed the Atlantic—and he decided to go to Chicago to participate in antiwar demonstrations at the Democratic National Convention. On the weekend before the convention, the Mad Scientist went strolling through Lincoln Park, asking, "Do you know Abbie Hoffman?" Eventually, he asked Abbie himself, and before you could say hidden laboratory, there was one. The lab consisted of long tables, spread out with hundreds of packages of Bugler tobacco. The hash oil was cut with pure grain alcohol, put in atomizers and sprayed on the tobacco, which was then placed back in the packages and given away as Yippie cigarettes.

For those who preferred a healthier version, the hash oil was mixed into jars of honey. This was strong stuff. The Fugs were completely fugged up. Ed Sanders described the grass he was walking on as "a giant frothing trough of mutant spinach egg noodles." Tuli Kupferberg took a big taste, and friends had to carry him by the armpits back to the apartment where he was staying.

"They're delivering me," he explained.

I swallowed two tablespoons of honey and stayed in the park. I was on my knees, holding on to the grass very tightly so that I wouldn't fall up. The Yippie leaders were all zonked out of their minds. A group of us were driving around Chicago when we realized that we were being followed by another car. It was like beng in a slow motion chase scene. But could this merely be paranoia as a side effect of the hash oil? I suggested that we go the wrong way down a one-way street. Then, if the other car was still following us, we could be sure that they were following us.

We stopped in front of a guy sitting on bench. I got out and told him that we thought we were being followed. We would drive around the block, and if he saw that this other car was in fact following us, he should give us a signal. So we circled the block, the other car followed us, the guy on the bench gave a signal, and we continued on, figuring that now the two men who were tailing us had to wonder what this guy had just accomplished that he was signaling us about, and should they maybe follow him instead?

The previous day, we had been refused service at a diner. I told the manager, "You're about to have your first Yippie sit-in," and they finally served us. Now we stopped there again, shook hands with the manager and told him there were no hard feelings, even as he was being put on the suspect list by the cops who were following us.

We also stopped at an art supply store where we had been treated rather rudely, and got them listed as accomplices too. Finally we parked. So did the other car. Two men in suits were sitting in front. We got out of our car and walked back to theirs. They tried to appear nonchalant.

"Hey," Abbie said, "are you guys following us"

"Yeah." Reluctantly.

"Are you local or federal?"

"We're plainclothes officers with the Chicago Police Department. You're under twenty-four-hour surveillance."

"Wow," I said, with perverted pride, "three shifts, just for us."

"No, we're short on manpower. We're on two twelve-hour shifts."

"Well, it's an honor just to be nominated."

We introduced ourselves and shook hands with the cops. Their names were Herbie and Mac. We offered them official Yippie lapel buttons.

"No, thanks, we're on duty."

I explained that if we happened to lose them in a crowd, we'd be able to spot them more easily if they were wearing Yippie buttons, so they accepted the buttons and pinned them on their jackets. But this kind of communication is a two-way street, so the cops asked us if we were planning to eat soon, because they had been following us for a while and now they were hungry. Although we had terminal dry mouth from the hash oil, maybe lunch would stimulate our salivary glands. We were new in town and asked the cops to recommend a good restaurant.

"Well," said Herbie, "the Pickle Barrel in Old Town has pretty good food."

"And," Mac added, "their prices are reasonable."

It felt like we were in a TV commercial of the future, where all the authority figures are cops.

"Okay," I asked, "what's the best way to get there?"

"Follow us."

This was indeed a rare and precious moment, to be embedded in amber for posterity. We obediently got back in our car and followed the cops. I thought they were going to try and shake us, but we managed never to lose sight of them. It was as if someone had pushed the rewind button, and now our slow motion chase scene seemed to be running backwards.

I expected to see the cops stop at the art supply store, and the diner, and then a guy sitting on a bench would give them a signal. But instead we just followed them straight to the Pickle Barrel. We sat at separate tables.

Morning Glory Seeds / Rex Weiner

When I was fifteen, the word was, you could get high from eating morning glory seeds. So one fine morning, I went to the garden store and bought ten packets.

At home, I sat down in the kitchen and poured them into a bowl. They were hard polygonal little black things. I tried chewing one and it nearly broke my tooth. I tried to mash a handful with my mom's rolling pin, but at that moment she came home. So I hurriedly poured all the seeds into my pocket, and got busy making myself a salami sandwich. When my mom walked in, that's all I was doing—making myself some lunch before going outside "to play."

In the woods nearby, I sat down with eager anticipation of a psychedelic afternoon in the midst of glorious nature. I poured the seeds out of my pocket and tried pounding them with a rock, intending to take the powder and eat it. But they just sort of splintered when I hit them.

They pissed me off, those little black seeds, and I was impatient to get high. So I took out my salami sandwich, pulled open the bread, and piled on the seeds. A lot fell out, but the mustard held most of them very nicely.

I consumed the sandwich and was picking the little black buggers out of my teeth for about fifteen minutes when suddenly a stabbing pain seared my gut like a blowtorch, and I keeled over, puking furiously. I was sure I was going to die.

When I looked down, my puke was in technicolor. For the next five hours, I was flat on my back, hallucinating like crazy, and I just hung on for the ride until I could finally walk home.

But forever afterward, I could not eat salami or mustard or even think of them without feeling queasy. And the sight of anything small, black, and seedlike made me sick to my stomach, even a dotted line on a piece of paper, even thinking about it more than thirty years later.

Rex Weiner is the author of *The Adventures of Ford Fairlane*.

Mustard Gas / Ted Kane

When I was in high school, there was this guy (let's call him Mark) that we hung out with who wasn't all that bright. One day before school, Mark came up and said, "Hey, I found a new way to get high last night."

So, naturally we were interested, and were like, "Yeah, yeah, what is it, what did you do?"

And he said, "Well, I was doing my laundry, and I saw on the bottle of bleach where it says 'Hazardous when mixed with ammonia,' and so I figured that it would give me a good buzz. So, I got a metal bowl, I mixed some bleach and ammonia, and I put my head down there and sniffed it."

He beamed at us, proud of his discovery. Meanwhile, those of us who actually paid attention in history and/or chemistry class were stunned. Finally this guy Brian spoke up and said, "Uh, Mark, what you made is mustard gas. Mustard gas is what they used in World War I to kill people." Anyway, apparently mustard gas will give you a good buzz.

Cough Medicine / Olu Karib

A quarter after 10 p.m., with jets droning overhead and thin walls of a cheap room vibrating, the four of us sit down with a small magical bottle, and I am given the honor of twisting the cap and killing the poison. The thick syrupy liquid is new to my tongue, though I am by no means new to getting stoned. Of my several LSD trips, a few transported me to a literal paradise that I vowed to hold onto, but always lost when I came down. Heroin was good, too; it inspired a surreal calm and a feeling of omnipotence. They called it Girl back in the day. Made me feel affable, irresistible. I also tried mescaline and other stuff, and smoked a ton of hashish as an airman in Trebizond, Turkey. But the surprise of my getting-high life comes tonight via this little bottle of insanely bittersweet cough syrup.

The year is 1970. I am living in a weekly room-rental dump of a place, formerly a motel-by-the-hour, situated on the south side of Century Boulevard, a few blocks down from Hollywood Park race track and a few miles up from the LA airport. I am gainfully employed, however, and I wear cowboy boots to my job as assistant manager of a quick-chicken place. The boots are de rigeur, I figure, for riding my red-and-silver Honda 175 mph along the avenues of Watts. Got my motor runnin'!

The three dudes I'm sitting and sippin' with, the ones who turned me on to Robitussin CF, insist that they are from Gary, Indiana. Their black Buick Electra, which they say they stole, has Illinois plates. They move in to one of the downstairs rooms, hit me up to buy beer for them because I'm of age, and the next thing you know, we're going to lunchtime strip joints together and watching white babes who pretend to be nurses and secretaries and stewardesses taking off all their clothes.

"Let's go boostin' out at the airport," one of the criminally inclined Gary brothers says one evening. And I'm like, "Boostin'? That's stealing. No, sorry, not me."

So what we finally end up doing is purchasing two bottles of cough syrup, Robitussin. Not regular Robitussin, but Robitussin CF, the one with the heavy dose of phenyl-propanolamine, PPA, the stuff you find in pep pills. PPA in combination with the other ingredients in the syrup Robitussin CF "may cause drowsiness." They should write on the label, "May cause strokes or comas." We're sitting in their room, sipping, passing the bottle, and the next thing I know, my body is sitting there by itself. Nobody's inside-skin, bones, clothes, internal organs, and stuff—just sitting there on the edge of the bed. The other part of me—call it soul, consciousness, spirit, whatever you like—is moving about the room in slow motion.

Or maybe everything's moving at the speed of light and, like Einstein predicted, things just seem slower. Chairs and tables and the bedside lamp and the walls and other objects in the room are swimming, floating, like they do when you're on acid. Except I'm not see-ing colors and shit. But I am hearing sounds. Street traffic out on the boulevard is a melody.

"As good as LSD," someone utters from within my corpse.

"Yeah, but not as dangerous," says a voice from one of the boys from Gary. "LSD can make you lose your mind, make you think you can jump off a building and fly. This is just plain old cough syrup. Nothin' to worry about."

Later, outside in the parking lot sometime between deep night and first light, one of the Gary boys says to me, "Damn, look at how slow you're moving. You're stoned. Here, give me your keys, and I'll help you up the stairs and open the door for you."

"No, thanks. I can make it on my own. I'm in no hurry."

Somehow the word *perspicacious* enters my faltering consciousness. It's a big word, a good word, so I know that I'm not brain-dead, not yet.

Kif / Ronald Gordon

All right, everybody, get closer to the fire, and I'll tell you about my experience with drugs in Istanbul. Now this was before the *Midnight Express* era, though on the other hand, this could be what caused it. One of the more fascinating things about traveling through Europe in '65 was seeing what the last country I had been in was now doing. Most of them were kicking out the beatniks, as we were still being called then. This was kind of amusing and, I'll admit, it filled me with a small bit of antiestablishment pride.

By the time I got to Istanbul, I had just begun to locate the drug scenes. In Italy, where I had met Tom, we talked about how much fun pot was, which we had both recently discovered. And that's as far as it went in Italy. In Yugoslavia we didn't even talk about it. In Turkey we finally found it. At least that's what the guy said, from whom we got it.

"It's kif." (Rhymes with thief, perhaps for a reason.)

"Oh," said we, who were previously only familiar with grass and hashish. "I guess that explains why it's green powder."

We smoked it. Well, we attempted to smoke it, on the ship that took us from Turkey to Israel. But we had no rolling papers. No, wait, we did! I rolled it in a ticket to the Pope's summer home. Something that's never failed to give me a small kick. Unlike the green powder. Well, maybe it was the fact that powder doesn't draw very well. Or maybe it's because Pope tickets don't make the best rolling paper.

Mace / Todd Miller

Someone says mace, the food seasoning, will do the trick. It's got to be French's mace, though, because that's the freshest. Four of us unhesitatingly agreed to take two full teaspoons of this sawdustlike powder, quickly followed by a glass of water to wash the stuff down. Then we sat and waited. Nothing. For about an hour and a half . . . nothing. Bored, three courageous souls went their separate ways while I manned the home front.

Two hours later, I started getting phone calls asking if I felt what the others felt—if I saw the funny bright lights they saw, heard the wobbly, nonsensical voices they heard—but especially they asked, from various unknown scattered points in the East Bay, how the hell to find their cars and how to get back to the commune. "No, no," they'd say. "You don't understand . . . I parked the car by the big tree . . . like the one on the UC campus where the stream goes by . . . you know, the one with diamonds glistening in it." I heard three similar stories within a half-hour, but since I didn't think they were humans talking to me, I quickly hung up. I guess a mace high sort of waits by your bloodstream and slowly hitchhikes its way to your brain.

Rug Cleaner / Mark Groubert

In the summer of 1969, I was a ripe fourteen years old and ready for further adventures at Levine's Bungalow Colony. My parents went off to Europe or something and left me in the care of my grandparents. I was very happy to get off of Long Island, let me tell you that.

Grandparents are just that. They're grand, but they are no longer parents. They've lost it. They've retired from the parenting business. They're two generations away from their grandchildren. It's kinda like a double generation gap. If you can get away with some things with your parents, you can get away with twice as much with your grandparents. To put me in their care for a summer was a complete mismatch. Now, my grandfather was no slouch. He was tough. Physically and socially, he seemed like a cross between Archie Bunker and James Cagney. But still, too much time had passed him by. Things were changing much too fast for him.

Just like millions of other adults, the long hair thing drove him crazy. No one could figure why the youth of America were lengthening their locks at such a lightning pace. They just couldn't figure it out. Why? It was a magical summer and why not? It had already been a magical year. The Jets led by Broadway Joe Willy Namath shocked the world by upsetting the Colts and winning the Super Bowl in January. In July, Neil

Armstrong was immortalized when he took one small step for man, one giant leap for mankind. For that, even we had to find a TV that could give us reception clear enough to see the first moon-walk. At the beginning of August, the Miracle Mets were starting their run at the National League pennant, that would culminate in October with a World Series victory over the Baltimore Orioles. Bad year for Baltimore all the way around.

This was all going on while the whole country raged over an atrocity called the Vietnam War—1969 was already turning out to be one helluva surreal summer. That was also the summer I met Shag. He was my first rock 'n' roll hero. He had long blond hair, kind of like Duane Allman, and dressed in tight white jeans, black cowboy boots, and usually a black cowboy shirt. He fronted a band called Shag and the Savage Reaction. I never saw them play and, come to think of it, I never met anyone in his band. But he did have a red hollow body Gibson guitar and an amp.

As far as I know, Shag, who must have been around seventeen, played only one song. It was "Hey, Joe," the Jimi Hendrix ballad that was popular at the time. I had never heard anyone perform on guitar and sing live. All my references for "real" rock stars came from records. To me Shag was soon to become a real rock star. He was a local guy from up there, raised around Monticello somewhere, which made him far more interesting than the summer transplants like myself.

Shag was also a drugstore cowboy, petty thief, and all-around criminal. His specialty was grave-robbing. He and his friends would look in the local paper for recently deceased citizens, and after they were buried, they would dig up the body and remove any and all jewelry that might have been left on the corpse. Usually rings and things. Shag would describe in matter-of-fact detail how, after digging in the night, they would uncover a body, notice rings on his or her fingers and try to remove them. Occasionally, this would entail having to remove fingers and things as well. It was all extremely fascinating to someone like myself. Not that I could ever do that, you understand, but just the thought of it was enough to give me nightmares for months.

The first drug I ever did was also supplied by Shag. Well, it wasn't actually a drug. More like a rug cleaner. Well, actually it was a rug cleaner. It was called Carbona. I think it was manufactured in the Bronx. At least that's where Shag said he got it. From a fat gay guy named Mitchell Budine. (Back then there where a lot of fat gay guys for some reason—today they're quite extinct.) The getting-high process involved rubbing the liquid substance on a T-shirt (which in our case substituted for a rug) and then bringing the shirt to your face and inhaling deeply and repeatedly. Slowly and surely. Deeper and deeper . . . oh, sorry. Carbona was all the rage in the Summer of '69.

Years later, with the help of *Please Kill Me* co-author Legs McNeil, I was to learn and hear that the BQE-bred punk group The Ramones recorded a super revved-up homage to their rug cleaner of choice entitled "Carbona, Not Glue." (The tune was censored by their own label and only exists on bootlegs.) Carbona was fast, cheap and effective. You didn't have to "cop" at a specialized toy store like you did with glue. Nah, there it was right in the household goods department of Grand Union, Waldbaum's, and the A&P. It was sandwiched between such old family favorites as Brillo, Comet, and Pine-Sol. No one was hip to Carbona—except maybe the marketing people at the company, who must have glared more than once at those unusual sales figures coming out of Mott Haven, Pelham, and the Van Courtland Park section of the Bronx.

Although I had nothing to compare it to, I can tell you that Carbona, when done right and frequently, would indeed alter your mood. The high was loopy, dopey, and kinda Ludey, if you know what I mean. I later graduated to airplane glue, which practitioners will tell you is a much different high altogether and must be inhaled from a paper bag to be thoroughly enjoyed. The glue high was more spacey. More light headed. Closer to the early copy-toner buzz we copped from the primitive duplicating machines in the school's administration office.

In retrospect, I guess Carbona was a "gateway inhalant." In the early '80s, head shop suppliers tried to capitalize on the earlier success of Carbona with commercial products named "Locker Room" and "Rush"—inhalants that, while well-intentioned and actually directed to the inhalant audience of America, couldn't come close to those early heady days in the summer of '69 when Carbona, however briefly and boldly, was the mood alterer of choice for the yet-to-be-named Pepsi Generation.

Dramamine / Jim Tranchida

Dramamine is a motion-sickness pill, and for some reason there was an urban legend circulating in the early 1970s in Elmhurst (a Chicago suburb) that it contained a fair amount of belladonna, which we regarded as an exotic psychoactive drug, even more potent, gothic, and alien than LSD.

The lowdown was that three packs of Dramamine (thirty-six tablets, no more, no less) would deliver enough belladonna for you to experience a genuine medieval trip. We had no fear of overdosing on anything in those days, yet very few of us ever took the Dramamine challenge. One of our club members, Swede, was the first we knew of who was willing to test the wild claims of the belladonna theorists.

His lone companions were Steve and me. We escorted him up to the local Walgreens, where he shoplifted the required amount of over-the-counter hallucinogen. Outside the store we watched as, without trepidation, Swede consumed three packages worth of Dramamine. Then we walked to the park where we sat and eagerly awaited the results of his experiment.

Swede grew tired of our persistent questioning: "How do you feel?" "Are you off yet?" "What's it like?" He also grew very silent, which was unusual for Swede, even when tripping. Eventually, he got restless enough to insist that Steve and I take a nice nighttime stroll with him through downtown Elmhurst. Perhaps he had grown hungry, because as we walked along, he would occasionally grab some leaves from nearby trees and chew contentedly on them.

When we got into town, an odd thing happened. Swede began walking on cars. Now, he was a shoplifter, and he would sometimes snatch a Mercedes hood ornament for the hell of it, but he did not engage in pointless acts of vandalism. Yet, as we walked down the brightly lit main street, not two blocks from a police station, Swede began treading on vehicles. He would hitch up a leg and take one giant step up onto the trunk of a car, proceed smoothly across the roof, then down onto the hood and out across to the trunk of the next car in line.

Steve and I pointed out that this was foolish activity and asked him to stop, but he wouldn't speak to us or heed our warnings, continuing calmly and silently across the rugged terrain of his own private landscape. Less than two blocks later (roughly, the distance of ten cars), a squad car squealed to a stop alongside of us, and we were busted.

Swede remained orderly in the face of the law, which was not normal behavior for him. During one police raid at the park just as he was beginning to eat a cheeseburger, it became apparent that the cops were going to bring him in on some charge or other. In a bold act of defiance before being taken away, he removed the slice of cheese from his burger and slapped it squarely down on the cop's shiny black shoe. This was forever after known as "the Cheeseburger Bust."

Now the two cops searched the three of us by the curbside. There were no drugs to be found. In fact, the only item of interest to the officers was my 99-cent plastic Bullwinkle wallet. "Trippy," I had thought to myself when buying it. The cops had a different opinion. "Hey, look at this," said one scornfully, as he held it up under his flashlight, sniggering. "Bullwinkle!" And they both snorted in derision.

Apparently, Swede had not done any property damage, but the cops, disappointed in the lack of contraband on our persons, decided to take him in anyway. Steve and I followed along to the station house about a block away and were allowed to wait in the lobby. Swede, the only real item of interest to them, was hauled away for a strip search and further questioning. He was gone about a half hour.

Swede's apparel included numerous roach-clip necklaces, many rings around his fingers, and a plastic skull dangling from his belt. The last image I have of that night is of Swede, confused and disheveled, coming down the stairs from the interrogation room, seemingly having just been searched and released. As he descended he was fumbling with the belt on his jeans, trying to fasten it, while his plastic skull dangled. And as he drew even with the receptionist behind the plate-glass window of the radio room, his fingers slipped and his pants dropped to his ankles, and the plastic skull clunked on the steps. Without skipping a beat, Swede hoisted them back up, and we all three disappeared back out into the night.

Kanemanol / Doug Bertrand

One of the more stupid things I've done was a substance called Kanemanol, that was supposedly half cocaine and half librium, but which I later found out was probably animal tranquilizer. Shortly after shooting up at a friend's house, and just barely being able to keep up a facade of normalcy in front of his parents, I left for home. On my way, I felt I needed some nourishment and stopped at a restaurant. Everything was fairly okay until I got my table. From that point on, I was in trouble. I had great difficulty selecting anything from the menu—more than usual, anyway. When the food arrived, I had trouble figuring out how to consume it. Knowing that I'd better get out of there fast, I got up and staggered to the cash register, leaning on tables and chairs for support. I handed my money to the cashier and hoped she would be kind enough to give me my correct change; I was in no shape to tell. Driving home, I felt most comfortable by taking a complex, mazelike route.

The next thing I knew, I was safe in my apartment, but I didn't know how I'd gotten there. I sat in a chair and read *Magick without Tears* by Aleister Crowley, but the words had a tendency to fly off the pages. It was nearly impossible to concentrate. An ash from the cigarette I was smoking fell like a slow, whistling bomb, and hit the page of the book with an audible crash that I "heard" with my eyes!

It scared me to be so stoned, and I wondered if this was to be a permanent condition. If so, how would I conduct my normal daily affairs? I was alarmed and didn't know what to do. I crawled into my bed and lay there searching for a solution. I went backward through my life, in vivid detail, until I reached approximately age two. Then I stopped. It occurred to me that what I was doing was trying to find a way out of my mess by delving into everything I knew or had ever experienced. The amazement I experienced then had a relaxing effect. I quit panicking and escaped into slumber land.

Comet / anonymous

One time I was at a party, and this dude got so messed up that he actually snorted a line of Comet cleanser. It made him kinda sick, and he said that the drainage sucked. But he didn't die, and he caught a killer rush.

DPT / Jeremy Davis

DPT—Dipropyltryptamine, an analog of DMT and psilocybin—is the sacrament of the Temple of the True Inner Light. Interestingly enough, the church has not run into the legal obstacles that face many psychedelic religions. They do ceremonies and rituals with impunity (as of yet). They use DPT freebase and smoke it on raspberry leaves from a hookah. DPT is euphoria, squared. The best comparison I can come up with would be 500 mics of LSD plus 250 mgs of MDMA.

A few weeks ago, I decided that it would be a nice day to go to the renaissance festival and experiment with the last of my supply of DPT. I'd had a few interesting experiences smoking it, but nothing totally world shattering. I had never snorted DPT, having read that the drip is very bad, but I figured that, with the last of the gram, I might as well go for the gusto.

I drove out to the park where the festival was (about a half hour from my house) around 8:30 a.m. (I'm an early riser—mornings are always so refreshing in Florida in February.) When I got there, I parked my car and pulled out a neuropsychopharmacology textbook (that I'd found in a thrift store for two dollars), my bottle with the remaining amount of DPT, and my driver's license.

I figure I had around 225 mg or so. I cut the amount into two equal lines on the book and snorted one and a quarter of the lines. Immediately I was hit by a sneezelike reflex. I can't accurately explain it, but it was intensely disgusting, and I almost blew the other 75 mg right off the book with the force of the reaction. Luckily, I didn't. I had some water that I started guzzling, and then I got out of the car. I grabbed my book bag and headed off for wonderland.

It took between fifteen and forty-five minutes to go from first alert to full immersion. During that time, and for the remainder of the trip, I had a feeling of toxicity, and I sensed the DPT was somehow eating away at the mucous linings in the back of my throat and nasal passages. I set up a tie-dye blanket by the shore of a beautiful park lake right in the middle of the magic of imagination floating by, with, and through the festival.

Once the DPT had fully hit me, the visuals exploded across my vision. Everything was moving, and all the energies and vibrations going on around me were plainly visible. Colors washed across everything, and I was reminded of the most beautiful and transcendent moment of a high-dose mushroom trip. I was swimming in a sea of beauty that was the same as, but so much infinitely more than, me. I was a brush stroke on God's canvas, small but absolutely existent. I knew that everything in the world was moving exactly as it should, that everything was a thread in the fabric of reality that all things from the past flow through and all things of the future flow into.

All of a sudden, I closed my eyes and got a vision of a simple lavender and silver image that twisted gracefully in the breezes of my mind. As this image came to me, I got this overwhelming feeling of riding a cresting technicolor wave. When people talk about fan-

tastic, terrific, earth-shattering sex, they use images of fireworks and symphonies playing . . . . I had the most unbelievable, crowning sensual experience of my entire life.

I heard every instrument in the orchestra singing with all the might of the heavens in
praise of all that is beautiful and good. There was nothing but fireworks exploding before
my eyes, and what can only be called a cosmic psychedelic orgasm flowed from within
me, out every pore in my skin and from every part of my body, out and back into the
cosmos.

During this sequence, an image of Susie and me appeared. We had broken up about
a month before, but were still friendly. I hadn't really thought much about us as an item
for a couple of weeks, and I didn't recognize that I had any really deeper feeling for her.
For Susie to manifest as the image of the Divine Beauty in my vision was very surpris-
ing. And after the initial orgasm (still only a figure of speech), all of sudden I was tired,
just like it is for me in sex, and I felt as if I would go to sleep for a moment.

Suddenly, another wave of the DPT intoxication crashed over my consciousness, and
I was swept into reverie about Susie and me. I saw all kinds of beauty in the future for
us and was quite frankly very surprised at the intensity of my feelings for her. As I was
thinking about her, someone left a message on my voicemail, so I couldn't tell who it
was from my pager, so I decided to go to my car to get thirty-five cents to call my voice
mail and check my message. I had a dollar in my pocket that I could've changed to use
the phone, but I didn't really want to talk to anyone just yet; I still felt kind of vulnerable from such an opening experience. Besides, I knew that it would be a fun mission
to the car and back.

As I walked through the festival, I saw all kinds of weird and cool things. Everyone
was in costume dressed in renaissance clothes, talking in funny fake accents and generally having fun. Everywhere I looked were smiling faces and a cacophony of floating
sounds. A big red troll popped out of nowhere and scared a lady on my right. A troupe
of teenaged girls were dressed in fairy costumes, painted head to toe in glitter, fairy
wings, and mischief.

On the way, I passed an entrance guarded by a woman dressed as an archetypal Mother
(Gaia, Enchantress, Sorceress, The Fates). She told me it was one dollar to enter the
enchanted forest. Hey, I just couldn't wait! I came upon a small gathering of faerie folk
who gave me a handful of faerie dust (glitter). I also ran into a dragon and—well, it's
been a couple of weeks, I kinda forget what else I saw. As I walked the main road to the
front gate, I heard people saying, "Look at the faerie dust! Look at the faerie dust!" I
looked down, and the ground was covered in what seemed at the time to truly be faerie
dust. The earth was dressed in jewels that couldn't contain their own beauty. The
ground sparkled and shone with all the intensity of a million rainbows and radiated
warmth, energy, and love.

Eventually I reached the front gate, got my hand stamped for reentry, and walked outside. I packed a bowl of some glowing, crystallized, kind buds and went for a walk.

Usually, I would probably have been smoking more, but the festival had a lot of kids, and it just wouldn't have been totally cool to light up inside the event. The festival didn't take up the whole park—it was actually a very large park—and I went for a walk on a nearby trail. I thought more about Susie and what just occurred, and wondered about the significance of the two being juxtaposed.

Soon I remembered that I was on a mission and started back in the direction of my car. When I got in and sat down, it felt sooooooooooo good that I thought I might spend the rest of the day right there. Sooner or later I got myself up and headed back to the festival to check my message from the nearest pay phone. As I walked back in, I could hear bells playing a beautiful melody. I turned a corner and came upon a giant instrument made of huge bells, declining in size and hung in order. It was played like a piano, with keys that caused the bells to ring. It was being played by a guy dressed all in black robes and a black hood over his face. The melodies were haunting and eerily beautiful. I was totally enraptured.

As I was walking to the phone, I passed a jewelry maker's shop and saw a necklace that I had once owned a copy of. It was just a silver key with a heart at the top hung from a black nylon cord. My old one, was really, really, really important to me, but alas, on the wings of reality all things doth fly and no longer was the key to be mine. But here it was again, miraculously, right in front of me. I searched through my pockets and came up with six dollars. I grabbed the necklace from the rack and brought it to the guy who owned the shop. I said, "Will six dollars be enough for this trinket?" He looked at me, looked at the necklace, and said, "No." So I put the necklace back and went on to find the phone. I called my voicemail, and it was Susie, of all people . . . smiles . . . I wandered around for an hour or so until it was time for another excursion outside the front gates to reexplore the kind buds' effects.

The herb complemented the DPT nicely and created a good introspective frame of mind to relax in after all the day's events. I was able to put a lot of thought into the situation between Susie and me. It manifested itself as a major, and what I consider the most important, part of the trip, as it led to the reestablishment of a relationship that I hadn't seen anything in. It revealed a secret magic to me that I hadn't even known existed. Sometimes the greatest good and the most beautiful things exist behind guarded and hidden realities. I actually feel that the DPT was in effect a supreme therapy, opening closed doors in my psyche and clearing away emotional mildew that was building up for who knows how long. After a long walk through the forest and my "breath of fresh air," I went back to the festival.

I was determined to get the jewelry maker's business card, so that I could get the necklace at a later date. I wasn't ready to let it slip so easily through my fingers. I went back to the shop, and there was another man working the booth, a younger man. I grabbed the necklace from its place and approached the new guy. "Will six dollars be enough for this trinket?" I asked, hopefully.

"Uh, yeah, that's cool," he said . . . smiles again . . . so now I had found my lost key. I felt a renewed wholeness of self.

Eventually I wandered off and made my way back home. First, though, I called a friend and invited him to come sample the last 75 mg of DPT if he wanted. He also reported having a very significant experience. He threw up. (I had felt a passing nausea but never regurgitated.) He said that it felt like everything toxic from his whole life came flowing out of his body in the, well, vomit. But his story, is his story, and that's a whole 'nother story. The feeling of toxicity that pervaded much of the experience makes me extremely reluctant to try it again.

2-TC-2 / S. Rogan

It's kinda like Ecstasy, kinda like acid, but not as intense as either," Martin says, pulling out a small vial from the nightstand. "It doesn't mess with your serotonin levels so you won't feel like shit tomorrow."

"What is it?" I ask, shaking fine white powder that could be anything.

"2-TC-2."

"Never heard of it."

"Doesn't really have a catchy street name."

"How much does it cost?"

"Don't worry, you can afford it."

"It's been a while since I've done anything like this."

"Perfect. Welcome back."

He measures out 11 mg in a glass of water. I gulp the slightly bitter liquid down and remember a junior detective novel in which bitter almonds figured prominently. Cyanide smells like bitter almonds, and I wish my brain didn't make such bizarre automatic associations.

Twin Peaks is in the VCR, and we settle on the couch until sepia tones overshadow Leland Palmer's face. The waiting is hardest. Anticipation always is. Martin rubs his fingernails over mine, blackberry nail polish swirling with periwinkle glitter in a glampunk cosmetic tie dye. His cats are asleep and lavender escapes from the curtains. We look at each other unblinking through the diluted haze of blank candlelight and pharmaceutical auras.

"I'm so glad you're here."

"Me too. Right now."

"I'll get tired of you someday. But not for a long time."

"Someday doesn't matter. What about now?"

He pulls out a bottle of Astroglide. It doesn't hurt. Actually, it's quite pleasant. It doesn't feel like a man on top inside me, just warm pressure radiating throughout my body, the heavy warmth right before a sleeping foot mutates into pins and needles.

"My God, what did gay men do before silicon lubricants and synthetic drugs? I can't imagine doing this with only Vaseline and poppers. The '80s just seem so archaic. Where do we have to be tomorrow?"

"Nowhere. Welcome back."

Nitrous Oxide / Kent Manthie

When I was eighteen and just out of high school, I was starting what would be my party animal phase, which eventually tapered off about four or five years later.

By the age of eighteen, I had already been into all of the usual vices available to someone my age: marijuana, acid, mushrooms, coke, and beer—lots of beer!

Then, what must've seemed like an epiphany to me at the time, an old high school buddy (who, I guess because he couldn't handle the awful pain and heartache of growing up, hanged himself a few years ago) came up with a new scheme for getting high: nitrous oxide—N_2O, laughing gas, whippets. Remember sucking all the gas out of those seltzer-water cartridges? Or sucking dry those Redi-Whip bottles? Well, that was nothing compared to what he had conjured up.

This was the plan: my friend, Chris, somehow was able to convince this auto-supply store in St. Paul (I lived in Minneapolis) that he was a racer of nitrous-powered dune buggies, and I think he even had the forged papers to prove it. Anyway, they asked a minimum of questions and, next thing we knew, we were racing, all right. Our brains were going about 150 mph!

Well, even though we were out of high school, some of us had day jobs and others went to school, so we couldn't be partying every single night. So it was usually on the weekends or the occasional midweek party. But basically, wherever there was a party, you could count on Chris being there. What we would do is, after getting the tanks, we would buy a bag of jumbo balloons. Then at the party we'd just fill up the balloons with the laughing gas the way you'd fill up a balloon with helium. Basically, if you've ever been to one of the later Grateful Dead shows, then you know what I'm talking about, as they were big sellers there (about two or three dollars would get you a huge-sized full balloon that would give you around six blasts).

Talk about a rush! It was a fabulous feeling. Not the kind of rush you'd get from doing poppers, which give you a headache, but almost an out-of-body experience. Everything went into slow motion, and we could see what we were doing. It's hard to explain in detail—you just have to experience it—but it is very intense.

Of course, it wasn't long before capitalism took over this enterprise, as it usually does most enterprises. Meaning, the first circle of friends we were doing this with were okay, but as the crowd got to be more and more, then with all the demand for it the money idea came over Chris—and you can't blame him entirely—it did cost money to fill those things up, and well, he had to pay for it somehow. But at least he did take care of his real friends.

After a while, we started taking it for granted. We always showed up at a party expecting Chris to be there with a couple of tanks full. And, of course, we had to experiment. I can't remember all the combinations we tried, but the one I remember the most was taking a big blast of nitrous oxide while on LSD—that was a real rush! Wow! I felt like I was zooming into outer space, and it was almost as good as the real thing. Then, when I came down for the descent back to earth, it was a nice, gentle float back to the ground; like landing in a field of daisies. Not a free-fall screaming back to reality, but a very smooth ride indeed.

Unfortunately, as most good things do, this too came to an end. After almost two years, the proprietors of the auto-racing supply shop started getting a little suspicious. Although Chris did have some sort of documentation stating that he had the authority to buy tanks of nitrous oxide for his racing hobby, they finally cut him off for good. Now, I'm not sure why he was cut off—whether it was because of their suspicions or beacuse of external pressure from the authorities, some oversight committee, industry watchdog, or plain ol' flatfoot cops. But somehow it all came to a screeching halt.

But to tell you the truth, I wasn't really that brokenhearted. In fact, if he hadn't gotten cut off when he did, I probably would've gotten sick of it pretty soon anyway. It's not like taking LSD or mushrooms or even a phenobarbitol or quaalude—you don't get high for very long, if at all—you just get a nice head rush that is the most intense head rush available.

I would definitely recommend nitrous for someone who hasn't tried it before, but don't end up like my friend Chris did. Who knows why he killed himself? He had definite issues—a bipolar disorder for one and possibly schizophrenia to boot. I know that he had been in and out of institutions a few times during his short life. But he was still a decent guy. A little psycho, but wouldn't you have to be to go through what he did just to get access to laughing gas?

MDA, Nitrous, and Quaaludes / Paul Krassner

Robert Anton Wilson, in his book *Sex and Drugs: A Journey beyond Limits*, writes that "The 'experts' are forbidden to do research in this area, while those who have done the research are criminals and, hence, regarded as untrustworthy—yet they must know things that the experts do not, since they have had the experience."

Since I have long been just such an untrustworthy criminal, allow me now to share with you a few excerpts from an unscientific survey of my own experiences in combining sex with psychoactives.

1. MDA was a synthetic drug, manufactured in Canada. I had tried it a few times. It felt like a combination of mescaline and amphetamine, acting as an extraordinary energizer and, if you were with the right person, as a powerful aphrodisiac.

One time I took it with my girlfriend. We were supposed to go out for dinner with another couple, but the MDA was so overwhelming, we stayed home instead, screwing our asses off on the kitchen table. Why the kitchen table? Because it was there.

2. I completely forgot about this until an ex-girlfriend reminded me of the time she had obtained a tank of nitrous oxide. I had previously taken nitrous at my dentist's office, where along with the numbness of novocaine it acted as a pleasant painkiller. But instead of dental work, my girlfriend suggested performing fellatio on me while I breathed the nitrous from a tube attached to the nozzle of the tank.

It was a terrific sexual experience, although my orgasm was accompanied by an explosion of utter hysteria as I savored the preposterous image of my penis being sucked by my girlfriend while I was simultaneously sucking a rubber tube. They don't call it laughing gas for nothing.

The next time I went to the dentist, I started thinking about this incident, and while a cavity in my tooth was being filled, to my surprise, I got an inadvertent erection.

3. I had sequential affairs with two young women who were friends with each other as well as with me. One night at a party, they decided that we three should go home, take quaaludes, and have ourselves a delightful little orgy. I was bursting with anticipation as my fantasy began to become a reality.

The three of us undressed partially and got into bed as the quaaludes began to take effect.

And that was the last thing I remembered. We had all fallen asleep. In the morning we had appointments to keep. But I would not forget this, and I remain haunted by an awareness that nothing happened . . . unlike my having forgotten the nitrous-oxide incident.

And the moral of this story is: Sometimes a blow job is not as memorable as a blown opportunity.

Heroin / Preston Peet

There isn't anyone out anywhere. Thomas has been to all the spots. The Green Man pub, the bus stop, the old shabby apartment he'd been taken to on one occasion—there isn't anyone or any dope, anywhere. But as he's heading back home, he remembers one more stop he can make, one of the Jamaican dealers he'd hoped to find on the street, who happens to live just blocks from the squat where Thomas is living, halfway between the Kennington tube station and the squat. Though he doesn't expect to catch him there, he decides it can't hurt to try.

Ringing the bell gets an answer fast. The dealer's girlfriend lets him up with hardly a word through the intercom; just a "Who's that," a click of the door, and he's in and climbing the stairs. He's sick, and the lack of dope makes him feel exhausted, worn out, making the climb more difficult than it should be, especially since fresh out of the tube from busking, he has his guitar with him. The door is open when he arrives, but he finds her alone.

"He'll be right back, he just went to pick up," she tells him. "Have a seat."

He rests his caseless guitar against the arm of the sofa and sits, making small talk, trying to ignore the nausea he feels, not wanting to throw up on the living-room floor in front of his hostess, who is being very nice. She gives him a glass of water and, seeing how ill he appears, offers him some of her filters, the now-dried bits of cotton she's been drawing her gear through when she cooks up a shot in her spoon. He's about to accept, when the dealer arrives.

"Check this out," the dealer tells the two of them as he opens up a packet of white, floury powder. "China White, totally fantastic stuff." His own eyes are already pinpoints, almost no pupil whatsoever. "Don't need lemon, don't need heat; just put it in the spoon, stir, and stick it right in your bloody vein," he says, giving them both a wicked grin.

Just looking at it sitting there, at least a quarter ounce of dope, as sick as he feels, makes him break into a sweat, and he wants to yell at the guy, "Hurry the fuck up," but it doesn't pay to yell at one's dealer, so he bites his lip and waits. It doesn't take the dealer long to measure Thomas out twenty quid's worth of dope, two-tenths of a gram, weighing it on his triple-beam scale right in front of him, which Thomas really appreciates, as most pushers sell their shit prewrapped so one never knows exactly what, or how much, one might be buying.

"Could you put half of it in a paper for me, and give me the other half to do now please?"

The dealer agrees and hands him one half wrapped and folded closed in a square of paper, the other half in an open square, and a spoon with his other hand. Thomas wastes no time. Sitting back down on the sofa, he pulls the glass of water the dealer's girlfriend had given him closer. He puts the spoon down and pours the dope in. Next comes his water, and sure enough, the dealer wasn't lying. As soon as the water hits the dope, it begins to melt, breaking down immediately. Usually, he has to squeeze a couple drops of lemon juice into it and cook it to break the dope down, to get it to mix with the water and get him high. This is very different.

He's only done China White, real China White, once or twice before, and never in his arm, only up his nose, or smoking it—"chasing the dragon." His mouth is watering as he draws it up into his rig, getting every drop, wiping the bit of cigarette filter around and around in the spoon, soaking up every bit of moisture, then pushing the needle's tip sideways down onto the cotton he draws the last bit of fluid into the rig, watching the filter turn white as the fluid leaves it, becoming bone dry. "Oy, watch it with that stuff, it's really, really fucking good. I'm telling you, mate, careful." The dealer is watching Thomas as he finishes tying off above his elbow, tapping his arm to get the vein to rise. "Put it in slow."

Thomas concentrates as he finds the vein and registers, a ribbon of bright red blood twirling and swirling up into the clear plastic tube, clearly visible in the solution inside, then he shoves the plunger, forcing it all in. Never one to tarry once prepared, he has to go all the way, as fast as he can, every time. Takes a lot to kill the pain he carries inside. Then he hears what the dealer said, at the exact same moment he smiles. "Holy shit, this is good," he just manages to slur before he falls back, toward the back of the sofa, into another place, never feeling himself land.

Instead he finds himself outside walking along the sidewalk with no idea what time it is or where he is exactly; he only knows that he is no longer sitting in the living room at his dealer's. The traffic is sparse, but loud, unnaturally so. His mouth tastes funny, both dry and sticky at the same time, with an overabundance of thick saliva. Thomas begins to feel like he can't get his breath around the mouthful of spit, so he puckers up his lips, leans forward, and spits it all out in front of himself, onto the carpet at his dealer's feet.

That isn't what brings him back. Although his brain is trying to tell him there isn't something quite right about what he's just done, it is not his own awareness that brings him to, but rather the disbelieving guffaw, the laughter and cry of "Jesus Christ, man, you are fucked up!" He opens his already open eyes, and the picture shifts in front of him, the street losing focus and the living room almost instantaneously, but not quite, replacing it, with the dealer's white-toothed smile and outstretched rag to clean up the spit on the floor looming before him.

"Don't tell me I just spit . . . ," he trails off. It's obvious he did, that he just spit a huge gob right at the feet of his dealer, in the middle of his dealer's living-room floor. Thomas almost feels humiliated, but the dealer and his girlfriend seem to be handling it okay, more glad he is still alive and not overdosed on their sofa than angry for his spitting on their carpet. Plus he is so stoned it'd be very hard to really feel much of anything, much less shame. He manages to clean it up, now that he is awake again, but he is utterly wiped out.

Before he'd felt tired and drained, now he feels completely removed from any sort of care about anything, and feels no pain, none at all, physical, or mental. His cramping muscles have relaxed, his stomach is no longer heaving, and he is feeling a warm soft glow all over, almost like a huge comforting hand holding him close. After he gets the spit off the floor, he takes the other envelope of dope and puts it deep in a pocket of his shirt, under his sweater and jacket, then heads back out into the cold mid-November London air, his bag and guitar over his shoulder. As he heads toward the squat, he remembers that Emma is always on the lookout and lives only blocks from the dealer's house as well, just like himself. She'll be really mad if he tells her about this dope later, if he doesn't try to let her know now that it is around. The dealer already told him he won't be able to get it for long either, so Thomas stops at the first phone box he sees.

Getting into the thing causes him some problems at first, as he pulls the door open right into his face, almost knocking himself out, hitting his forehead on the door. He finally gets in after a brief argument with the uncooperative door, puts down the guitar, and picks up the phone. Placing the receiver against his ear, Thomas lifts a coin towards the coin slot.

"Hey, wake up, mate. You all right?" Thomas opens his eyes. He is in the phone box still, but on the ground, under the phone, the receiver dangling over his head. "What'd you take?" Crouching down over him, wearing one of the tall, silly-looking, dome-shaped Bobby hats, is a London officer of the law, a cop. Thomas struggles to wake up. What in the hell happened, he wonders silently to himself. He doesn't remember a thing, except getting ready to put the coin into the phone, and now there's this cop he's got to deal with. Gotta think fast.

"Uh, I didn't take anything. I'm just really tired. I spent the night with a friend and haven't slept in two days. Just fell asleep," Thomas tells him, trying to get a grip on the shelf above his head to pull himself erect. It isn't easy. He feels way off balance trying to explain the situation to this cop while sitting on his ass on the floor of the phone box. The cop gives him a hand up, looking straight into his extremely pinned eyeballs.

An old girlfriend once told him not to come into the bar where she worked in Rotterdam due to the fact that his eyes look "like fucking billboards" when he's on dope, advertising for all the world, "Hi, I'm on heroin." It's no different now in front of this cop, but for some reason the cop doesn't tell him he knows that Thomas is lying, though it is obvious to Thomas, even as fucked up as he is, that the cop knows. While Thomas is helped to his feet, a second cop is going through his shoulder-bag, and finds two rigs, one brand new one and one that's open and floating around inside his bag without a cap over the tip. Good thing the cop didn't stab himself. No cop is ever friendly after that. "What's this then?" The cop holds out both needles in his hand, the plastic-wrapped and the open-tipped, out in front of the three of them standing there facing one another on the late-afternoon sidewalk.

"Uh, those are a friend's. She gave them to me last night to hold, and I forgot to give them back to her this morning," he lamely tries to explain. The cops just stare at him without a word for a moment. Thomas is upright, but his eyelids are only barely the same. He valiantly forces them to remain open, and the cops sense this, it seems, and decide to take pity on him. There is no other explanation for what they do next. "All right, you can go. Go on, get out of here, go home." The cop stuffs the rigs back into the bag and hands the bag to Thomas, who is stunned motionless at first. "What?" he stammers at the cops, who repeat, "Go on, that's it. You sure you're okay, right?" The cops stare at him some more. "Sure." Thomas takes the hint. Picking up his guitar, he crosses the street right away, and walks to his squat, just another block up the sidewalk.

He only manages to get into one of the big ripped-up easy chairs in the living room in front of the fireplace in the big, ramshackle Victorian building he's squatting in with friends. The fire passes shadows flickering over his face, he passes out again, out to the world, lucky to be alive, but completely unaware at that moment of the fact.

Datura / Heather Ripley

It was at the Rainbow Gathering at Knockengorroch, Scotland, in 1997. I had been smoking datura most of the day before, as most other drugs had run out, and we'd spent a week three miles off-road at the Clannach up a mountain in a bog in the pouring rain with a bunch of upper-middle-class wankers, and finally made it back from the Clannach to the relative sanity of my trailer at the base camp where most sensible people had stayed all week. Lillian and I had been playing wicked Irish trad with a mean fiddler, and we unknowingly drank large quantities of fly agaric tea supplied by Geoff.

Lillian began a haunting ballad to the Goddess, giving it full volume with a voice that can make mountains tremble, and I, with no inferior vocal capacity, joined in, in harmony. I remember as we reached crescendo, dancing and playing bodhran, leaping over the flames, and feeling when we finished that this was as best a finale to the evening as ought to be delivered. Then I lay down on top of my wax coat by the fire and closed my eyes, having given Lillian a hug and said goodnight, while the fiddler continued playing, which lulled me to sleep.

Next thing I knew, I awoke in thick mist by the fire beside Geoff. Geoff was not actually there when I woke up; he'd gone back to his van after making the tea, before it had even been passed around. Although he was a part of my experience, he did not, in fact, have anything whatsoever to do with it. Neither did the tea, I think.

I was unable to see much more than a few feet. My right arm was almost hacked in two, a wound I remembered that I had suffered at the Clannach, up the mountain, where Geoff and I and a couple of others had been involved in a bloody battle we were lucky to escape from, running three miles or so for our lives, the night before.

I was a man. It was at the time of the highland clearances, I was dressed in a plaid, and we had returned to our family and clansmen late the previous evening to find that the Cambells had slaughtered every man, woman, and child at the Clannach. Our entire family—wives, children, grandparents—all had been slain. My first realization on regaining consciousness was an indescribable and unbearable pain as I realized what had happened.

Insane with grief and demented, I headed for the river to either drown myself or bathe my arm, the forearm of which was hanging by a piece of swollen sinew and was already turning black, the bone shattered by a claymore. I found it incomprehensible that a clan of my own race had committed this atrocity. I stumbled down the bank, past the horse-drawn wagon and Bramble the Lurcher guarding Jon's fire pit.

At this point, I began to gain a sense that there was a large camp of some description farther on, but as a strange, unnatural shape loomed before me, I was gripped by the kind of awe and fear that one could only imagine one would experience coming across a spaceship. It was a car, but I had never seen a car ever before and had no idea what it was. Something in my rational mind was whirring like a hard drive installing a program, and my mind was like a computer searching for a file it knew was somewhere on disc.

I somehow knew which direction to stumble in and, as I continued through the mist, climbing over a familiar dry stone dike and through the trees, I found my trailer. It was still an object I had never seen before, but something told me how to gain access through this strange door made of a material I didn't recognize, and when I entered, there were my sleeping children, not the cold butchered bodies I remembered finding the night before in my blackhouse, but warm, breathing, alive—not cold and dead corpses, just live, grumpy, sleeping wains.

I fell onto the bed hugging them and sobbing, "Thank God, thank God, I thought you were dead, are you all right, I thought you were dead, oh my God, my weans"—until they told me to fuck off and shut up a few times, then consoled me, assuring me I was drunk, that I'd had a nightmare and ought to go to sleep, as everything was fine, and I should stop taking weird drugs and get a grip.

Sean had come in very late the previous night, a night after smoking datura all day, crying and terrified, gibbering on about Egypt. I had been half asleep and got up and put him to bed, assuring him he was okay. The next day he didn't want to talk about it, but realizing that I was experiencing something very similar to his experience the previous night, he got up and made me a whiskey coffee, rolled me a joint, and seemed relieved that it must have been the datura, which evidently takes twelve hours or more to send you into a previous existence.

When I woke much later that afternoon, I realized I was damp around the crotch and thighs. I was wearing leathers, which seemed to be dry outside, and the bed was dry, so evidently I hadn't lain on anything wet. I stripped off to discover to my horror and disgust that my pants and leggings were soaked in piss. I went down to the river to wash, and on returning past the same dike I'd clambered over the night before, I suddenly had a flashback where I clearly remembered stopping to take my penis out from under my plaid to pee the night before.

This memory was so clear that I could remember in exact detail the colors and pattern of my plaid as I cast it aside, and the size of my member—even the part of the wall I'd pissed on, and the relief of midstream combined with the images of the night before I'd experienced while pissing (wondering if the camp I sensed ahead was ours or the Cambells). I have no memory whatsoever, and my mother will testify, I never once in my life pissed my pants before, even as a child.

No matter what stage of inebriation I have ever been in, none has caused me to lose control of my bladder—I just have that control—so it was a confirmation to me that the experience of being a man at that time was much, much more real than anything I have ever experienced before. I have taken loads and loads of acid, from age fourteen, massive amounts of mushrooms, done "regressions" into previous lives, hypnotherapy, you name any altered state possible. This was different!

I really went back to a previous life. I know I did—I knew everything about my family and clan and history; I was that man, I had lived that life. I went to the guy who owned the land, as I knew he knew the history of the Clannach, and he told me the slaughter had happened—before I told him why I wanted to know what happened up there.

It could be I was temporarily possessed by a ghost who had experienced this—that these weren't my memories but someone else's—but the experience was much more real than simply a trip. I relived a part of history and can still remember to this day what it felt like. The memory will never leave me. Memories of amazing hallucinogenic trips have faded or gone completely, but that memory is as vivid now as it was the day after.

Flagyl / Rodenta D'Amore

All right, I will confess to having been part of what was surely one of the stupidest attempts to get high ever made. Persuaded by a friend we called Dr. Bill, a whole group of us one night tried to smoke Flagyl. Flagyl is a medicine prescribed for vaginal infections; it comes in the form of a white pill, and taking it orally has never made anyone high.

Most of the women present knew this from experience, and their significant others would have known it too, but that didn't really occur to us at the time. Dr. Bill said it would get us high, so we set about grinding up all the Flagyl we could find. I think we made several different attempts to smoke it in a pipe, mix it with grass, and roll it in a joint. Perhaps some hardy soul even tried to snort it. It was horrible, of course. I don't think Dr. Bill took even the teeniest toke.

Over time, friends and I had responded to rumors and reports of novel, cheaper, and more legal ways to achieve an altered state by smoking virtually every herb in the spice rack, eating countless heads of lettuce, chewing on tough morning glory seeds, swallowing nutmeg, and, yes, when Donovan sang "E-lec-trical banana," we scraped the white part from banana skins, dried it in the oven, and tried to smoke that too.

We also enclosed ourselves in sensory deprivation chambers, listened to oscillating tones through earphones, placed little pyramidal grids under the bed, stared at strobe lights without blinking, and listened to the sound of silence in earphones.

That we were, for the most part, all well educated, reasonably intelligent human beings, seems hard to believe. I think you'd have to have been there. The only explanation I can offer is that it is an intrinsic part of human nature to seek changes of consciousness.

The first time a group of friends and I attempted to get high, I was in third or fourth grade, and we hyperventilated in the parking lot of our grade school at recess. The technique was to breathe in and out really fast, while your friend stood behind you ready to squeeze the breath out of you on the count of ten. Everyone took turns being the squeezer and the squeezee.

Hashish / Paul Krassner

I was fortunate enough to be there with a bunch of Merry Pranksters when the Grateful Dead performed in Egypt in 1978. The Dead were scheduled to play on three successive nights at an open-air theater in front of the Pyramids, with the Sphinx keeping watch. Bob Weir looked up at the Great Pyramid and cried out, "What is it!" Actually, it was the place for locals to go on a cheap date. The pyramids were surrounded by moats of discarded bottlecaps.

A bootleg tape of Dean Martin and Jerry Lewis doing filthy schtick served as a preliminary sound check. Later, an American general complained to stage manager Steve Parish that the decadence of a rock 'n' roll band performing here was a sacrilege to 5,000 years of history. Parish said, "I lost two brothers in 'Nam, and I don't wanna hear this crap." The general retreated in the face of those imaginary brothers.

But there were a couple of real injured veterans.

Bill Kreutzmann had fallen off a horse and broken his arm, but he would still be play-ing with the band, with a single drumstick, or, as an Arabian fortune cookie might point out, "In the land of the limbless, a one-armed drummer is king."

Basketball star and faithful Deadhead Bill Walton's buttocks had been used as a pin-cushion by the Portland Trailblazers so that he could continue to perform on court even though the bones of his foot were being shattered with pain he couldn't feel. Having been injected with painkilling drugs to hide the owners' greed rather than to heal his injury, he now had to walk around with crutches and one foot in a cast under his extra-long galabia.

Maybe Kreutzmann and Walton could team up and enter the half-upside-down sack-race event.

One afternoon, Mountain Girl, Goldie Rush, and I decided to score some hashish at a courtyard in the oldest section of Cairo. It came in long thick slabs, and we eagerly sat down on benches to sample it. The official task of a teenage boy was to light the "hubbly-bubbly," a giant water pipe which used hot coals to keep the hash burning. He circled the area to honor the locals' toking privilege, and in lieu of a tip, he took several hits himself.

The custom was to blend the hash with tobacco, but never having been a smoker of cigarettes, I opted to smoke the hash straight. It left me extremely dizzy and sweating profusely. To the Egyptians, *not* cutting the hash with tobacco was considered to be a blatant waste. Nevertheless, disclosing a streak of competitive machismo, they followed my lead, resulting in severe fits of coughing, then laughing at their own coughing, until they managed to get it under control.

When we departed, it was with a certain sense of paranoia. The alleys seemed espe-cially sinister, with Arabs whispering to each other as they stared suspiciously at us while we walked gingerly past them. Maybe they simply weren't used to seeing a guy with two women—and Goldie was a blonde—who were not covered from head to toe by the tra-ditional chador with only their eyes showing.

The night of the first concert was permeated by an air of incredible excitement. Never had the Dead been so inspired. Backstage, Jerry Garcia was passing along final instruc-tions to the band: "Remember, play in tune." The music began with Egyptian oudist Hamza El-Din, backed up by a group tapping out ancient rhythms on their pizza-sized sitars, soon joined by Mickey Hart, a butterfly with drumsticks. Then Garcia ambled on with a gentle guitar riff, then the rest of the band, and as the Dead meshed with the percussion ensemble, basking in total mutual respect, Weir suddenly segued into the forceful beginning of Buddy Holly's "Not Fade Away."

"Did you see that?" Ken Kesey shouted. "The Sphinx's jaw just dropped."

Every morning, my roommate, George Walker, climbed to the top of the pyramid. He was in training. It would be his honor to plant a Grateful Dead skull-and-lightning-bolt flag on top of the Great Pyramid. This was our Iwo Jima.

In preparation for the final concert, I was sitting in the tublike sarcophagus at the center of gravity in the Great Pyramid, having smoked hashish in my hotel room and ingesting LSD that a Prankster had smuggled into Egypt in a plastic Visine bottle. I had heard that the sound of the universe was D-flat, so that's the note I chanted. It was only as I breathed in deeply before each extended Om that I was forced to ponder the mystery of those who urinate there.

I had a strong feeling that I was involved in some kind of lesson. It was as though the secret of the Dead would finally be revealed to me, if only I paid proper attention. There was a full eclipse of the moon, and Egyptian kids were running through the streets, shaking tin cans filled with rocks in order to bring it back.

"It's okay," I assured them. "The Grateful Dead will bring back the moon."

And, sure enough, a rousing rendition of "Ramble On, Rose" would accomplish that feat. The moon returned just as the marijuana cookie that rock impresario Bill Graham gave me started blending in with the other drugs. In America, Graham used to wear two wristwatches, one for each coast. Now he wore one wristwatch with two faces.

This was a totally outrageous event. The line between incongruity and appropriateness had disappeared along with the moon. The music was so powerful that the only way to respond was by surrendering to it. When the Dead played "Fire On the Mountain," I danced my ass off with all the others on that outdoor stage as if I had no choice. Ordinarily, I belonged to a vast army of secret dancers who only dance when they're alone.

The next day, a dozen of us had a farewell party on a felucca, an ancient, roundish boat, a sort of covered wagon that floats along the river. Garcia was carrying his attache case, just in case he suddenly got any new song ideas. There were three guides who came with our rented felucca: an old man whose skin was like corrugated leather, a younger man who was his assistant, and, of course, a kid whose job was to light the hubbly-bubbly.

We were all completely zonked out of our minds in the middle of the Nile. The Egyptians kept us stoned on hash, and we in turn gave them acid. The old man mumbled something—our translator explained, "He says he's seeing strange things"—and the old man gave me the handle of the rudder to steer, which I was able to do despite, or maybe because of, my stupor. The felucca was a vehicle for our cultural exchange.

"You know," Bill Graham confessed, "last night was the first time I ever danced in public."

"Me too," I replied.

That was the lesson.

Mouse Turds / Paul Krassner

When my daughter Holly was eleven years old, she decided to come stay with me in San Francisco for a whole year. This was a courageous move for her— a new city, a new school, new friends. Our apartment was halfway up a long, steep hill, and in the back was what Holly called "our magic garden." States Street was just off the intersection of Castro and Market—the heart of the gay ghetto—and there was a Chinese laundry at the foot of the hill called the Gay Launderette, which, even though it had changed owners several times, always kept that name. There was a clothing store named Does Your Mother Know? a bulletin board announcing an "Anal Awareness and Relaxation Workshop," and gays told jokes about themselves, like, "Why do the Castro clones all have mustaches?" And the answer was, "To hide the stretch marks."

I met Harvey Milk and watched him develop into the gay equivalent of Martin Luther King. Had former cop Dan White not assassinated him—along with Mayor George Moscone, who, as a state senator, had been the author of a bill to decriminalize marijuana—Milk himself might have been elected the first gay mayor.

Holly's best new friend was Pia Hinckle, whose father, Warren, was then editor of *City* magazine, published by Francis Ford Coppola. It was the film director's brief foray into print journalism. The girls used the *City* color photocopying machine to reproduce dollar bills. Holly and Pia enjoyed playing tricks. Once, they rolled a marijuana joint for me, only they filled it with herbal tea. Actually, I had a healthy stash of pot in my desk drawer, but mice kept getting inside and eating right through the baggie in order to get their cannabis fix. I would find mouse turds in the box each day. We had no mousetrap, but Holly had an idea.

"Doesn't the mouse get the munchies after eating the marijuana?"

So we left on the floor of our kitchen a large paper bag containing a piece of cheese and a lollipop. Sure enough, in the evening we would hear the mouse rustling inside the paper bag, and I would capture it by closing the top before it could get out. Then we would bring the bag with the stoned mouse out to an empty lot across the street and let it go free, only to be caught sooner or later by a stray cat, who in turn would get zonked out from having eaten the stoned mouse.

Although we had literally invented a better mousetrap—a nonviolent one, at that— the world was not exactly beating a path to our door, as promised by the folklore of the capitalist system.

I had been performing stand-up comedy, and naturally that little experience turned into a bit on stage. I would weave an imaginary story about how I had found myself becoming especially stoned on this stash, but I could not figure out what made it so powerful. Then I decided to send a sample to Pharm-Chem, a sort of People's Food and Drug Administration, and they informed me that a preliminary test showed there was an unknown additive in my marijuana. They could ascertain only that it was organic. But further testing indicated that it was mouse turds. So I began to entice the mice by leaving marijuana out and capturing them with the old lollipop-in-the-bag ploy. I would collect their turds until I had enough to roll a dynamite joint. I had discovered a new and cheap way of getting high: smoking mouse turds.

I decided to present a comedic equivalent to Tony Orlando and Dawn. What stand-up comic had ever featured back-up singers before? I held an informal rehearsal with Holly and Pia for the debut of Paul Krassner and Dusk. They choreographed their own dance steps to perform behind me, singing the appropriate doo-ah doo-ahs, while I proceeded to tell the tale of my discovery of a new way to get high at no expense except for a lollipop and rolling papers, culminating with a spectacular musical chant by Dusk—"Mouse turds! Mouse turds! Mouse turds!"—as they rhythmically flailed their arms in the air.

At a local "No Talent Contest" sponsored by *Rolling Stone*, I decided to play my musical saw for the first time publicly. As I was putting rosin on my bow, I confessed to the audience, "This is slightly humiliating for someone who was a child prodigy violinist—me, the youngest concert artist ever to perform at Carnegie Hall, when I was only six years old—but . . ."

And then, having diligently smoked mouse turds, I surrendered to an impulse. Instead of playing "Indian Love Call," as I had been practicing, I simply sawed my bow in half. The audience was stunned for an instant, then laughed and applauded my bizarre performance. Holly berated me for wasting money like that, and I promised never to do it again.

We spent that Christmas with Ken Kesey at the family farm in Oregon. They all lived in a huge, sectioned-out barn, with a metal fireplace that hung from the living-room ceiling. Ken's brother Chuck ran a creamery, and he brought over a large supply of homemade ice cream blended with two kinds of liquor. I ate so much (the coldness and sweetness covered up the taste of alcohol) that, without even knowing it, for the first time in my life I got drunk—on ice cream—throwing up and passing out.

Later, I explained, "I never take any legal drugs."

Acknowledgments

"Further Weirdness with Terence McKenna,"
"False Alarm," "Smoked Lennon," "The Zen Bastard Goes to Ecuador," "Remembering
John Lilly" and "Mouse Turds" were published in *High Times*.

"The Day the Lampshades Breathed" is excerpted from *Famous People I Have Known*.

"The Honeymooners to the Rescue" is excerpted from *The 99th Monkey*.
"Chub Chub" and "Frisco, Baby, Frisco" are excerpted from *Awake*.

"Incident at Mar Vista" was published in *(sic)*.

"That's the Way It Is" was published in *Whole Earth Review*.

"Psychosis in the Park" and "Heroin" were published in *New York Waste*.

"The Animal Free Alternative" was downloaded from BBspot.com.

"Hash Oil" was published in *Penthouse*.

"Rug Cleaner" is excerpted from *Memoirs of a Maniac*.

Also
by
Paul Krassner

How a Satirical Editor Became a Yippie
Conspirator in Ten Easy Years

Tales of Tongue Fu

Best of *The Realist* [Editor]

Confessions of a Raving, Unconfined Nut:
Misadventures in the Counter-Culture

The Winner of the Slow Bicycle Race:
The Satirical Writings of Paul Krassner

Impolite Interviews

Sex, Drugs and the Twinkie Murders:
40 Years of Countercultural Journalism

Pot Stories for the Soul [Editor]

Psychedelic Trips for the Mind [Editor]

Murder at the Conspiracy Convention
and Other American Absurdities